Personal Identity and Ethics

To Marie, my better self.

Personal Identity and Ethics
A Brief Introduction

David Shoemaker

BROADVIEW GUIDES to PHILOSOPHY

Library and Archives Canada Cataloguing in Publication

Shoemaker, David, 1964-
    Personal identity and ethics : a brief introduction / David Shoemaker.

Includes bibliographical references and index.
ISBN 978-1-55111-882-6

    1. Self (Philosophy). 2. Identity (Philosophical concept). 3. Ethics.
I. Title.

BD450.S45 2008   126   C2008-904149-6

Broadview Press is an independent, international publishing house, incorporated in 1985. Broadview believes in shared ownership, both with its employees and with the general public; since the year 2000 Broadview shares have traded publicly on the Toronto Venture Exchange under the symbol BDP.

We welcome comments and suggestions regarding any aspect of our publications—please feel free to contact us at the addresses below or at broadview@broadviewpress.com.

North America
PO Box 1243, Peterborough, Ontario, Canada K9J 7H5
2215 Kenmore Ave., Buffalo, NY, USA 14207
Tel: (705) 743-8990; Fax: (705) 743-8353
email: customerservice@broadviewpress.com

UK, Ireland, and continental Europe
NBN International, Estover Road, Plymouth, UK PL6 7PY
Tel: 44 (0) 1752 202300; Fax: 44 (0) 1752 202330
email: enquiries@nbninternational.com

Australia and New Zealand
UNIREPS, University of New South Wales
Sydney, NSW, Australia 2052
Tel: 61 2 9664 0999; Fax: 61 2 9664 5420
email: info.press@unsw.edu.au

www.broadviewpress.com

This book is printed on paper containing 100% post-consumer fibre.

PRINTED IN CANADA

Contents

Acknowledgments

Despite the many lonely hours I have spent working on it, the overall production of a book like this is far from a solitary task. Many others have contributed to it in one way or the other and they deserve mention. For her original suggestion that I put together such a project, I'm grateful to Broadview's Tania Therien. For his early encouragement and helpful editorial guidance, I thank Ryan Chynces. For his later encouragement and helpful editorial guidance, I thank Alex Sager. I also wish to thank the rest of the wonderful team at or associated with Broadview Press, including especially Bob Martin, Piper-Lee Bradford, and the delightful Don LePan. I am also deeply grateful to an anonymous reviewer, who helped me make the manuscript immeasurably better. I did all of my revisions while on a research fellowship during the academic year 2007-2008 at the Center for Ethics and Public Affairs, part of the Murphy Institute at Tulane University. Thanks, then, both to the Murphy Institute for financial support, and to my home institution, Bowling Green State University, for supporting my academic leave during that period. Finally, my thanks to the late great Greg Kavka for starting my earlier self down the personal identity path way back when.

Introduction

Motivation

Consider the following six cases.

Case 1: Gretchen has been in a terrible motorcycle accident, which has caused such internal damage that she will die in just a few days. A lifelong atheist and advocate of the view that "once you're dead, you're dead," Gretchen now begins to wonder if she'd been wrong all along. She would, after all, very much like to be able to anticipate some kind of continued survival after the death of her body, but such anticipation will be rational only if it's possible for her to survive the death of her body. But is it? Her body and brain will in fact cease to exist in a few days (she has requested cremation after she dies), so how could it even be remotely possible that she, Gretchen, will survive if her body and brain won't?

Case 2: Carlos and Tanya are having a discussion about abortion. Carlos says, "Abortion is wrong. It would be wrong to kill me, wouldn't it? Well, that fetus from which I developed was also me, so it would have been wrong to kill it as well." "I disagree," says Tanya. "While you certainly developed from a fetus, that fetus wasn't you, just like an acorn isn't an oak tree. What you are is a person, after all, a being with the capacity for not only consciousness but also self-consciousness, whereas an early-stage fetus, say, has neither capacity. Thus, insofar as you aren't the same sort of things, it could be wrong to kill you without being wrong to kill the fetus from which you grew."

Case 3: When Meredith is 55 she is diagnosed with early-stage Alzheimer's. She knows exactly what the disease does to one's mind, since she watched her mother

1

die from it. She thus signs an advance directive instructing doctors that they are not to use any extraordinary means to keep her alive if she gets seriously ill after becoming demented. But once Meredith actually gets to that demented state and contracts pneumonia, it turns out that she is perfectly content and, when asked, expresses a preference to stay alive. Whose wishes are to be honored here, the early-stage patient or the late-stage patient?

Case 4: Howard and Annie are top-notch reproductive scientists. Annie has made a breakthrough in her research that would enable her to clone an adult human being, that is, to take one of his cells, coax it back into an undifferentiated state, combine it with an egg whose nucleus has been removed, and then implant the resulting zygote in a woman's uterus, from which a human being with the same genetic structure as the original cell donor will eventually be born. Howard is horrified by the prospect of cloning, however, and objects by saying that cloning someone would be wrong insofar as it would rob the clone of his own unique identity; instead, he'd just be a copy of someone else. Annie scoffs, noting that human identity has nothing to do with genetic or physical structure; instead, it's entirely about psychology, and given that the clone would grow up in a very different environment from the original, he'd certainly develop psychologically in very different ways from the original, leaving them both with two distinct identities.

Case 5: Sitting around with his family after Thanksgiving dinner, a slightly tipsy Phil laughingly brings up an old family story about how when he was ten years old he caused his younger sister Jen to fall out of a tree, breaking her arm. "I still blame you for that," Jen says, suddenly quite serious, "I get angry at you whenever I think of it." "Oh, c'mon, Jen," replies Phil, "it was thirty years ago and I'm nothing like that ten-year-old anymore. Surely you can't still be mad at me for what that stupid little ten-year-old did!" "Oh, I am," mutters Jen, "because no matter how much time has passed or how much you may have changed, you are still the one who pushed me out of that tree."

Case 6: Darren and Samantha have two young sons, Brad and Albert. Brad is perhaps the cutest baby of all time, and so his parents allow him to model infant clothes and, as he gets older, toddler clothes. Brad has very sensitive skin, though, and the clothes he models aren't made from very good fabrics, so he gets a skin irritation every time he does a modeling job. Nevertheless, he gets paid a lot of money, all of which his parents save in a special account. Albert, on the other hand, while not terribly cute, is obviously a budding genius. Darren decides one day that, when the boys get older, they should take all the money earned by Brad's modeling career and give it to Albert so he can afford to go to the best schools: it will make the most good come out of that money. Samantha vociferously disagrees, saying that Brad was the one who sacrificed for that money, and so he's the one who should get it as compensation. Giving it to Albert would simply be unfair, she thinks.

All of these cases are in some way about the relation between personal identity and ethics. **Ethics**, very generally, is about the way(s) in which we ought to live our lives. This includes the actions we ought or ought not perform, the attitudes and concerns we ought or ought not have, and the character traits we ought or ought not develop. Many people take the term "morality" to be interchangeable with the term "ethics," and that will be fine for our purposes.[1] In addition, for many the term "ethical" is interchangeable with the term "practical," and this is also a substitute you will see throughout the book. In particular, one might construe this book as being about the relation between personal identity and our **practical concerns**, those practices and patterns of caring that are central to the living of our lives, both with respect to our treatment of ourselves—call these our **self-regarding practical concerns**—and our treatment of others—call these our **other-regarding practical concerns**. The relevant self-regarding practical concerns here include our anticipation of the future, the special sort of caring we have only for ourselves, and our concern to survive into an afterlife. The relevant other-regarding practical concerns here include our attitudes toward specific moral issues like abortion, cloning, advance directives, and so forth, as well as our more abstract commitments to various practices of moral responsibility, compensation, and fair distribution of resources.

---

1   Others think ethics is better construed as the *study* of morality, where morality consists of the principles and standards that guide action and character. This is a narrower understanding of "ethics" than we will employ.

Now the cases described above are about the various interesting and fruitful ways in which considerations of personal identity may be particularly relevant for these practical/ethical concerns, be they self-regarding or other-regarding. To see this, consider the cases in more detail.

Case 1 is about the relation between identity and the rationality of anticipating survival in some sort of afterlife. It seems, after all, that for Gretchen rationally to anticipate surviving her death, it has to be possible for there to exist someone in heaven (or hell!), say, who *is* Gretchen, and who is not just a replica of her. But this way of putting the matter implies that, in general, it is rational for me to anticipate only *my own* future experiences, which on its face seems quite true: surely I can't anticipate *someone else's* experiences! So while I may worry about what it will be like for you to undergo some experience, or even have a genuine understanding of what it will be like for you, I cannot look forward to *having that experience* in the way you can. And closely aligned with anticipation of experiences is a special kind of concern, a concern you have, it would seem, only for yourself; indeed, it's what we typically call "self-concern." Now to appreciate the "specialness" of this type of concern, suppose I tell you that I've managed to create a full blown replica of you in the next room, an actual human being who's exactly like you in every respect, and I further tell you that tomorrow morning I'm going to torture him for several hours. Surely you'll be concerned for him, perhaps even fearful on his behalf. But notice the difference in the attitude you'll have were I to tell you instead that I'm going to torture *you* tomorrow morning. Now the type of concern you'll have is of a different sort, and its difference seemingly consists in your being able to anticipate the experiences of the torture victim in the second version of the story, but not the first. The basic lesson, then, seems to be that both rational anticipation and this kind of special concern depend in some crucial way on personal identity, on the anticipator and anticipatee, the concerned and the concerned-for, being one and the same person.

Cases 2–4 are all about the relation between personal identity and various issues in the field called **applied ethics**, wherein one attempts to apply abstract moral theories and principles to concrete, real-life cases. *Case 2* focuses on the key issue of personhood and our essential nature. What am I, precisely? Was I ever actually a fetus, or did I—a person—come into existence at some point after that fetus, that is, did I develop *from* a fetus? If the former, then given my obviously significant moral status now (I have a right to life, surely), wouldn't such moral status have to be shared as well by all the parts of my past, lending moral protection to fetuses generally? If the latter, then wouldn't my moral status as a person simply be fundamentally different from that of fetuses, so that what it's wrong to do to me would not apply (or would at least carry less weight) with respect to fetuses? The import of these questions for our general topic is that the correct theory of personal identity itself seems to depend on what the actual nature is of those individuals whose identity is being tracked; that is, we can't put together the proper theory of our identity (and its relation to ethics) unless we first understand what we are. And this is a source of great controversy.

Case 3 raises different sorts of issues. Normally, it is assumed that the authority of an advance directive to determine the care of some patient stems from its being the directive of the patient herself, that is, the *signer* of the directive and the *subject* of the directive are one and the same person. If this is true, then in Meredith's case she is expressing two contrary preferences, one at the time of the signing, and one at the time of the illness. Which preference thus has authority here? Many people think that, in the case of advance directives, the preferences of the earlier self are authoritative, but this reaction seems to conflict with the way in which we treat past preferences in most other contexts. Suppose that you and I have been friends since we were 20, and when I was 21 I told you, "If I'm not a professional poet by the time I'm 40, I want you to take out an ad in the *New York Times* proclaiming what a failure I am." But now that I am forty, and not a poet, I'm likely to say something like, "Do you remember that crazy demand I made of you at 21? Please just forget about it—I'm so embarrassed by my pretentiousness back then." In this case, we are likely to think the earlier preference is no longer binding; the preferences I have *now* are what counts. So why not think this in Meredith's case? Why not think the preference of her demented self, given that it is expressed *now*, is binding? Of course, one (serious) difference is that Meredith's later self is indeed demented, so it may be that we need to decide what would be best for the patient in a way we don't do when it comes to the poet promise, say. But *who* is the precise subject here? Is it simply the unit comprised of the Later Meredith (LM) and the months she has left? Or is it the unit comprised of Meredith's entire life, in which case these last few months are a kind of tragic coda, which will, if allowed to occur, undermine many of the goods of Meredith's life as a whole? How we answer this question will go a long ways towards determining how Meredith is to be treated here.

On the other hand, it may be that LM and Earlier Meredith (EM) are actually different persons, or that LM *isn't even a person at all*. Consider the former possibility: even if LM and EM are different persons, that doesn't yet answer the question of which one's preferences are authoritative. For while it's true that I typically have no say in the medical care someone *else* is to receive, this isn't always the case. After all, I *do* have a say in the medical care my child, or another close relative, is to receive. And so it may be the case that, even in the absence of identity between EM and LM, EM's directive is authoritative. What, though, if LM isn't a person at all? Wouldn't this then imply that the preferences of EM—a person—are authoritative? Maybe not. After all, even if LM isn't a person, that doesn't yet mean that EM and LM aren't still *identical*, as intimated in our brief discussion of *Case* 2: if what we are essentially *isn't* in fact persons, then the fact that some stage in my life isn't a person may be irrelevant to determining which preferences are authoritative.

Case 4, on cloning, is really about the relation between personal identity and *uniqueness*. Uniqueness is something many of us value, and we think that what makes us unique *just is* what determines our personal identity. On this view, however, cloning me would rob both the clone and me of uniqueness, and thus rob us each of a personal identity. But is genetic identity what matters for *personal* identity? If so, then wouldn't all identical twins lack both uniqueness and a personal identity? Perhaps, though, the intentional creation of a clone is a relevant difference here, or perhaps identical twins *do* lack an important kind of uniqueness. At any rate, more needs to be said to identify the essential features, if any, of a person's (unique?) identity.

Case 5 is about moral responsibility, something that seems to depend on a principle about personal identity: one person can be morally responsible only for his own actions, and so he cannot be morally responsible for the actions of someone else. The dispute between Phil and Jen, however, isn't over this principle—a principle they both accept; rather, it's over whether or not Phil is in fact the same person as the little boy who pushed his sister out of the tree. Jen insists that of course he is; who else could that boy have been? Indeed, doesn't Phil now say things like "Remember when *I* pushed you out of that tree"? Phil, on the other hand, while perhaps agreeing that, in one sense he was that little boy, disagrees that that's the sense of identity that *matters* with respect to things like moral responsibility. Instead, Phil is suggesting that the type of identity that matters is in some crucial way merely psychological. In other words, when a person changes a great deal psychologically, his identity (in this different sense) changes, and so he may no longer be responsible for what he did prior to the changes. And many people would agree with respect to legal responsibility as well: when a hardened criminal is genuinely converted to Christianity while in prison, there are many who would advocate absolving him (the "new" him) of his (the "old" his) crimes. So which sense of "identity" is appropriate for cases of moral and legal responsibility? Furthermore, is *any* sense of "identity" appropriate? After all, perhaps what Phil is suggesting is that, while he is in fact the same person as that little boy, that fact about identity is just *irrelevant*, given the abundant psychological changes that have taken place since then. What matters for attributions of responsibility, then, might instead be about the psychological relations—or perhaps even some *other* kind of relations—between the blamee and the original agent.

Case 6 is about compensation. Here, most of us would agree that compensation is something that, once again, presupposes personal identity: I can truly be compensated only for my own past sacrifices, and I cannot be compensated for burdens I have undergone by benefits being given to someone else. This is, after all, the principle Samantha clearly seems to accept in maintaining that benefiting smart little Albert wouldn't count as compensation to cute little Brad for the sacrifices Brad made as a child. But not only is she making a conceptual point, she is also maintaining that it's *wrong* to benefit Albert for the burden undergone by Brad, that, more generally, uncompensated sacrifices are just unfair. Darren, on the other hand, disagrees, maintaining that it's not immoral to benefit Albert with the money made from Brad's burden, given that this distribution will actually make the world a better place (perhaps Darren has noticed that Brad has become a bit of a slacker these days, and so would just squander the money). This is a true ethical dispute, but it's a dispute that nevertheless may depend on the truth about personal identity, in several different ways. First, if it turns out that 18-year-old-Brad is actually a *different person* than two-year-old-Brad—given the vast psychological and physical differences between them, say—then Samantha's worries about compensation are moot: giving the money to Albert would not be unfair, given that two-year-old-Brad no longer exists. Second, even if the two "Brads" are indeed the same person, that fact may simply not be very *morally* important, given the vast psychological and physical differences between them. In other words, the moral importance of personal identity may vary in proportion to how *strong* the identity relation actually is— perhaps, after all, identity comes in degrees and so perhaps the tighter the various relevant psychological or physical strands are, the more morally important Samantha's principle of compensation becomes. Finally, there is clearly a sense in which the two "Brads" are the same person, and if this is the sense of identity that matters morally, and if Samantha's principle about compensation is indeed an important moral factor, then it is difficult to see how Darren's view is very tenable.

These are just a few of the many interesting and important issues that arise at the intersection of personal identity and ethics, but they should be enough to motivate our project. In general, people are led to investigate the nature of personal identity precisely because of its relation to our practical concerns, but, as we will see, what they find might surprise them, perhaps even pushing them to reconsider the nature and significance of the practical concerns with which they began the investigation. In other words, what would seem to be a straightforward relation between personal identity and ethics may turn out to be anything but. In what follows, then, we will explore in detail this tangled and multifaceted relation. In doing so, we will try to sort out and understand the various contenders for the "true" theory of personal identity, along with the implications each theory would have for our practical concerns.

Before embarking on that project, however, we need to take the time to discuss some crucial concepts and distinctions, which we will do in the remainder of this Introduction. The book from there on out is divided into two parts, each focused on a different domain of ethics. In Part A, "Personal Identity and Self-Regarding Ethics," we will focus on identity and the practical concerns we have regarding what we ought to do and care about with respect to *ourselves*. In Part B, "Personal Identity and Other-Regarding Ethics," we will focus on identity and the practical concerns we have regarding what we ought to do and care about with respect to *other people*.

In Chapter One, then, we will begin our exploration of the relation between personal identity and self-regarding concerns, motivated by the issues raised in *Case 1* about the rationality of anticipation and the possibility of immortality. In doing so, we will lay out four rather crude theories of personal identity, theories focused individually on souls, memories, bodies, and brains, and we will discuss crippling problems with all four. In Chapter Two, then, we will attempt to develop two much more sophisticated theories of identity—the Psychological Criterion and the Biological Criterion—still with an eye towards their relation to self-regarding concerns (in particular to anticipation and self-concern), and we will discuss various strengths and weaknesses of each theory. In Chapter Three, spurred by a kind of standoff we'll be left with in Chapter Two, we will investigate two much more radical approaches to the issue, namely, a view called "narrative identity," and a view that personal identity is in fact not what matters for anticipation and self-concern. While there will be problems with these two theories as well, they will join the Psychological Criterion and the Biological Criterion as legitimate contenders for the "right" theory to anchor the relation between identity and ethics throughout the remainder of the book.

We will then turn to our other-regarding concerns in Part B. We will begin, in Chapter Four, with some important identity-related moral conundrums at the beginning of life: abortion, stem cell research, and cloning. We will then talk in Chapter Five about genetic intervention (both prenatal and postnatal genetic therapy), and any obligations we might have regarding bringing entire populations of people into existence. In Chapter Six, we will turn to a discussion of a couple of important moral issues at the end of life, including advance directives and causing the "deaths" of multiple personalities during therapeutic treatment of that psychological disorder. In Chapter Seven, we will explore the issue of moral responsibility, which has been the main focus of many people interested in the topic of personal identity over the years (and was the subject of our *Case* 5). In Chapter Eight, we will turn to a discussion of the relation between personal identity and ethical *theory*, which will include not only a discussion of the compensation issue of *Case 6*, but also a discussion of which theories of identity bolster the plausibility of which theories of ethics.

In the brief concluding chapter of the book, we will switch gears rather dramatically in order to discuss outright an important abstract question that hangs implicitly over the entire enterprise, namely, what is the right or best *method* for investigating the relation between personal identity and ethics? There are three assumptions about method made by most writers on this relation. First, they assume that the *motivation* for an investigation into the nature of personal identity comes from our practical concerns, that it's because we want answers about various practical questions that we are led to explore identity. This is not the only motivation available, however, for someone might be interested in personal identity solely insofar as it's an interesting metaphysical issue *independently* of our identity-related practical concerns. It's quite possible, though, that these different motivations may yield different results, about both the nature of identity and its implications for our practical concerns. Now it should be obvious that we are adopting the more popular assumption here, given that we have started off explicitly with cases of practical concerns to motivate the project. But it will be worth keeping in mind the alternative route into the project, and in the last chapter we will discuss whether or not we should be worried by possible conflicting methods here.

The second methodological assumption of most writers is that personal identity is prior to ethics,[1] so that our practical concerns ought to answer to, and so be revised in light of, the correct theory of identity. This will also be our default method. We will thus be applying various plausible theories of identity to our ethical issues, assuming that if one particular theory is true, it will have one set of implications for our practical concerns, but if another theory of identity is true, it will have a *different* set of implications for our practical concerns. Nevertheless, this method may be questioned. Instead, one might believe that ethics is actually prior to personal identity, so that our theories of identity must answer to, and so be revised in light of, our practical concerns. This conflict will arise in Chapter Eight, on identity and ethical theory (given that it's a challenge presented by some ethical theorists), and we will address it both there and in the concluding chapter.

The final assumption of most writers on this topic is that what we are seeking is *the* relation between identity and ethics, that we are seeking one theory of personal identity that can stand in the same relation to all of our practical concerns, both self-regarding and other-regarding. So, one might think, if there is a relation between identity and ethics, it's going to be between all of our practical concerns and a psychological-based theory of identity, say, or between all of those concerns and a biological-based theory of identity. And this is the default assumption we will work with as well. But as we proceed, we will come to question this assumption, given that one theory of identity will do really well at relating to some of our practical concerns but do poorly with some others, themselves which will seem more closely related to a different theory of identity altogether. We might well wonder, then, whether or not different theories of identity are relevant to different practical concerns, whether there just is no single criterion of identity that bears the appropriate relation to all our practical concerns.

---

1   This means that decisions must be made about identity first; only then can ethical issues which depend on these decisions be considered.

These are the three difficult methodological questions we will take on explicitly in the final chapter. Indeed, the book as a whole gets more difficult as it progresses, primarily because of the increasingly abstract nature of the topics. My aim, though, will be to make those more difficult aspects of the book as clear and accessible as possible and to prepare the reader throughout the journey for the challenges to come.

Concepts and Distinctions

Before we launch into the metaphysical investigations of Chapter One, we need to get clear on a few important concepts and distinctions, some of which are specific to our project, and others of which we'll run across occasionally that have general philosophical importance. What we are looking for, in working out the first part of the relation between identity and ethics, is a criterion of personal identity. Unfortunately, the terms "criterion" and "identity" are actually ambiguous. Consider the latter term first. Suppose that, when handed a photograph by your mother of your five-year-old self, you sigh and say, "I'm afraid, mom, that I am no longer the same person as that little child you loved so much." What are you saying, exactly? Now there's a sense in which you *aren't* the same person insofar as you are different (likely psychologically) from that child. But there is clearly another sense in which you *are* the same person as that child, given your clear implication that *you yourself* have changed, where change is compatible with identity.

This ambiguity in the phrase "same person" stems from an ambiguity in the more general term "identity," so it's with reference to that term that we need to make our first essential distinction:

X and Y are **qualitatively identical** if and only if they have exactly similar qualities.

X and Y are **quantitatively identical** if and only if whatever is true of X is true of Y and vice versa.

The best way to explain this distinction is by considering examples. If you bought two brand new copies of this book (go ahead, try it!), they would likely be qualitatively identical, that is, all of their qualities—shape, size, pages, words, cost, and so forth—would be exactly similar to one another. But the books nevertheless could not be *quantitatively* identical to each other. Why not? Well, for one thing, they occupy different points in space-time, so whatever is true of one (namely, its particular location in space-time) could not be true of the other. To make this point even more explicit, you could simultaneously hold one book right side up and the other upside down.

Each copy of the book, then, will be quantitatively identical *only with itself.* Quantitative identity is also known as **numerical identity**, and in both cases the relevant quantity, or number, is *one*, as in *one and the same thing*. So if "X" refers to the copy of the book held steady in your right hand, say, at *this* precise moment in time, and "Y" refers to the copy of the book still in your right hand at this *later* moment in time, then X is quantitatively identical to Y insofar as it is one and the same thing as Y. Notice further that quantitative identity, unlike qualitative identity, is compatible with qualitative changes. So if you were to take your copy of the book and then fold up the corner of the title page, it would still be the same book—quantitatively—as the book you bought, even though one of its original qualities (an unfolded title page) had changed.

One of the main questions we will be concerned with, then, is about *quantitative*, or numerical, identity: what makes me the same person as the child in that photo, even though we're not qualitatively identical to one another (we in fact share very few, if any, qualities)?

This leads to the second distinction we need to make. Again, what we'll be looking for is a criterion of personal identity across time, but "criterion" has two senses as well. To draw the appropriate distinction, we will use some standard philosophical terminology that is, unfortunately, rather unwieldy:

X is a **metaphysical criterion** of Y just in case X provides an explication[1] of what Y consists in, an explication of Y's nature. (*Metaphysics* is the

---

1 An *explication* is a detailed, formal explanation, with attention to theoretical issues and implications.

philosophical study of the principles of existence—of beings in general, or of particular kinds of things.)

X is an **epistemological criterion** of Y just in case X provides a way of identifying Y. (*Epistemology* is the philosophical study of knowledge: what it is and how you get it.)

To understand this distinction, suppose I tell you that what makes you the same person as that child in the photo is that you both have the same *soul.* You then respond, "Well maybe, but how could we ever *know* that I have the same soul as that child? After all, the soul is supposedly nonphysical, but because we can have evidence only for the existence of physical objects, we could never have any evidence whatsoever for the existence of souls, so we could never determine whether or not I have a soul, whether or not that child had a soul, and whether or not my soul and that child's soul are the *same* soul!" While this would be an important claim to consider, it would not be directly responsive to my initial assertion, and that's because we are each discussing a different kind of criterion of personal identity. On the one hand, I have offered a *metaphysical* criterion: the nature of personal identity, I say, consists in persistence of the same soul. On the other hand, you have denied the existence of a particular *epistemological* criterion of identity: we have no empirical means of identifying souls, you're saying. But then what we're doing is just talking past one another. For even if we could never know whether or not your soul now is the same as the soul had by that child in the photograph (if you even actually have a soul at all), it could still be true that personal identity consists in sameness of soul, that what would *make you identical* to that child is the identity of your (shared) soul. And alternatively, what provides the means for our identification of the bearer of identity may be in place (or not) regardless of what actual metaphysical criterion of identity is true.

So what sense of "criterion" are we going to be interested in here? Clearly it's the metaphysical sense of the term: we want to know what the *nature* of identity consists in, regardless of whether or not we could ever know if that nature obtains in any individual case. Nevertheless, as we shall see, some people have insisted that there should still be a close relation between the nature of personal identity and how we can come to identify when it obtains. If, after all, I could never actually know when some (metaphysical) criterion of personal identity obtained, could it really be the right criterion? We make what seem to be justified judgments of identity all the time (for example, every time we recognize our friends). Could these really be unjustified, though? If our ordinary judgments of identity don't (or can't) track what some theory tells us is the true nature of identity, that theory may lose some points. We will say more about this problem in the first chapter.

While we will primarily be interested in a metaphysical criterion of personal identity across time, there is a somewhat related criterion that will crop up occasionally as well, and it will be good for us to say something in detail about it right away. This is a **criterion for membership in a kind**. A "kind" is just a grouping of items that all have something in common. So staplers, lamps, tigers, and pearls are all *kinds*. A criterion for membership in a kind, then, is going to tell us what makes X a member of a kind Y, all of whose members share some identifying feature.

Now there are two relevant sorts of question we might ask, both of which seem related to identity. On the one hand, we might see some object and ask, "What kind of thing is that?" Or we may ask a more specific version of this question: "I know that's an animal (i.e., it's a member of the kind "animal"), but what kind of *animal* is it?" Or even more specifically, "I know that's an animal and that it's a squirrel, but what kind of *squirrel* is it?" On the other hand, we may ask "Is that the same thing/animal/ squirrel we saw here the other day?" The first sort of question is about the kind-identity of some object, whereas the second is a question about the numerical identity across time of some object. Each of these questions relies on a different criterion to answer it: a criterion for kind membership will tell us what it takes for some object to have an identity as a member of a particular kind, and a criterion of numerical identity across time will tell us what it takes for some object to be one and the same thing at different times. On its face, then, it would seem that these are quite distinct sorts of criteria.

Consider an example. Suppose a rich person built an elaborate building in 1850 that served as his family homestead until he and his family all died off, at which point it was bequeathed to a neighbor who in 1900 turned it into a church. Fifty years later it was sold to a historical society, and they transformed the building into a museum. Fifty years later in 2000 they sold it to a private group that turned the building into a nightclub, which it remains to this day. Suppose you visited that building in 1901, remembering it having been the old homestead of the rich guy's family, and you ask, "What makes this building a church?" You're asking a question about kind-membership, about what makes this object (the building) a member of the kind "church." And fifty years later you could well ask what now makes the building a museum, and fifty years later (my, how you've grown old), you could ask what makes it a nightclub. In each case, the answer will have something to do with the intentions of the owners and attendees, as well as the functions served by the various parts of the building with respect to the intended end.

The question of kind-membership identity will call for a different sort of answer than the question of numerical identity across time. Suppose that in 1949 you returned to the site and asked, "Is this the same church as the one I saw in 1901?" What makes a building the same church across time may be quite different from what makes it a church to begin with. To be the same church may involve preservation of the same basic physical structure, or at least some kind of continuity of form of that structure, across time, whereas being a church itself may simply be a product of the intentions of some owner(s) in determining the function of some physical space. And so it may go with respect to identity and persons: the question of what makes me the same person across time asks for something different than the question of what makes me a person to begin with.

Nevertheless, the questions asked (and the criteria produced) are related, and some authors we explore will attempt to exploit their relation in the following way. There may be good reason to think that what makes for membership in a kind will actually be an essential ingredient in a criterion for identity across time of its members. So to be a member of the kind *church*, a building will have to have several parts that function in "church-like" ways per the intention of the owner. So it will have to have a gathering area, and pew-like seats, and a stage, and perhaps a pulpit-like area, and so forth. But if these are the properties that *make it* a church, it might be thought that those properties will be necessary to its ongoing preservation, so that it cannot lose them without also losing its identity. This suggests that kind membership provides a crucial condition for identity across time: what makes X a member of kind Y is also what must be preserved in order for X to be the *same* Y across time. So it may be with us: if what makes me a member of the kind "person" are certain psychological capacities, then those capacities must be preserved in order for me to be the *same* person across time.

Nevertheless, as we will see in Chapter Two, there is a powerful argument available that shows that this truth applies only to kinds whose members are *essentially* members, things that simply wouldn't exist at all if they weren't members of that particular kind. So while the building is a member of the kind *church* once the owner cleared out the congregation space, built the pulpit, and so forth, the building itself could still exist—and did, in our example—even after it ceased to be a church: the building is not *essentially* a church. In other words, the building exists before, during, and after the existence of the church, and so the criterion for membership in the kind *church* does not in fact give us the identity conditions for the *building*. Those identity conditions will instead come from the criterion for membership in the kind *building*, which will likely have something to do with a thing's having an intentionally-shaped physical structure.

How, then, does all of this relate to the question of *our* identity? Some authors think that being a person is like being a church, where what *I* am is not essentially a person but something much more fundamental, something that exists before, during, and after its incarnation as a person. What is this thing? A particular sort of animal, a biological organism. But if this is what I am essentially, then my identity conditions must have their source in that *biological* nature, which means that what preserves my identity across time may have nothing whatsoever to do with what makes me a person, with my psychology. This also suggests that *my* identity, the identity of the individual that I am, may not necessarily be a *personal* identity after all. That is, for these authors, the issue of "personal identity" has been mislabeled: instead of being about whether or not a person at one time is the same person as a person at another time, it is really about whether or not something that is a person at one time is identical to *something*—person or not—at another time. Realizing this distinction, they say, enables us to resolve all sorts of problems.

More on this argument in Chapter Two. What matters for now is just that, while there is an important distinction between one's numerical identity across time and one's identity as a member of a kind, these two sorts of identity are nevertheless related in very interesting and subtle ways, and it will be important for us to keep this in mind as we go.

One final distinction before we conclude. There is a crucial philosophical distinction that will crop up repeatedly as we go, a distinction between *necessary* and *sufficient* conditions. Here is the gloss on each:

> X is a **necessary condition** of Y just in case there could be no Y without X.

> X is a **sufficient condition** of Y just in case X in and of itself guarantees Y.

> X is a **necessary and sufficient condition** of Y just in case if there's X there's Y, and if there's Y there's X.

The easiest way to explain this distinction is by means of example. Start with necessary conditions. It is a necessary condition of a person's being the President of the United States that he or she be born in the United States. One can't be President of the U.S. without being born in the U.S. Nevertheless, this isn't a sufficient condition of being President, for there are millions and millions of U.S.-born citizens who aren't President: being born in the U.S. isn't enough to guarantee that one becomes President; far from it. When X is a necessary condition for Y, we say, "Y, only if X."

Now consider sufficient conditions. Suppose you are six feet tall. Being 6'2" is a sufficient condition for being taller than you, then. And so is being 6'5" or being 6'1/2". Are any of these *necessary* conditions for being taller than you? No. It's not as if I wouldn't count as taller than you if I were 6'8", say. When X is a sufficient condition for Y, we say, "If X, then Y."

Finally, consider necessary and sufficient conditions. Together these provide a guarantee of the presence of some thing that also couldn't be present without the conditions in question. So the necessary and sufficient conditions of someone's being a lesbian, say, are that (a) that person is a woman, and (b) that person has a predominant sexual interest in women. Note that neither of these conditions alone is sufficient (although they're each necessary): just being a woman isn't enough to guarantee you're a lesbian, and neither does just having a sexual interest in women (you could be a heterosexual male, for instance). But whenever someone meets these conditions she will be a lesbian, and wherever there's a lesbian she will meet these two conditions. When X is a necessary and sufficient condition for Y, we say, "Y if and only if X."

Given all of these important distinctions, then, the first question we will pursue may be put as follows: *What makes person X at some time (t₁) quantitatively identical to person Y at a later time (t₂)?* This is a question about the nature of the quantitative identity relation, not the membership in a class relation. It also seems to be demanding both necessary and sufficient conditions, although both conditions may not turn out to be essential for what we need in some cases. And of course this general formulation itself may not survive throughout our entire inquiry—there are many who think it's just the wrong formulation of the identity question, as we will see in both Chapters Two and Three—but for now it gives us enough, namely, a clear entrée into the puzzle of personal identity. And that is the topic to which we can now, finally, turn.

PART A

Personal Identity and Self-Regarding Ethics

CHAPTER ONE

Personal Identity and Immortality

Gretchen Weirob, a philosophy professor, has gotten into a terrible motor-cycle accident, and she now finds herself in the hospital with only a day or two left to live. Despite being close to death, however, she is lucid, and is thus able to carry on an extended conversation with her two friends, Sam Miller, a chaplain, and Dave Cohen, her former student. Weirob is a lifelong atheist, but as her death approaches, she wonders about the possibility of immortality, and yearns, as many of us would, for the comforts of being able to anticipate surviving the death of her body. Through the next three evenings, right up until her death, the three friends discuss the nature of personal identity and immortality, with Miller and Cohen trying desperately to find a way to provide Weirob with the comfort she seeks (within the demanding strictures of reason), but to no avail: Weirob dies believing that there is simply no way for her to survive the death of her body, and thus no reason to anticipate immortality.

This is the "plot" of John Perry's imaginative *A Dialogue on Personal Identity and Immortality*,[1] and insofar as it is a terrific introduction both to the most historically influential theories of personal identity as well as to the motivation many people have for becoming interested in personal identity in the first place—worrying about the possibility of life after death—we will take it as our initial guide in this chapter. Along the way,

---

[1] Bibliographical information on this and other writings referred to in this book will be found at the end of chapters.

we will critically evaluate the various theories discussed in the dialogue, as well as a few variations the dialogue participants overlook. By the end of the chapter, we will see not only how difficult it is to come up with a coherent criterion of personal identity that allows for the possibility of immortality, but also how difficult it is to come up with a coherent criterion of personal identity at all.

BACKGROUND

Weirob wants the comfort of being able rationally to anticipate surviving the death of her body. What is involved in this sort of rational anticipation, though? There are two elements. First, it cannot be rational to anticipate the occurrence of something that's just impossible. So in order for it to be rational for Weirob to anticipate surviving her body's death, it must at least be possible for her to survive her body's death. Further, this is all that Weirob demands: she is not asking whether or not she will definitely survive her body's death, nor is she asking whether or not such survival is probable. Instead, she simply wants to know if it's *possible* to survive, that is, if it's conceivable without contradiction or serious absurdity (one might think of this as **metaphysical possibility**). This is a very minimal constraint, it would seem, although as we will see it's actually a constraint that turns out to be very tough to meet in this case.

The second element Weirob assumes is that personal identity is a necessary condition of **rational anticipation**. What does she mean by this, though? In general, to anticipate something is to look forward to it. So I may anticipate the end of the current war in Iraq, say, or I may, as in the old commercial, anticipate the ketchup's finally coming out of the bottle onto my hot dog. But Weirob has in mind a very specific form of anticipation that involves *looking forward to actually having certain experiences as occurring "from the inside."* Think here of what it's like to remember some recent experience: you have a representation of a past you lived through, so you relive the sights, sounds, and even smells of what it was like to actually undergo that experience from the inside, as the experiencer of that event. Anticipation is just this aspect of remembrance cast into the future: to anticipate some experience is thus to have an imagined representation about what some experience one expects to have will feel like from the inside.

Furthermore, to *rationally* anticipate some future experience, for Weirob, is to do so in a way that is correct, or that makes sense. So suppose Cohen and Miller could establish not just the *possibility* of heaven, a "place" where there are lots of happy people communing with God for all eternity, but heaven's actual existence. This wouldn't yet be enough for Weirob to rationally anticipate anything: she wants it to be possible, not only that there will be persons existing in an afterlife setting, but that one of those persons *will be her*. After all, how could it be rational for her to anticipate the experiences of a stranger in heaven? Indeed, even if that stranger were exactly like her in every way, if that person weren't in fact *her*, then how could she rationally look forward to the experiences that that person would undergo in heaven? Instead, it seems what's necessary is that, for such anticipation to be rational, it must be possible for there to exist someone in heaven who is identical to—who is the same person as—Weirob on Earth.

In general, someone has the burden of proof in an argument if the claim that that person is advancing is not obviously true. Weirob holds that the claim "survival of death is possible" is certainly not obviously true, and she makes explicit that her dialogue partners have the burden of proof here by reiterating an uncontroversial fact: her body will eventually cease to exist. And we can make this even more explicitly true by stipulating that her body will be cremated immediately after she dies. Given this fact, she asks, how could *I* still exist? Now this way of formulating the question indicates that she holds a **materialist** conception of the "I": it is *physical*, consisting of matter. In putting the challenge in this way, Weirob also gives us our first criterion of personal identity, what she takes to be the default view that Miller and Cohen have the burden of replacing:

> **The Body Criterion**: *X at t1 is the same person as Y at t2 if and only if X's body is the same as Y's body.*

While we will discuss the subtleties of this view later, for now it should be obvious that, if it's true, and if the rationality of anticipation depends on personal identity, and if one's body does indeed cease to exist after death, then it would be irrational to anticipate surviving the death of your body, because such survival would be *impossible*. After all, if your body is destroyed upon your death, then no one could have your same body after that death, and so no later person could possibly be you—even if both God and heaven exist.[1]

The gauntlet Weirob throws down to Miller and Cohen, then, is to show her that things could possibly be otherwise. More specifically, she presents

> **Weirob's Challenge**: *come up with an alternative criterion of personal identity that (a) could provide a means, a mechanism, to enable Weirob to rationally anticipate surviving the death of her body, and (b) does not yield a contradiction or deep absurdity, that is, it's actually possible.*

A theory fulfilling both of these conditions would thus allow her rationally to anticipate the afterlife, giving her the comfort for which she is so desperate in her final days, and, not inconsequentially, giving each of *us* some reason to hope that there's more to our own lives than this merely mortal coil.

---

1   Peter van Inwagen has actually concocted a scenario, however, in which immortality is possible (and thus it could be rational to anticipate survival in the afterlife), even assuming the truth of the Body Criterion. The way in which he accomplishes this is actually by denying Weirob's so-called uncontroversial fact. He maintains it is possible that, just as you are about to die, God whisks your body to heaven and replaces it on earth with an exact replica that then dies in your place. This would make the person's body in heaven thus continuous with–the same thing as–your body on earth, and so would make that heavenly person you. See van Inwagen, *The Possibility of Resurrection and Other Essays in Christian Apologetics* (Boulder, CO: Westview Press, 1998), Chapter Three, "The Possibility of Resurrection," pp. 45-51. While this scenario might indeed be metaphysically possible, it remains unclear just what this process of "whisking" involves, and so it remains unclear just what would make that body in heaven the "same" as the body on earth. It would also, more disturbingly, turn God into a deceiver, someone who allows us to think that we and our loved ones will die, when in fact all those who actually die are imposters.

The Soul Criterion

After some initial misunderstandings about the nature of the challenge, the chaplain Sam Miller offers a familiar and expected alternative criterion:

> **The Soul Criterion**: X at t1 is the same person as Y at t2 if and only if X's soul is the same as Y's soul.

How would this answer Weirob's challenge? The soul is ostensibly your essence, and something that is different from, and can exist independently of, your body. Thus, the soul could provide a means to enable Weirob to rationally anticipate surviving the death of her body in the following way: her soul could continue to exist after her body dies, and perhaps be transplanted into another body in the afterlife. And so, more generally, if the soul is your essence, and a soul doesn't have to die along with your body, then *you* could continue living after that body dies. The Soul Criterion thus seems to meet the first demand of Weirob's Challenge. What about the second demand, though? Is it actually possible for things to work this way?

Before answering this question, we have to do some basic philosophical spadework, that is, we have to get clear on just what we're talking about here. What exactly *is* a soul, after all? It turns out this is a rather vexed question, one that has yielded many different sorts of answers throughout history. Consider just the two most influential answers. Plato took the soul to be what a person really was, which he thought was an essentially non-physical thing, so that persons were the incorporeal occupants, perhaps even the prisoners, of their bodies. Aristotle, by contrast, took the soul to be merely the formal design, the organizing principle, of a living body. Persons on this conception, therefore, are like coins, whose essence consists in both their formal design (shared by all coins) and their particular physical manifestations.

Now obviously whether or not you can establish the possibility of immortality by means of souls will depend on what you think the nature of souls actually is. If you accept Aristotle's view, then the soul just isn't a substance, a *thing*, that could ever even exist independently of a particular living body, so once your body dies, its soul would have to be no more (destroyed coins simply have no design). This is why, for example, Thomas Aquinas, a Catholic theologian and philosopher who accepted Aristotle's conception of the soul, insisted on the resurrection of the *body* in the afterlife, for without their bodies, persons could not survive their deaths. So it looks like the only conception of the soul that has a chance of enabling immortality is Plato's (a conception also shared, more or less, by Descartes).

But even on this conception of the soul as purely incorporeal, some questions remain. What is its nature, after all? Is it a purely psychological substance—a thing whose whole essence is to think (as Descartes maintained)—or is it a substance that, while *having* a psychology, is in principle separable from it? Furthermore, is a soul something I *have* (distinct from me), something I *am*, or something else entirely? These are very hard questions, and it's quite unclear how to answer them. Indeed, once we allow that the soul would have to be incorporeal, we are more or less resigned to the problem of having no direct and reliable way of determining whether or not they exist or what they'd be like, given that we can directly and reliably know about the existence and nature of only those substances we can experience with our senses. But then, if we cannot directly determine the existence or nature of souls, how could they play any real role in personal identity, which often involves precisely such direct and reliable judgments?

Indeed, Weirob raises a version of this problem herself in the following argument (**Weirob's Soul *Reductio*[1]**):

1. If the Soul Criterion were true, we could never have the grounds to judge that X is the same person as Y.

2. Sometimes we *do* have the grounds to judge that X is the same person as Y.

3. Thus, the Soul Criterion is false.

---

1   The term "*reductio*" here is short for *reductio ad absurdum*, a Latin phrase meaning, roughly, "reduces to absurdity." Running a *reductio*, then, involves showing that someone's argument has implications that are either contradictory or absurd, which itself implies that their original argument is either false or implausible.

In other words, if we believe, as Miller does, that sameness of incorporeal souls is what preserves persons' identities across time, but we have no direct way of reidentifying souls (given that we can't sense them), then we would also have no direct way of reidentifying persons either. But surely this is false, given that we directly reidentify people all the time and seem to do so for very good reasons. When I return home every evening and greet the person standing there with a kiss, I'm judging that this person is my wife, the same person I married and the same person I kissed goodbye in the morning. But if what made the morning and the evening person identical were just their identical souls, I would have absolutely no direct and reliable way to determine that they in fact were the same person (and so perhaps I should be withholding those kisses!). This can't be right, though. These sorts of common, immediate, everyday reidentifications must have rational grounds, if anything does.[1] Thus, any theory that implies that these sorts of ordinary reidentifications are groundless *must* itself be false, given that it implies a contradiction with the facts of ordinary identity attributions. The Soul Criterion, it seems, cannot pass the possibility condition of Weirob's Challenge.

How might a defender of the Soul Criterion respond? What one needs to do is find some intermediate link between the grounds we use in ordinary judgments of reidentification and the identity of those incorporeal souls, and there might be two ways to do so: (a) via bodies, and (b) via psychology. The first response might go as follows. Ordinarily, we reidentify people visually, by reference to their bodies. But what bodies might do is simply serve as an *indicator* of the soul "inside," such that same body implies same soul. We thus infer the existence of the same soul upon seeing the same body. Ultimately, then, what preserves your identity across time is your ongoing soul, and while we cannot reidentify souls directly, we can reidentify them *indirectly* via their bodies, which always carry within them the same soul.

---

1   This is not to say that I couldn't be *mistaken* in my reidentifications. If my wife has an identical twin, they might occasionally play a trick on me by switching places, in which case I might judge that some person is my wife when in fact she isn't. This would be a case in which I was mistaken about what my grounds for reidentification actually were, however—they have to consist in more than mere physical similarity, it would seem—not a case in which there were no such grounds.

Unfortunately, this won't do, for how could we ever establish a principle like "same body, same soul" in the first place? In other words, why think that there's a one-to-one correlation, or *any* direct correlation, between bodies and souls at all? In driving home this point, Weirob offers Miller a box of chocolates, and he picks out one that has a swirl on top, given that it indicates the presence of caramel inside. Miller, then, operates on the principle "same swirl, same filling." The question, though, is how he could ever have established a principle like that, and the answer is that he's observed both sides of the equation: he's actually been able to bite into a swirl-on-top chocolate repeatedly, and he has then *tasted* the caramel inside each time. But this method simply won't work to establish the principle "same body, same soul," given that we can never directly experience both sides of the equation, that is, we can never *taste* a soul. So it's just impossible for us to *establish* the correlation Miller wants between bodies and souls.

The second attempt to link ordinary reidentification to the identity of souls comes via the intermediary of *states of mind*. Ordinarily, of course, we reidentify people via their bodies. But bodies alone are merely *indicators* of identity, and although usually reliable, they could mislead. If the person with the body of your best friend suddenly started talking and behaving precisely in the manner of your worst enemy, or like a complete stranger (even failing to recognize you), you might begin to have doubts that she was indeed the same person as you knew before, despite your judgment that this person has the same body as your friend. So while our grounds for reidentifying people make reference to their bodies, this is just a shorthand way of reidentifying their psychologies, their states of mind. And given that states of mind are simply states of *soul*, according to Miller, reidentifying someone's psychology is a reliable and indirect method of reidentifying her soul. Consequently, what makes X and Y at different times the same person is the presence of the same soul in both, and what enables us to reidentify X as Y is the sameness of psychological characteristics, which themselves bear a one-to-one correlation to souls, and which are themselves (typically) reidentified via reidentification of bodies.

This last attempt fails as well, however, as Weirob demonstrates with a discussion of rivers. Suppose an expert on a few local rivers could reidentify them solely on the basis of the state of their water. So some rivers have cloudy, brownish water, while some rivers are crystal clear. One might think, then, that the expert reidentifies the rivers according to the principle "same water, same river." But of course, the water the expert points to in reidentifying some river isn't the *same* water he's seen before—that's all long downstream. Instead, it's just *similar* water, or in similar states to the water he's seen before. So the same river at different times consists in different, albeit similar, water.

Analogously, then, the same person could consist in different, albeit similar, souls (or minds). It's perfectly possible, after all, that similar (but distinct) states of mind are attached to similar (but distinct) souls, which would be, remember, substances we couldn't see, touch, smell, taste, or hear. But because it's impossible for us to reidentify souls directly, any number of hypotheses about their relation to me is fair game: I could indeed have had one soul attached to this body and psychology since birth (or before), but I might also have gotten a new, exactly similar soul during my mid-life crisis, or every year on my birthday, or even have had a constant river of exactly similar souls flowing through me. Notice, then, how correct judgments of personal identity would have to depend on which of these scenarios occurred, if the Soul Criterion were true, but because we cannot establish any clear linkage between bodies, psychologies, and souls, we cannot ever know if our judgments of personal identity are correct. But again, this seems clearly false, given our confidence in the grounds of the many reidentifications we make in our ordinary lives. The overall conclusion, then, is that the Soul Criterion, while meeting the first part of Weirob's Challenge, cannot meet the second part: it does not provide a possible mechanism to get her (or us) to the afterlife, given the contradiction it yields with respect to our ordinary judgments of identity.

What are we to make of this overall argument, Weirob's Soul *Reductio*? Notice first that Weirob does not deny the existence of souls. Instead, she grants that they might indeed exist, but insists that, due to their allegedly incorporeal nature, they simply couldn't play any role in our judgments of identity. This way of putting it, though, reveals that the Soul

Criterion may not be false after all. Indeed, what Weirob seems to be doing is confusing the two senses of "criterion" discussed in our introductory chapter, the metaphysical sense and the epistemological sense. The Soul Criterion, as given, is a purely metaphysical criterion, purporting to explain what *makes* X and Y identical. Weirob's objection, though, is epistemological, complaining about how we could never *know* that X and Y are identical if the Soul Criterion were true. But for a defender of the Soul Criterion, such an objection might well be irrelevant, for souls could still constitute the identity-preservers for persons, even if we had no means of tracking their trajectories through space-time. This would constitute a straightforward rejection of the second premise of Weirob's Soul *Reductio* (which maintains that we do indeed have the grounds to make judgments of reidentification), and it would allow that it still might be possible for me to survive the death of my body via my soul.

Still, there remains something compelling about Weirob's objection. She claims that she hasn't based her "argument on there being no immaterial souls..., but merely on their total irrelevance to questions of personal identity, and so to questions of personal survival,"[1] but this isn't quite right, as we've just seen. Souls may be *quite* relevant to the question of personal identity itself. What they're not relevant to, however, are the *practical concerns* we have that are related to personal identity. In other words, all of the prudential and moral cases discussed in the Introduction that seem to depend on personal identity actually presuppose that we *can* make correct judgments about when that identity relation obtains. Holding people responsible, compensating them, determining the moral relation between fetuses and the adult humans into which they develop, determining the moral relation between early- and late-stage Alzheimer's patients, and (what's most relevant to the present chapter) rationally anticipating some future experience(s)—all of these practical concerns and commitments presuppose our ability to identify and track whatever criterion of identity turns out to ground them; they presuppose a tight connection, that is,

---

1   Perry, "A Dialogue on Personal Identity and Immortality," in Joel Feinberg and Russ Shafer-Landau, eds., *Reason and Responsibility*, 12th edition (Belmont, CA: Wadsworth/ Thomson Learning, 2005), p. 371.

between the metaphysical and epistemological senses of "criterion of personal identity." Consequently, any theory of personal identity to which we lack this kind of epistemological access is just going to be *practically* irrelevant.

And this is precisely the case with the Soul Criterion. *It could be true*, of course. But given that we in fact reidentify people via their bodies or their psychologies (what else could we do, either reliably or directly?), and given that souls would have no necessary connection to *either* (as Weirob correctly points out), it's very difficult to see what the point of appealing to souls in a metaphysical criterion of identity could possibly be. So we can either (a) allow the truth of the Soul Criterion, in which case we have to allow both that there's a disconnection between the nature of personal identity and our practical concerns, and also that our reidentification practices are likely ungrounded and potentially wildly mistaken, or (b) we can insist on a tight connection between the nature of personal identity and our practical concerns, and thus reject any theory of personal identity—like the Soul Criterion—that denies this connection. Because (a) would have wildly unsettling implications for many aspects of our daily lives, there are good practical reasons for adopting (b), and thus rejecting the Soul Criterion.

Note what we both have and have not done here. There are many compelling arguments that have been given to deny either the existence or the coherence of souls. Obviously, if these arguments succeed, then the Soul Criterion is false—if identity is ever preserved across time, it couldn't be because of some non-existent substance. But we have not appealed to these sorts of arguments. Instead, we have suggested that, even if there are souls, they aren't relevant to the *practical* questions we are asking, and so any criterion appealing to them just misses the point of the general inquiry. Is this a satisfactory dismissal of the Soul Criterion? This is the sort of very abstract matter we will take up in the final chapter. But for now, it's important to see how the Soul Criterion fails to meet Weirob's Challenge in a different way than Weirob herself thinks it fails: while Weirob thought the soul could have been a mechanism warranting rational anticipation of survival but the criterion of identity appealing to the soul couldn't possibly be true, we have suggested instead that while such a criterion could in fact be true, the soul couldn't actually be a mechanism warranting rational anticipation of survival. Imagine, for instance, that there could be someone in heaven with my soul, but who had neither a body nor a psychology anything like mine, someone who didn't remember my life or experiences at all. What possible reason could I have to anticipate his experiences, *even if he is me*? It would be no different from my anticipating the experiences of a complete stranger, and so its possibility would surely fail to provide Weirob (and us) with the comforts of anticipation being sought.

Nevertheless, it may still be rational to anticipate the possibility of surviving death, even without reference to souls. How so? One might appeal to a criterion of identity that is more closely connected to our ordinary practices of reidentification but that is in principle separable from one's body. And that's just what Miller tries to do in the second night of the dialogue.

The Memory Criteria

In arguing that the Soul Criterion fails, Weirob makes reference to the ordinary practice of reidentifying other people: we simply make no reference to souls when engaged in that everyday practice. Nevertheless, third-person reidentification isn't the only sort of reidentification we engage in; another kind is *first-person*. So when you groggily and gradually wake up in the morning, you know who you are—you reidentify yourself, for example, by thinking that *you* should have gone to bed earlier last night, or getting angry with yourself for having forgotten to study for today's exam when *you* had a chance yesterday. Now what are your grounds for such first-person reidentification? Do you check to see if your soul is the same as that of the person who got into bed so late last night? Of course not, but we already knew the Soul Criterion was a dead end. But here's the kicker: you also don't check to see if your *body* is the same as that of the person who got into your bed last night.

In fact, you can imagine waking up in a totally different body, yet still remaining "yourself." Indeed, this sort of thought is familiar from a variety of literary and cinematic flights of fancy. The opening line of Franz Kafka's *The Metamorphosis*, for example, is as follows: "One morning, as Gregor Samsa was waking up from anxious dreams, he discovered that in bed he had been changed into a monstrous verminous bug."[1] Notice that our reaction is not that this is incoherent, or utterly incomprehensible. Instead, while acknowledging the exceedingly unusual nature of the metamorphosis, we can still grant that it's *conceivable* and, for all we know, perfectly possible. This is also true of the numerous popular "body swapping" movies made over the years, such as *Big, Vice Versa,* and *Freaky Friday.* All of them assume that it's possible for a person's identity to be preserved (and known about first-personally) regardless of any particular body that person might have. If all of this is true (and Weirob is skeptical), then there simply is no *substance* underlying personal identity, that is, it necessarily consists in neither souls nor bodies. Instead, it consists in various relations among the various stages of persons, relations to which we have access from the first-person standpoint.

To illustrate, suppose you attend a baseball doubleheader (two baseball games played back to back), and you get up in the middle of the seventh inning of the first game, during a one-to-one tie, to buy a hot dog. As it turns out, the line is fairly long, and you don't get back to your seat for another hour. Upon your return, you see that the score is one-to-one, but you ask the person next to you, "Is this the same game I was watching when I left?" It's equally possible, after all, that the first game ran long or that the second game already started and the teams are once again tied. Now what would identity of games consist in? That is, what is the nature of the question you have asked? Are you asking about *souls*, in some sense, about whether or not this game has the same "spiritual essence" as the game you'd been watching? Clearly not: we certainly don't think that anything of the sort underlies a baseball game. Are you instead asking about *bodies*, in some sense, about whether or not these are the same players or the same field as before? No. It's possible, for instance, that the same game could proceed without *any* of the same players and on a different field.

---

1   Franz Kafka, *The Metamorphosis,* trans. by Ian Johnston. Available as e-text on the web, at http://www.mala.bc.ca/~Johnstoi/stories/kafka-E.htm.

This would be the case, say, if there were an earthquake in the fourth inning of a World Series game that stopped play and damaged the stadium, such that they had to complete the game in the opposing teams' stadium, where both managers, in an attempt to fire up their teams, replaced all the starting players with the benchwarmers. What, then, are you asking about with your question?

You're asking about the *internal relations* of the game, about how the parts of the game—its various events, like strikes, hits, outs, runs, and so forth—relate to the *whole* game. What you're asking is whether the out one team has just recorded counts as an out in the first game or the second. A baseball game, as a whole, is simply comprised of all its various individual events, and as long as the parts are connected *in the right way*, then it's still the same game. What counts as the right way? Well, that's to ask for an actual criterion of identity for baseball games, and to answer, we would have to make detailed reference to the rules: there are nine regularly scheduled innings (although sometimes more are played if there's a tie, and sometimes only eight and a half are played when the home team's ahead), and each of these innings is comprised of three outs per team, and some outs consist in catches of fly balls, and other outs consist in a batter swinging at and missing a pitch three times, and so forth. But at any rate, when one baseball-event is related to various other baseball-events in the right way, given the rules of the game, they are all parts of the *same* game.

What Miller thus suggests to Weirob is that a person is like a baseball game: a person, as a whole, is simply comprised of all its related parts, and is not some underlying substance, such as a soul or a body. What thus allows you to know who you are in the morning is not your reidentification of some persisting substance, but is instead your awareness of the relation that connects your various parts into a single whole, the true relation of personal identity. But what exactly is this relation? It is clearly psychological, and Miller borrows from the seventeenth-century philosopher John Locke to make it more specific: what unites our various stages are *memories*. We can start afresh, then, with a new theory of identity based on this insight:

Memory Criterion #1 (MC1): *X at t1 is the same person as Y at t2 if and only if Y remembers the thoughts and experiences of X.*

Could this criterion meet Weirob's Challenge? On its face, it easily meets the first demand. It is certainly possible that 1000 years from now there will be some person in heaven who remembers Weirob's life (from the "inside"), thinking of Weirob's past as her own, in the way we all do upon waking up in the morning. If she did this, she would, on this criterion, *be* Weirob. And just as it's rational for me now to anticipate the thoughts and experiences of the person who will wake up in my bed tomorrow and who will remember my thoughts and experiences today, so too it would be rational for Weirob to anticipate the thoughts and experiences of this person in heaven who will remember her life on earth. This would, in effect, be like Weirob's finishing her "baseball game" on a different field.

Can MC1 meet the second demand, though? Could the criterion be true without implying any contradictions? As it stands, the criterion runs into two immediate difficulties, noticed by two critics of Locke's original view in the century after its publication. First, as Joseph Butler pointed out in 1736, MC1 implies that if I cannot remember some past experience, then that experiencer could not be me. In other words, I have existed, on this criterion, only during those moments I now remember. But this must be false: just because I don't remember having lunch last Thursday doesn't mean that none of last Thursday's lunch-havers were me! Surely identity can persist through some memory loss.[1]

A related, but potentially more devastating, problem came from

---

1   One thing to consider is that this point is an objection to the *necessary condition* of MC1, claiming that my remembering some past experience isn't necessary for making that past experiencer me: he may be me even if I *don't* remember his experiences. All Weirob really wants, though, is a criterion that provides a *sufficient condition* for identity, identifying some substance or relation that, if present, will ensure her survival. So she would be perfectly happy if a memory of some past experience was enough to guarantee that the rememberer was identical to the experiencer, even if memory wasn't necessary for identity, for that could still allow her a mechanism to survive the death of her body: as long as someone in heaven remembered Weirob's life and experiences, that person would be Weirob. Nevertheless, our interests are wider than Weirob's, for we'll ultimately want a full-fledged criterion of identity that explains what it *always* requires, and for this task the objection above is relevant.

Thomas Reid in 1785, from the **Brave Officer Case**. Suppose that, at 10, a boy steals some apples from a neighbor's orchard, and then at 40, as a brave officer, he steals the enemy's flag in battle, and then finally, at 80, he's a retired general. Furthermore, suppose that, as the 40-year-old is stealing the flag, he fondly remembers stealing the apples as a 10-year-old, and as the 80-year-old is relaxing in his rocking chair, ruminating about his life, he fondly remembers stealing the enemy's flag, but—and here's the troublemaking part—he has no memories whatsoever of stealing the apples. What does Locke's view say about the relation between the retired general and the apple-stealing kid? Because the brave officer (BO) remembers the experiences of the apple-stealer (AS), the BO is the same person as the AS. And because the retired general (RG) remembers the experiences of the BO, the RG is the same person as the BO. But then if AS = BO, and BO = RG, then AS = RG; in other words, logic demands that, given Locke's theory, RG is the same person as AS. Nevertheless, RG doesn't remember any of the experiences of AS, so Locke's theory also implies that RG is *not* the same person as AS. Consequently, Locke's theory implies a contradiction—RG both is and is not identical to AS— and so the theory itself cannot be true.

Both problems, however, can be resolved with a fairly easy patch-up job, for all we need to do is amend MC1 by having it appeal to an overlapping chain of direct memories, rather than to a direct memory link itself. In other words:

> **Memory Criterion #1a (MC1a):** *X at t1 is the same person as Y at t2 if and only if Y directly remembers the thoughts and experiences of X, or Y directly remembers the thoughts and experiences of some Z, who directly remembers the thoughts and experiences of some Q (who remembers R, who remembers S, who remembers T, as needed)...who directly remembers the thoughts and experiences of X.*

I remember what my yesterday's self did, and he remembers what *his* yesterday's self did, and so on, back to last Thursday's lunch-haver. So while I now have no direct memories of what I had for lunch last Thursday, I'm connected via this chain of memories to someone who *does* remember, and this is all that's needed to respond to the first objection. Furthermore, this amendment can also easily deal with the Brave Officer Case, for now the RG will be identical to the AS, given the chain of overlapping memories between them, even though the RG has no direct memories of the AS's experiences, so the contradiction is dissolved.

Nevertheless, there is another serious problem: how does MC1a distinguish between *seeming* to remember and *actually* remembering? Consider, for example, the psychiatric patient who thinks he's Napoleon: he seems to remember fighting the Battle of Waterloo and sleeping with Josephine. He is obviously deluded. But now notice the problem for MC1a as it pertains to immortality: suppose there's a person in heaven 1000 years from now who seems to remember my thoughts and experiences. What's to prevent this from being just like the Napoleon case, one in which there's someone who is *deluded* into thinking he's me?

Any successful memory criterion of personal identity will obviously have to refer only to *genuine* memories. What's needed, then, is a way to distinguish between genuine memory and merely apparent memory: what makes one person's memories genuine, after all, and another's merely apparent? Suppose, then, that Y at t2 seems to remember the experiences of X at t1. One might very well be inclined to say that Y's memories are genuine if and only if Y *actually had* the experiences he now remembers. Indeed, how could I have genuine memories of anything other than *my own* experiences; isn't this just what the nature of memory consists in?

Unfortunately, this is a deeply problematic response, for it renders the overall enterprise circular, and so undermines the establishment of MC1a. Here's why. Suppose we've got a person in heaven at t2 who claims to be Weirob. What would make this person Weirob? On MC1a, she is Weirob if and only if she remembers Weirob's thoughts and experiences. Now suppose this heavenly person does indeed seem to remember Weirob's life. It remains possible, given the Napoleon case, that she could be deluded, so we now have to ask, "What makes her memories genuine?" Well, goes the possible response above, she was the person who actually had those experiences she now remembers, that is, *she was*

Weirob. But now the problem should be obvious: what makes her Weirob? She remembers Weirob's life. What makes her memories of Weirob's life genuine? She was Weirob. But what makes her Weirob? And round and round we go.... The problem is that it looks as if genuine memories *presuppose* identity, that you cannot have genuine memories of someone else, that memories by their very nature (when genuine) *reveal* your own past to you. But if that's the case, memories cannot constitute the identity relation, for in order for my memories of some past experiences to be genuine, I *already* have to be identical with that past experiencer.

Nonetheless, is it necessarily the case that I can have genuine memories of only my own experiences? It may not be. Consider the following possibility (drawn from arguments given by Sydney Shoemaker and Derek Parfit). Suppose scientists develop a way to copy a memory trace of your European vacation into me, such that I seem to remember standing underneath the Eiffel Tower (even though I have never been to France). Further, suppose I know that I've never been to France, but I know you have, and I further know that the scientists have performed this procedure on me. My memory would thus not be a delusion (for I wouldn't think *I* was the one who'd been to Paris), nor would it be of an experience that happened to me. Why couldn't it thus count as a genuine memory, an accurate memory of some experience that nevertheless didn't presuppose identity? If so, then what makes it a genuine memory would be a purely causal matter: the memory must be caused by *the experience* that I now remember. Genuine memories thus simply have to have an orthodox causal history. They must be caused by an experience of the remembered event and so be a product of the ordinary causal chain: an experience causes a trace in the brain, a trace which is then later tapped into in one's remembrance of the experience. What makes a memory merely apparent, then, is that it wasn't caused in the right way, that is, it wasn't caused by the experience that's being remembered. So, for example, the Napoleon guy may seem to remember fighting the battle of Waterloo, and while that memory will have a cause (perhaps a trauma in childhood), its cause will not be the *experience* of fighting in the battle of Waterloo, rendering it merely apparent.

These remarks thus yield a new version of the Memory Criterion:

Memory Criterion #2 (MC2): *X at t1 is the same person as Y at t2 if and only if (a) Y seems to remember the thoughts and experiences of X (either directly or via an overlapping chain of memories), and (b) Y's seeming to remember is caused in the right way.*

Can this criterion thus pass Weirob's Challenge?

In articulating the view, we have suggested that for Y's memory to be caused in the right way, it must be one that has been stored in Y's brain. But if that's the case, then MC2 can't pass the first part of Weirob's Challenge, for it wouldn't seem to provide a mechanism for immortality. After all, if my brain is what houses my genuine memories, and it is destroyed along with the rest of my body upon my death, then I simply couldn't survive the death of that body. So while there could be a person who exists 1000 years from now in heaven who seems to remember my life, he couldn't be me, given that his "memories" wouldn't have an orthodox causal history. They would have been caused by God, not by memory traces preserved in the same brain.

Nevertheless, why think that sameness of brain matters here? After all, what we really want in demanding genuine memories is that *the storage of information be reliable,* not that the process of storage take the same route every time. So normally, of course, an experience occurs, which causes a trace in the brain, and the experience is later retrieved from that brain as memory. But it seems the process could just as well go as follows: an experience occurs, which causes a trace in your earth-brain, the information of which is downloaded by God upon your death onto a Divine Flash Drive (DFD), which is then plugged into a new body in heaven, the information is uploaded into the new brain, and this newly activated person in heaven now remembers the experiences of the earth-you. As long as God and the DFD are reliable, why should we care that the process of transfer is a bit out of the ordinary? Sure, there may be no God, or if there is a God he may not care about helping us survive our deaths. But it's *possible* that God exists, and that God cares, and that God could store the information from our memories on earth reliably. And given these possibilities, we would have a mechanism to get us from here to there.

Is this really possible, however? Can the criterion relying on this mechanism avoid contradictions? As it turns out, it can't, and in seeing why we will run across a very famous and puzzling thought experiment, one that we will return to many times throughout the book. It is a case of *fission*, and one way to illustrate it comes from consideration of a possible heavenly case, what we will call **Divine Duplication**. Suppose that, upon Weirob's death, God did the downloading process described above, and then uploaded all of her memories into a newly created body's brain in heaven. This person thus "wakes up" thinking she is Weirob, that she has survived her death, and according to MC2, she'd be right: her memories would be caused in the right way, namely, via reliable information storage. Call this person Weirob 1.0. But now suppose God likes the results so much that he creates another new body and plugs the DFD into it, uploading Weirob's memories again. Now MC2 directly implies that this person—call her Weirob 2.0—is identical to the original Weirob as well. But if both versions 1.0 and 2.0 are identical to Weirob, then, by the transitivity[1] of identity, they must be identical to *each other*. But clearly they are not: they each occupy different locations in space-time, for one thing, and they could go on to lead very different lives after this, maybe even going on to reside in opposite sides of heaven. To insist they are the *same* person is simply to stretch the concept of personhood into something unrecognizable.

What we have, then, is the following problem for MC2:

1. If MC2 is true, then the products of the Divine Duplication of Weirob would be identical with one another (by transitivity).
2. Both resulting people would *not* be identical with one another (given their different locations in space-time, for one).
3. Thus, MC2 is false.

---

1   *Transitivity* is a property of certain relations, such that if A has that relation to B, and B has it to C, then it must be that A has it to C. An example of a transitive relation is *bigger than*: if A is bigger than B, and B is bigger than C, then it must be that A is bigger than C. An example of a relation that is not transitive is *is a friend of*. It could be that A is a friend of B, and B is a friend of C, but A is not a friend of C. It's often assumed that identity must be transitive: after all, if A is identical with B, and B is identical with C, then A must be identical with C.

The logical implication of MC2 cannot be true, so neither can MC2. It thus fails to pass the second part of Weirob's Challenge.

There is one remaining reply, however. What got MC2 into trouble was the duplication. If God made only *one* person in heaven with Weirob's memories, then that person would be Weirob, and it would be possible for her to anticipate surviving the death of her body. And it is perfectly possible that God makes only one version of each of us in heaven. So what we can do is simply stipulate that, where one copy is made, the original survives, and where any other number of copies is made, the original doesn't survive:

> **Memory Criterion #3 (MC3):** *X at t1 is the same person as Y at t2 if and only if (a) Y seems to remember the thoughts and experiences of X (either directly or via an overlapping chain of memories), (b) Y's seeming to remember is caused in the right way (via any reliable cause), and (c) no other beings satisfy conditions (a) and (b).*

Think of this as a **No Competitors** version of the Memory Criterion: as long as there's no competition, no other person whose memories of your life are genuine, you have survived. If there's no one in existence with genuine memories of your life, or if there exists more than one person with genuine memories of your life, you have not survived.

Unfortunately, as Weirob makes clear, this last-ditch attempt fails to meet the second part of her challenge as well, for it is deeply absurd. To see why, suppose that God is a bit of bumbler, and that sometimes his newly created bodies survive and sometimes they don't. Suppose, then, that he creates a new body in heaven upon Weirob's death on earth, and he uploads her memories into this new body. According to MC3, this person is Weirob. But then suppose God makes another body and uploads Weirob's memories into this person. Now neither person is Weirob, *even though the first person was Weirob for a day*. But this is just too weird.

Consider yourself, after all, from the first product's point of view. "I made it!" you might think, "I've been brought back to life by a kind and loving God. It's great to be alive and to be *me*, good old Weirob." But then suppose God creates the duplicate. Now you, the person who *was* Weirob, are no longer Weirob. Suddenly, you'd have to think "Well, I *was* Weirob, but now I'm someone else, a deluded imposter, someone who thinks she's Weirob but isn't." But now suppose the duplicate simply collapses and dies (it wasn't one of God's better efforts). Now what might you think? "Yes, I'm back! It's great to be me—Weirob—again!" But then suppose God resuscitates the duplicate. "*!$%#*, now I'm no longer Weirob, but just a deluded nobody once more!" And so forth.

The problem is that whether or not you're the same person would change as new competitors pop into existence. But this is terribly absurd. Surely my identity doesn't depend on what happens to other people! After all, it's perfectly possible that God has at this moment made a duplicate of me in heaven, or on the opposite side of the universe, or in Albuquerque. But then MC3 would imply that I have suddenly ceased to exist—even though I've undergone no physical or psychological changes at all—and at the moment of duplication I would have been replaced by an entirely new person, one who *thinks* he's Shoemaker, and has "memories" of Shoemaker's life, but who is just terribly deluded. But this cannot be right. Whether or not some future person is me must instead depend solely on the relations between us, not on the existence or non-existence of other people. And so, while we have found no straightforward contradiction here, we have found a deep absurdity, which, as Weirob says, has the same weight as a contradiction, and so this third twist on the memory criterion fails to pass the second part of her challenge.

The Body Criterion

Am I then just my body? If so, then immortality is impossible. And this is certainly what Weirob continues to believe, right up until her death, despite the best efforts of her friends to convince her otherwise. Once we start to examine this view closely, however, it too becomes difficult to believe.

Begin with the case of *Who is Julia?*, a work of fiction that's treated as if it were real in Perry's dialogue. The set up is as follows: as Julia attempts to save a young child, she is run over, and her body is left mangled, although her brain is fine. Meanwhile, the child's mother, Mary Frances, has a brain aneurysm at the scene, although her body is fine. Both people are rushed to the same hospital, where the remarkable Dr. Matthews is able to transplant Julia's healthy brain into Mary Frances's healthy body, resulting in one healthy person with Mary Frances's body and memories of Julia's life. What, then, has happened to Julia (and Mary Frances, for that matter)?

The general method behind the presentation of this sort of puzzle case (and we'll run across several others) is to identify and draw upon your intuitions[1] in various interesting cases, and then use those intuitions as the data for which a successful theory of personal identity must account. In this respect, then, a theory of identity will resemble a scientific theory, and, as in the science case, the better theories will be assessed as such, in part, by virtue of their explanatory power, that is, insofar as they are able to explain more of the data in a more adequate fashion. The *Julia* case is important to this end, as we will see, because it prizes apart two features that are ordinarily wedded together—our bodies and our brains—and it asks, "If they were separated, where would *I* go?" So what are your intuitions in this case? Who is the survivor: Julia, Mary Frances, or someone else?

Most people believe that Julia is the survivor: the resulting person would at least have apparent memories of Julia's life, would believe she was Julia, would recognize the people in Julia's life and fail to recognize those in Mary Frances's life, and so forth. Furthermore, there's no reason to believe that her memories are delusions, given that they would have been caused in the right way—the ordinary way—by having been preserved in and recalled from the same brain in which the experience was originally recorded.

Weirob, of course, disagrees, maintaining that the survivor is Mary Frances, a *deluded* Mary Frances, true enough, but Mary Frances nonetheless. Perhaps some plausibility for this position can come from consideration of other cases of organ transplants. If my liver were to fail and the

---

1   *Intuitions* are common-sense judgments that people would make prior to considering philosophical arguments and theories.

surgeons were to replace it with a donor liver, say, we would all agree that *I* was the survivor of that operation, that I'd just gotten a liver transplant. And if my heart were to fail and the surgeons were to replace it with a donor heart, we would certainly say once more that *I* was the survivor, that I'd gotten a heart transplant. Why not, then, say the same as well in the Mary Frances case, that *she* was the survivor, and that she'd just gotten a brain transplant?

But the brain isn't like those other organs, many of us want to say. It alone, after all, is what preserves our memories, and our psychology generally, and so for that reason it's in a very different category from the heart and the liver, at least with respect to *personal* identity. Sure, you might think, organs like the heart and the lungs keep me alive, but it's the psychology provided by the brain that is the *me* being kept alive, and while I could be kept alive by *any old* set of heart, lungs, and liver (and so could survive in Mary Frances's body), the me that's being kept alive is a psychological being, and that's what my uniquely important brain preserves.

If this is the intuition most of us share in the *Julia* case, and if such intuitions count as appropriate sorts of data, then we would have a powerful reason to reject the Body Criterion, for it would thus yield the wrong answer in this case. We would also have a condition any plausible alternative criterion would have to meet, namely, that it account for our intuitions that personal identity depends in some way on brain-based psychological relations.

Nevertheless, this isn't a knock-down objection to the Body Criterion, in part because some may share Weirob's intuitions on the case, and in part because there are, as we will see, seriously unclear or implausible features of the brain-based psychology view. Are there, then, other, less controversial, objections one might raise? There are two.

First, consider the real life case of the Hensel twins, Abigail and Brittany. (*See photo.*[1]) They are conjoined twins, sharing their internal organs below the waist, while having two spinal cords, two hearts, three lungs, and two stomachs. Nevertheless, they have only two arms and two legs,

---

1   Photo from http://www.search.com/reference/Abigail_and_Brittany_Hensel.

and their nervous systems are connected and partially shared, which allows them to coordinate their activities fairly well. They can run, ride a bike, swim, and play the piano.

What are we to say here? Given our ordinary conception of "body," it seems clear that Abigail and Brittany share a single body: they have one torso, after all, and they have two arms and two legs. How many persons are there, however? Clearly, there are two. The twins repeatedly stress that they are two distinct individuals, and it would be nearly impossible to deny that this is the case. Each writes separately in her own hand, they disagree with one another, they take pride in their individual accomplishments, and so forth. But if, as Weirob would have it, X and Y are one and the same person if they have the same body, and Abigail and Brittany have the same body, then Abigail and Brittany *are one and the same person*, which is clearly false. In this actual case, the Body Criterion gives the wrong answer, and so it is deeply flawed. (As we will see in the next chapter, the Biological Criterion, which is similar in certain respects to the Body Criterion, might have a way to deal with this case.)

A second problem comes from a more far-fetched case offered by Derek Parfit. An advocate of the Body Criterion must admit that your identity could be preserved through the loss and replacement of one of your fingernails. Similarly, it could be preserved via the replacement of your finger, your hand, your kidneys, and your heart. But there must be *some* point after which your identity would no longer be preserved, for if everything but your brain were replaced (as happens to Julia), Weirob insists you would no longer exist (or you would have gone wherever your body now was). But where precisely is the line at which your identity would be lost, before which the survivor would be you, and after which the survivor would be someone else? Is it at the 50% mark, so that if 49% of your body were replaced, you would survive, but if 50% were replaced, you wouldn't? Perhaps it's at the 51% mark?

We simply don't know. And, what's worse, we simply *could not* know. Even if we could actually do such large-scale replacement, and we could ask the person at the 50% mark who she is, why should we believe what she says? After all, the person with Julia's brain will say she's Julia, but an advocate of the Body Criterion wouldn't believe her; instead, this advocate would think that the survivor was a *deluded* Mary Frances. But then there would be no way in principle we could determine where the line was marking the difference between identity and non-identity, between life and death.

Nevertheless, there would have to be such a line. But then the deeper worry would be this: how could the difference between life and death consist simply in the replacement of a few cells? Suppose the 51% mark is the line in question (even though we could never know that), so that you'd be the survivor if only 50% of your body were replaced, but you wouldn't be the survivor if 51% of your body were replaced. This would make the difference between identity and non-identity, between life and death, depend on a very small amount of physical change: that 1% of bodily replacement would take with it your *entire* identity. But this is very hard to believe, especially in light of the fact that your identity would clearly be *preserved* through a 1% replacement at the *early* stage of the spectrum (getting a finger transplant, say).

The Body Criterion is thus in serious trouble. Sameness of body doesn't seem to be what preserves my identity across time. But there's a *part* of my body that may indeed do the trick, namely, my brain. Let us turn then, finally, to consideration of that possibility.

The Brain-Based Memory Criterion

Recall the insight that I can reidentify myself without reidentifying either my body or my soul (if I have one). This was the insight motivating the move from a substance-based criterion to a relational criterion, that is, the Memory Criterion. But as we saw, this view fell prey to the duplication objection: if there were two people in the future bearing the appropriate memory relation to me, according to this criterion they would both have to be me, and so by the transitivity of identity they would both have to be identical to one another, which they clearly would not be.

What got that view into trouble was its criterion of genuine memories, of what counts as a memory's being "caused in the right way." Because the advocates of the view in Perry's dialogue wanted to establish the possibility of life after death, they allowed that memories were like software and that memories would be genuine just in case the information they contained had been stored reliably.[1] This move allowed for God to download my earth memories onto the DFD, create a new body and brain in heaven, and then upload my memories into that new brain. But the metaphor of memories as software is what enabled the possibility of Divine Duplication, of that software being "uploaded" into two (or more) different "hard drives."

Nevertheless, this isn't the only way the view might go. Instead, we might think of memories in terms of a *hardware* metaphor, such that one's memories are genuine—caused in the right way—just in case they are

---

1   Of course, there may be good independent reasons to head in the direction Perry's dialogue participants do on this matter. One might, after all, simply be convinced by thinking about various cases that genuine memory is just a kind of accurate information storage and that any reliable vehicle for such storage would thus be sufficient to preserve identity. However, this position would be just as vulnerable to the duplication thought experiment as the one motivated by a desire to establish the possibility of immortality.

preserved *in the very same brain* in which the remembered experience was originally stored. What matters, on this view, is thus preservation of the same brain:

> **The Brain-Based Memory Criterion (BBMC):** X *at t1 is the same person as* Y *at t2 if and only if* Y *seems to remember* X's *thoughts and experiences (either directly or via an overlapping chain of memories), and* Y's *memories are caused in the right way, namely, via the same brain.*

This view eliminates the possibility of immortality, of course, but for now we're simply trying to come up with a plausible criterion of personal identity to account for rational anticipation in everyday cases. We'll return to discuss immortality in a bit.

The advantages of BBMC should be obvious. For one thing, it allows us to account for the intuition most of us share that Julia would be the survivor in the *Who is Julia?* case. The survivor, remember, would seem to remember Julia's life and experiences, and she would have Julia's brain. A second advantage is that, although we lose immortality on this view, we at least avoid the troublesome Divine Duplication case (and its earthly variants), insofar as one and only one brain could preserve genuine memories. A third advantage is that this view easily accounts for our intuitions in the Hensel sisters case: Abigail and Brittany are two different persons insofar as there are two different streams of memory provided by two different brains.

This view nevertheless has some significant problems, unfortunately, and they're brought out by consideration of some science-fiction cases. Suppose, first, that teleportation were possible. That is, suppose it were possible for you to step into a machine on earth that scanned and recorded the state of all your cells while zapping your body and brain out of existence, and then faxed that information to Mars, where another machine created, from new matter, a body and brain exactly like yours. In other words, your body and brain would be destroyed on earth, and moments later someone exactly like you in every single respect would walk out of the machine on Mars. Suppose the machine were 100% reliable. Would you consider using it?

One way to think of the question is this: would this be a way of travel-ing, where *you* would be going from earth to Mars in a matter of seconds, or would it be a case of death, then duplication? Many people's intuitions lean towards the former (perhaps from years of watching teleportation on *Star Trek* and other science fiction shows). But obviously, if you think you survive teleportation, that it's just a really fast form of travel, then you don't accept BBMC.

A second, and related, case casting doubt on the criterion is one to which Weirob refers, called Brain Rejuvenation, which is just an earthly version of the Divine Duplication case. Suppose your brain had weak blood vessels but that it was possible to replace it with a rejuvenated version, that is, possible to make a new brain, out of human tissue, that would be your brain's exact duplicate—it would consist in all the same psychologically relevant states—and then to replace your aneurysm-liable brain with the healthy duplicate. The resulting person would be exactly like you psychologically, seeming to remember your life and experiences, and thinking that he or she is you. Would you have the operation? *Should* you have the operation?

Your answer here will likely depend on where you stand on the ques-tion of whether or not the survivor would be you. But if you're an advocate of BBMC, both possibilities cause serious trouble. First, suppose you believe the survivor would be you. You've now abandoned BBMC, allow-ing instead that identity *doesn't* depend on sameness of brain, that the memories of the post-rejuvenation person would be genuine, despite not having been stored in and retrieved from the same brain of the person who experienced them. And beyond abandoning BBMC, you've now opened yourself up to the very same worries about duplication we ran into before, in the software version of the Memory Criterion.

On the other hand, if you believe the survivor *wouldn't* be you, you're sticking to your guns, but now you have some new questions to answer. First, it is unclear why preservation of the *very same brain* is so crucial to the preservation of identity in this case. Why think that it is? The resulting person would be exactly like you in every way, and he or she would still have a good 95% of your original body. Why think that that specific three pounds of gray matter is what makes the difference between your life and your death? Indeed, isn't it just the *memory* preserved by your brain that matters to your identity? Why, then, put so much weight on the mere *means* of preservation, as opposed to the *content* of the preservation? At the very least, more needs to be said to give us a positive reason for why the very brain that you have is so absolutely crucial to your identity.

Second, and more importantly, BBMC actually undermines the motivation for adopting a memory-based view in the first place. Recall Miller's point about everyday self-identification: we can wake up knowing who we are without having to reidentify any substances, either souls or bodies: I don't have to check to see if my body or soul is the same as those of the person who got into my bed the night before to know that that person was me. Miller took this fact about us to motivate a relational view of personal identity, arguing (alongside Locke) that what explains this fact about self-reidentification is the relation of memory one now stands in to the person (oneself) being reidentified.

But now suppose you agree to undergo the Brain Rejuvenation, just to see what it is like (your own brain is perfectly healthy, say), so you're now in the operating room, where the surgeons have already removed your brain (call it B1) and they have it sitting next to the duplicate brain (B2). Suddenly, one of the surgeons trips and falls into the table holding both brains, and they fall off the table with a squishy thud and then slide across the floor, bouncing into the wall and into each other. The surgeons rush over, pick them up, and sterilize them, but now they've lost track of which brain is which. After some quiet discussion, they agree simply to stick one of the brains into your cranium and stick the other into a different live body they happen to have in the next room, and they then agree never to speak of this again.

So now there will be a person who wakes up with your body and either B1 or B2 (call this person BrainyOne), and another person who wakes up with a different body and either B1 or B2 (call this person BrainyTwo). Now the original advantage of the Memory Criterion is lost: neither BrainyOne nor BrainyTwo will really know who he or she actually is. They'll be unable to engage in self-reidentification, the key capacity motivating a move to the Memory Criterion in the first place. Of course, they'll both *seem* to remember your life and experiences, but only one of them will have *genuine* memories of that life, insofar as only one will have your original brain, but neither will know – indeed, *no one* will know – which person is right and which person is wrong. So things simply become much more mysterious on this view, and BBMC loses much of its luster thereby.

We have now examined the same four possibilities for what preserves personal identity across time as Weirob and her dialogue partners: two types of substance criteria—a physical substance (the Body Criterion) and a non-physical substance (the Soul Criterion)—and two types of relational criteria—a software-based Memory Criterion and a hardware-based Memory Criterion. And all four theories were found seriously wanting. Indeed, it's very hard to believe that any of these theories could come close to making sense of rational anticipation. What we need to do, then, is either radically revise one or more of these theories or consider a very different type of identity altogether. In the next two chapters, we will pursue both strategies. First, however, we should consider where we stand on the topic that got us into this mess, namely, the possibility of making it into an afterlife.

The Possibility of Immortality

What, then, are we to say about immortality? Is it possible? Does Weirob, or do any of us, have any reason to look forward to it, to be comforted by it? Unfortunately, the prospects don't look very good. We have examined two general theories claiming to provide a mechanism for surviving the deaths of our bodies—the Soul Criterion and the software-based Memory Criterion—but neither of them, in any of their variations, could meet Weirob's Challenge: they were either irrelevant with respect to rational anticipation or led to contradictions or deep absurdity.

Does this mean, then, that immortality is impossible, and that we all ought to give up on looking forward to it? Not exactly. Indeed, we need to be very careful and precise about what's been shown here. It will be useful to remind ourselves of the basic conditions of the enterprise. According to Weirob, it is rational for me to anticipate the experiences of some heavenly person (HP) only if:

1. HP is me, that is, personal identity is a necessary condition of rational anticipation;
2. There is a criterion of personal identity accounting for why HP is me that yields no contradictions or absurdities; and
3. The mechanism of survival provided by this criterion of identity is (at least in part) what gives me a reason to anticipate the experiences of HP.

The Soul Criterion violates Condition 3: even if souls could possibly exist, and even if they could be the substances preserving one's identity across time, they would just be irrelevant with respect to rational anticipation. Given their incorporeal nature, we would have no direct means to track them or reidentify them, and so they could not be the basis for our direct judgments of identity, either in others' cases *or our own*. But if I could have no direct grounds to determine that some future person would be me, what reason would I possibly have to anticipate his experiences? Souls thus couldn't explain the rationality of *any* future anticipation, and so couldn't provide any reason to anticipate the afterlife.

One could, of course, simply deny Condition 3 and embrace the Soul Criterion. This wouldn't be a very promising move, however, for it would entail that a host of practices in which direct reidentification is essential—practices to which we are deeply committed, such as responsibility-attribution, compensation, and on-going personal relationships in general—are completely unfounded. But it is very hard to believe that these practices could be unfounded, that we're just *guessing* when we reidentify one another. Denial of Condition 3 would thus be far too radical for serious consideration.

Memory Criterion #1 (in both its variations) is incomplete, failing to incorporate a criterion of genuine memories. MC #2 and MC #3, however, while incorporating an account of genuine memories, nevertheless violate Condition 2 above: they cannot handle the possibility of Divine Duplication without either a contradiction or a deep absurdity. Of course, one could deny Condition 2, but this would be even less promising than denying Condition 3. Surely the mechanism constituting our identity must be possible!

Are there any criteria of personal identity that can meet these three conditions? It seems not, at this point. Given the uncontroversial fact with which we started, that our bodies will eventually cease to exist, any criteria meeting the afterlife conditions would have to rely on an essentially non-physical mechanism to get us from here to there. But either this mechanism will be provided by some kind of non-physical *substance* (with no necessary attachment to one's individual psychology)—a variation on the Soul Criterion—in which case it will violate Condition 3, or it will be provided by some kind of (non-physical) psychological software *relation*—a variation on the software-based Memory Criterion—in which case it will violate Condition 2 in dealing with Divine Duplication. In either case, then, it looks like what gets the view in trouble is its detachment from the earth-person's individual and unique *body*. But if viable theories of personal identity depend on the persistence of, or attachment to, that specific earth-body, then our prospects for immortality look particularly bleak.

There remains one last and extremely provocative response to the challenge, however, hinted at in Dave Cohen's final speech to Weirob. At this point in the dialogue, the participants have given up on the possibility of immortality, and they have focused instead on finding a way for Weirob to survive at least a few more years here on earth. As it turns out (in this fictional world), Dr. Matthews could perform a fascinating operation for her, transplanting her brain into another living body (a body currently without a brain). Weirob, however, refuses the operation, insisting that, insofar as it would be someone else's body, the resulting person would be someone else, despite the fact that that person would be, psychologically, exactly similar to Weirob. Cohen, unable to block Weirob's arguments for this view, makes one last appeal:

> Suppose you are right and we are wrong. But suppose these arguments had not occurred to you, and, sharing in our error, you had agreed to the operation. You anticipate the operation until it happens, thinking you will survive. You are happy. The survivor takes herself to be you, and thinks she made a decision before the operation

which has now turned out to be right. She is happy. Your friends are happy. Who would be worse off, either before or after the operation?

Suppose even that you realize identity would not be preserved by such an operation but have it done anyway, and as the time for the operation approaches, you go ahead and anticipate the experiences of the survivor. Where exactly is the mistake? Do you really have any less reason to care for the survivor than for yourself? Can mere identity of body, the lack of which alone keeps you from being her, mean that much? Perhaps we were wrong, after all, in focusing on identity as the necessary condition of anticipation....[1]

What Cohen is suggesting is that we should at least consider denying Condition 1 above. Perhaps what grounds rational anticipation isn't personal identity at all, but something else. And perhaps this something else is a mechanism that can survive the deaths of our bodies. If so, then while none of us can actually survive our deaths, it could at least be possible to rationally anticipate the experiences of some heavenly person, in the same way we may rationally anticipate the experiences of our future selves from day to day. But what could this "something else" possibly be? And do we really need to make such a radical move? Perhaps we can still get everything we want through a better-built theory of personal identity. In order to understand Cohen's suggestion and fully appreciate the motivation for it, then, we first need to analyze and evaluate the two most popular and sophisticated theories of personal identity around today, theories that have been designed to overcome many of the objections we have encountered to this point.

WORKS CITED OR REFERENCED IN THIS CHAPTER

Aquinas, Thomas. *Summa Theologica*. Translated by Fathers of the English Dominican Province. Benziger Bros. edition, 1947. Christian Classics Ethereal Library, http://www.ccel.org/ccel/aquinas/summa.html.

---

1   Perry, p. 383.

Aristotle. *On the Soul*. Translated by J.A. Smith. *The Internet Classics Archive*, http://classics.mit.edu/Aristotle/soul.html.

Butler, Joseph. "Of Personal Identity." In Perry, *Personal Identity*.

Descartes, Rene. *Meditations on First Philosophy*. http://oregonstate.edu/instruct/phl302/texts/descartes/meditations/meditations.html.

Harris, Barbara. *Who is Julia?* New York: Fawcett Books, 1977.

Kafka, Franz. *The Metamorphosis*. Translated by Ian Johnston. http://www.mala.bc.ca/~Johnstoi/stories/kafka-E.htm.

Locke, John. "Of Identity and Diversity." In Perry, *Personal Identity*.

Parfit, Derek. *Reasons and Persons*. Oxford: Oxford University Press, 1984.

Perry, John, ed. *Personal Identity*. Berkeley, CA: University of California Press, 1975.

———. "A Dialogue on Personal Identity and Immortality." In *Reason and Responsibility*, 12th edition, edited by Joel Feinberg and Russ Shafer-Landau. Belmont, CA: Wadsworth/Thomson Learning, 2005.

Plato. *Phaedo*. Translated by Benjamin Jowett. *The Internet Classics Archive*, http://classics.mit.edu/Plato/phaedo.html.

Reid, Thomas. "Of Mr. Locke's Account of Our Personal Identity." In Perry, *Personal Identity*.

Shoemaker, Sydney. "Persons and Their Pasts." *American Philosophical Quarterly* 7 (1970): 269-85.

van Inwagen, Peter. *The Possibility of Resurrection and Other Essays in Christian Apologetics*. Boulder, CO: Westview Press, 1998.

CHAPTER TWO

Personal Identity, Rational Anticipation, and Self-Concern

INTRODUCTION

Suppose that we persist in our commonsense belief that a necessary condition for my rational anticipation of some future person's experiences is that he will be me. After all, goes the normal thought, while I can imagine, be excited about, or have sympathy for the experiences of someone else, I can't *anticipate* that other person's experiences. So if anticipation is rational at all, it has to be (at least in part) because the person whose experiences I'm anticipating will be me.

The same, we might think, goes for the special type of concern known as *self-concern*. Suppose I find that my best friend will undergo torture this weekend. I will be very concerned about him. But if I find out that *I* will undergo torture this weekend, my concern is now of a different kind. What seems to justify this difference? It surely seems as if the justification has its source in the fact that in the second case the tortured person will be *me*, while in the first case he will not, which suggests that this sort of special concern is also grounded in personal identity.

If identity is really what grounds rational anticipation and self-concern, though, then we need to make a more valiant effort to see just what the right criterion of identity is in order fully to understand what implications it might have for these practical attitudes (as well as what it might imply about the possibility of immortality). In the previous chapter, we examined four such theories—Soul, Software-Based Memory, Brain (Hardware)-Based Memory, and Body Criteria—but saw that they were either false, seriously problematic, or just irrelevant to the issue of our practical concerns.

In this chapter, we will examine two much more sophisticated theories of personal identity, theories that, while similar in certain respects to the previous four, have nevertheless been designed to overcome many of the objections we launched against them. Most contemporary theorists support one or the other of the two theories we will examine here, and our job will be to see whether or not either one can truly avoid serious objections while also providing the grounding for anticipation and self-concern we have been seeking. We will also occasionally explore what implications they might have, if any, for the possibility of immortality. Let us begin, then, with the theory improving on the one many of you likely found most plausible in the first chapter.

The Psychological Criterion

Many of the problems we ran into regarding both the Body Criterion and the Brain-Based Memory Criterion (BBMC) were due to the difficulties both theories had in explaining our intuitive responses to certain cases, both real and science-fiction. So, for instance, the Body Criterion could not seem to deal with either the Hensel twins case or the *Who is Julia?* case. And while BBMC could handle both of those cases, it could not handle the teleportation and Brain Rejuvenation cases very well.

On the other hand, what seemed to handle all of these cases quite well was the software-based Memory Criterion, according to which personal identity is constituted by memory-relations, where memories are genuine insofar as they are caused by the remembered experience and the memory-information has been preserved reliably across time. The fairly devastating problem for this theory, however, came from the possibility of Divine Duplication. So is there a way we can preserve the advantages of this theory, while avoiding the duplication fiasco?

There just might be. In fact, the most popular contemporary theory of personal identity, until quite recently, has been a robust expansion of the Memory Criterion that simply stipulates away the problem:

> **The Psychological Criterion:** *X at t1 is the same person as Y at t2 if and only if Y is uniquely psychologically continuous with X.*

There are several elements of the view to explain. First, this criterion appeals to psychological continuity, rather than mere continuity of memory. One reason should be fairly obvious: most of us would believe that someone's identity could be preserved through a bout of amnesia, that memory alone isn't the be-all and end-all of personal identity. What the Psychological Criterion does, then, is incorporate several other psychological relations that seem important to identity. There are four relevant relations that might obtain between X at t1 and Y at t2: (a) present-past relations, that is, Y now remembers the actions and experiences of X; (b) present-future relations, that is, X now intends to perform an action that Y later carries out in action; (c) persistence relations, that is, X has a belief, desire, or goal that persists across time to be held by Y; and (d) resemblance relations, that is, X and Y have very similar characters.

X and Y may bear these relations to one another either directly or indirectly. When they hold directly between the two person-stages—as when Y directly remembers an experience of X—call the relation one of *psychological connectedness.* Now across time there may be any degree of connectedness that obtains between two person-stages. So Y at t2 may remember only one experience of X's at t1 and that's it (i.e., Y has no other memories, intentions, beliefs, desires, or character elements of X). This would still mean psychological connectedness obtains between X and Y, albeit of the most minimal degree possible. Alternatively, Y may remember all of X's experiences, as well as carry out X's intentions, believe everything X believed, desire everything X desired, and have a qualitatively similar character to X. Psychological connectedness of course obtains between them, but now to the highest degree possible. And one can imagine all sorts of degrees of connectedness in between that could obtain.

Of course, it's easy to imagine cases in which there are just *no* degrees of connectedness between two stages that are nevertheless stages of one and the same person. Consider the Brave Officer Case from Chapter One again, with a slight twist. Now instead of the eighty-year-old general not remembering any of the experiences of the 10-year-old apple stealer, suppose the retired general (RG) also bears no psychological connectedness of any kind to the apple stealer (AS). Nevertheless, we can still imagine that the RG bears a fairly strong degree of connectedness to the brave officer (BO). If psychological connectedness were what constituted numerical identity, we'd have the same problem on our hands that Locke did with his Memory Criterion, for it would have to imply that the RG both is and isn't identical to the AS: because the RG is connected to the BO, RG would have to be identical to BO, and because the BO is connected to the AS, BO would have to be identical to AS, and so by transitivity RG would have to be identical to AS, and yet because RG is in no way connected to AS, RG would also have to be *not* identical to AS.

We need, then, our account of numerical identity to appeal to overlapping chains of direct psychological connections to resolve this worry. But there is another worry to contend with. Suppose it were possible to transfer a memory trace of one of your experiences into my head. So perhaps I could wake up seeming to remember eating what you had for dinner last night. This would establish a minimal degree of connectedness between us. Would it establish any degree of *identity* between us, though? Clearly not: one connection does not identity make. What people emphasize in embracing a psychological theory of identity is that our identity across time is preserved only by there being an ongoing stream of *lots* of such connections. How many, though? This is a very difficult, if not impossible, question to answer. As Derek Parfit puts it, "[W]e cannot plausibly define precisely what counts as enough [connectedness]."[1] We seem to

---

1   Derek Parfit, *Reasons and Persons* (Oxford: Oxford University Press, 1984), p. 206.

think that one connection isn't sufficient to contribute what matters to preserving identity, that 100% connectedness is definitely sufficient, and that some amount less than 100% is also sufficient (given that we forget things about ourselves and change in various other respects as well). But identifying that amount precisely is just beyond us. So what we may do instead is stay rather vague on this point: with respect to its contribution to identity, what counts is **strong connectedness**, where this will just refer to *whatever* amount of connections we would typically agree is sufficient.[1]

Strong connectedness couldn't be our criterion of numerical identity either, though, for the simple reason that it's not a transitive relation, which any proper criterion of identity must be (the identity relation just being the "=" relation). Strong connectedness, after all, is also a matter of degree. To return to our brave officer example, the RG could be strongly connected to the BO, and the BO could be strongly connected to the AS, and yet the RG might not be strongly connected to the AS. So for strong connectedness to play any significant role in the identity relation, we must appeal to overlapping chains of it. As a result, when Y is strongly connected to an intermediate stage who herself is strongly connected to X, call the relation one of *psychological continuity*.[2]

The Psychological Criterion of numerical identity is thus constituted (in part) by the relation of psychological continuity, which can preserve identity even between very distant, minimally connected or altogether unconnected, stages. This seems plausible, for many of us likely think that one's 80-year-old self is one and the same person as one's 10-year-old self, despite their not being very closely psychologically related. After all, there is still a single *stream of psychology* running from the 10-year-old to the 80-year-old, and it's that stream the Psychological Criterion points to as providing the identity relation.

---

1 In *Reasons and Persons*, Parfit suggests a more precise criterion: "[W]e can claim that there is enough connectedness if the number of direct connections, over any day, is *at least half* the number that hold, over every day, in the lives of nearly every actual person" (p. 206; emphasis in original). But this could at most be a guess.

2 This is just one way it might work, a case in which there's only one link in the chain separating X and Y. For some people, however, there may be many intermediate stages providing many links in the strong connectedness chain.

What about the "uniqueness" clause in the original formulation? It is meant simply to stipulate that there can be no other person-stage at t_2, call him or her Z, who bears the same psychological relations to X that Y does. In other words, the relation between Y and X must hold uniquely in order for them to be the same person. Otherwise, for reasons discussed in the Divine Duplication case, Z and Y would have to be identical with each other, which they could not be. So the Psychological Criterion just eliminates this possibility by fiat: if there's ever a duplication that occurs, identity is lost.

Of course, this move is similar to the efforts of Dave Cohen when he presented Memory Criterion #3 to respond to the Divine Duplication problem, and you may very well think that Weirob's reply to it still applies here: this criterion would make my identity depend on the existence or non-existence of other people, which is absurd. Now on its face, this does seem rather crazy, but some advocates of the Psychological Criterion attempt to mitigate the craziness by making a very clever move to separate out personal identity from what *matters* in personal identity, so if it turns out that what matters in identity is preserved even in duplication cases, the fact that identity itself depends on the existence or non-existence of other people isn't as absurd as it might otherwise be. We will see how this move goes in the next chapter. For now, though, another response to the charge of absurdity might simply be that, while it may have this crazy implication, at least it doesn't yield any straight-out contradictions, as the Body Criterion does, and at least it provides a relation that's relevant and motivated, which neither the Soul Criterion nor the Brain-Based Memory Criterion are. So perhaps the absurdity involved is the least of four evils.

It's also worthwhile to emphasize the main advantage of the view, namely, it seems to account for rational anticipation and self-concern extremely well. If we continue with our assumption that personal identity is what grounds these prudential concerns and attitudes, then the Psychological Criterion makes a great deal of sense, for it looks as if I can rationally anticipate the experiences of, and have special concern for, only my psychological descendants. If some future person won't be connected to my current psychological stream, then it's hard to see how I could rationally anticipate his experiences or have that special type of concern for his well-being.

There might be thought to be yet another advantage of the view: in one of its versions, it allows for the possibility of immortality. Following Parfit, we may distinguish between two versions of the criterion, depending on what one takes to be the appropriate *cause* of psychological continuity. On the **Narrow Psychological Criterion**, psychological continuity must be provided by its normal cause, namely, the persistence of the same brain, in order to preserve identity. Obviously, this version of the view couldn't allow for one to survive the death of one's body. But why think the proper cause of psychological continuity must be the same brain? Isn't it just the preservation of that psychological *stream* that matters? If so, and if that stream could be preserved via a different brain, or via any other method, that should suffice for what we want. This is the version known as the **Wide Psychological Criterion**, according to which psychological continuity provided uniquely by *any* cause is both necessary and sufficient for personal identity. And on this version of the view, one could indeed rationally anticipate the possibility of immortality, for as long as it is possible that God exists, cares, and constructs a person in heaven—but of course only *one* such person—who is psychologically continuous with you on earth, it is thus possible that *you* will survive the death of your body, and so it could be rational for you to look forward to doing so.

Yet another advantage of the view is that it helps to explain ordinary cases of *self*-identification, for how it is that you can typically know who you are when you wake up in the morning without having to check on the status of any substances such as your body or your soul. Instead, your relation to the person who got into your bed the previous night is (typically) evident, available to simple introspection, and it is clearly the sort of psychological relation we have detailed, consisting in memories, intentions-to-be-fulfilled, persistence of beliefs/desires/goals, and similarity of character. And it seems clear that if last night that person had anticipated your experiences this morning, he or she would have been rational to do so given your status as his or her psychological successor. Now there are exceptions, of course, cases in which people are just wrong about what memories or character they have (e.g., the poor deluded fellow who thinks he's Napoleon), and it's possible that the psychological stream to which I have access doesn't hold *uniquely* between me and that person who got into my bed last night. Nevertheless, in ordinary cases our memories are genuine and we haven't been duplicated, so we can at least take it as the default position that what explains ordinary self-identification is the psychological continuity constituting the Psychological Criterion.

The basic thought behind the Psychological Criterion is rather simple: some past or future person cannot be me if that person is not *psychologically* related to me. This implies, then, that I cannot rationally anticipate the experiences of, or have reason for special concern for, those individuals to whom I won't bear that psychological relation. As mentioned earlier, this theory has probably had the most adherents among contemporary philosophers, at least until recently. It has declined in popularity over the past ten or fifteen years, however, because it seems to suffer from two general and serious problems: the **Method of Cases Problem** and the **Essence Problem**.[1]

The *Method of Cases Problem* is fairly straightforward, challenging the method by which people are typically moved to accept the Psychological Criterion. Think, for example, about just some of the far-out cases we have envisioned: teleportation, the *Who is Julia?* brain/body transplant case, the brain rejuvenation scenario, Divine Duplication, and the possibility of waking up as a giant insect. All of these cases pump the general intuition that persons go where their psychologies go, so when we project ourselves into these imaginary scenarios, we're inclined to dismiss the importance of our bodies. As a result, if what matters to personal identity in these sorts of scenarios—where our bodies are prized apart from our psychological streams—is our psychology, then (the thought goes) some form of the Psychological Criterion must be true.

There are at least two problems with this method, though. First, how are we to take these cases up in our imagination? There are two ways, each of which is problematic. On the one hand, we could consider them as scenarios in which we, *as we currently are*—with our current values,

---

1   Several philosophers have discussed these problems, including David DeGrazia, Mark Johnston, Eric Olson, and Kathleen Wilkes.

beliefs, physical construction, and technological know-how—undergo their imagined procedures. But as we currently are, these scenarios are simply physically and technologically impossible! We have neither the knowledge nor the means to bring them about. So we are being asked to think about what *would* happen to us in scenarios that *could not* happen to us, given the way we are and the state of our current understanding. Obviously, then, if something could not happen to me, the question of what *would* happen if it could is a nonstarter. On the other hand, we could consider these scenarios as occurring to creatures for whom they aren't physically and technologically impossible. But such creatures would be very different from us, so different it would be difficult to imagine what their lives could possibly be like. Yet on this way of understanding the method of cases, we would be asked to explain what would happen to *us* in scenarios in which *we would not exist*. Instead, it would be these other sorts of creatures that exist, and how could we have anything enlightening to say about what would happen to them? Thus we have a real problem: the scenarios would be possible only for creatures unlike us, in which case we couldn't draw any stable or illuminating philosophical conclusions from our imaginative consideration of them.

One possible response to this worry, however, is that there seems no reason in principle to think that the creatures who would exist in the technologically-advanced future couldn't be exactly like us in terms of our *values* and *conceptual knowledge*, and that's the similarity that matters for yielding viable results from these thought experiments. In other words, why can't we envision people psychologically just like us who simply happen to have a technology we don't currently have (perhaps we can imagine that aliens have just landed and given us the gift of teleportation)? If so, then why couldn't we learn something from these sorts of thought experiments? Surely we can put ourselves into the shoes of such creatures sufficiently to figure out what we would believe and how we would feel if these things were to happen. And that's all that's required from the method in question.

A second problem, however, is much more insidious: the Method of Cases, goes the charge, can actually yield contradictory intuitions. The objection here is based on a pair of cases first articulated by Bernard

Williams. In the first case, a person with what we'll call Body A will have his entire psychology downloaded to a computer, which will temporarily erase all the contents of his (Body A's) brain. Simultaneously, another person (with Body B) will have his entire psychology downloaded to the same computer, temporarily erasing all the contents of his (Body B's) brain. Then the first set of psychological contents will be uploaded into Body B's brain, and the second set of psychological contents will be uploaded into Body A's brain. What happens to each of the original people? This is, of course, just another version of our now-familiar "body swapping" thought experiments, and it's again one in which it seems clear that in each case the original person got a new body, going where his psychology went. So the person who originally had Body A now has Body B, and the person who originally had Body B now has Body A. Indeed, suppose you were the original person with Body B, and I were the scientist about to do the procedure, and I told you that after the downloading and uploading, I would give $1 million to the person who winds up with Body A and I would torture the person with Body B. You would likely be quite happy about this prospect, which indicates you think that you'd be the one with Body A after the procedure. So far so good.

But now consider a different case. Suppose you're kidnapped and a scientist tells you that he's going to torture you. "But first," he tells you, wild-eyed, "I'm going to erase your memories, beliefs, desires, intentions, and all the rest of your specific psychological characteristics!" "Oh great," you think, "I'll lose my mind, and then I'll be tortured." "But I'm not finished!" exclaims the scientist. "After I delete all your psychological characteristics, I'm going to implant in you all the psychological characteristics of your neighbor, constantly-stoned Fred!" "Wonderful," you now think, "I'll lose my mind, then I'll be deluded, and then I'll be tortured. What a lovely day I have in store." Then suppose the scientist tells you that, while this is going on, he'll be implanting a copy of your psychological characteristics into the brain of your neighbor Fred, and then he'll give Fred $1 million. This will not likely cheer you up. Notice, then, that you believe in such a case that *you* will persist through all these changes. But now the problem should be obvious, for all of this is just a different way to describe the exact same case from above, with you in the position of the Body B person. In that first case, though, your intuitions were likely that identity is preserved entirely by psychological continuity, whereas in this second case, your intuitions are likely that identity is preserved entirely by *physical* continuity. But now we've got seemingly contradictory intuitions *on precisely the same case*. A mere difference in description of a case shouldn't yield contradictory identity-judgments, and yet it does, which should lead us to have serious doubts about the viability of intuitions pumped by the Method of Cases generally.

Various replies have been given to this puzzle over the years, some of them fairly complicated. Given our purposes here, however, we might simply think about two questions. First, what should we think of the last inference given, that the Method of Cases *generally* is in trouble, given the troublesome pair of cases articulated by Williams? On its face, this seems quite a hasty generalization. Perhaps, after all, the Williams example is the only thought experiment, or one of the only few, that yields the contradictory intuitions. Without some more examples of the problem, then, we might still be justified in deploying the method to yield evidence from our intuitions in other cases like teleportation, Divine Duplication, and the *Metamorphosis*-style examples. And these cases still seem to produce intuitions in line with the Psychological Criterion.

A second question to consider, though, is this: how much support does the Method of Cases actually provide to the Psychological Criterion? Suppose, for example, that we take the Williams objection to be decisive against the Method of Cases. Does that mean we should *therefore* abandon the Psychological Criterion? Clearly not, for there are certainly other considerations in its favor. One is its facility in dealing with the self-identification phenomenon. Another is its facility in accounting for rational anticipation generally. And yet another might be its facility in handling certain real life cases, such as that of the Hensel twins. So we shouldn't think that, even if the Method of Cases is to be abandoned (and we have just seen reason to doubt the motivation for such a response), the Psychological Criterion is undermined as a result. One might think that one of its pillars of support has been lost, but that would not prevent the remaining pillars from providing nearly as much support as before.

The *Essence Problem*, on the other hand, discussed briefly in the introduction, is far more troublesome. It is also rather complex. It begins, however, with a seemingly simple question: what am I? This is, of course, a question about *membership in a kind*: to what *kind* do I belong? Now as it turns out, you and I (and all other readers of this book) are *many* kinds of things. Speaking for myself, I am an adult, a professor, an author, a husband, a stepfather, a driver, a voter, a homeowner, and many other things. More generally, I am a human being, an embodied mind, a biological organism, and a person (as are you all). But which of these many kinds in which we're all members is most fundamental? Is there some kind of thing that, if we weren't *that*, we wouldn't exist at all? This is to ask the question of essence: what am I *essentially*? What we are looking for may be called a **basic kind**. And there's a truism among metaphysicians that a determination of the basic kind to which a thing belongs—determining the essence of that thing—yields the necessary *identity conditions* of that thing as well. After all, if some object O has some essential property X, a property without which it couldn't exist, then in order for O to continue to be the same object over time, it must continue to have X.

Here's an illustration of the dependence of identity conditions on a determination of what kind a thing belongs to. Imagine that there's a statue in the park made of a big lump of bronze; after a while, people get tired of it, and the statue gets melted down and the melted-down lump is dumped in a warehouse. Now suppose somebody asks you: "That thing that used to be here in the park—does it still exist?" You might answer, "No, that statue was melted down and doesn't exist any more." Or you might answer, "Yes, that lump of bronze still exists, now gathering dust in a warehouse." Whether the thing that was in the park is identical with the thing now in the warehouse depends on what kind of thing the thing in the park was most fundamentally. If it was fundamentally a statue, then it couldn't be identical to the thing in the warehouse, for it would no longer exist; if it was fundamentally a lump of bronze, then it would be identical to the thing in the warehouse, for its very essence has survived. So which is the *right* way to think of the park-object? That depends on what its essence really is, that is, it depends on what we couldn't conceive it to exist without. Once we figure this out, we'll know the basic kind of the park-object.

So what is my basic kind? What am I essentially? I can very clearly conceive myself as not being an adult, professor, husband, stepfather, driver, voter, and homeowner. Indeed, when I was a young teenager, I was none of these things. So none of these is my basic kind. And the same goes for the rest of you. Perhaps then our basic kind is one of the more general kinds mentioned earlier. But which one?[1]

Advocates of the Psychological Criterion seem to suggest an answer: what I am essentially is a person, and persons are, by definition, psychological beings, which means that my identity across time must necessarily involve the persistence or continuity of my psychology.[2] Here advocates of the Psychological Criterion follow John Locke, who famously defined a person as "a thinking intelligent being, that has reason and reflection, and can consider itself as itself, the same thinking thing, in different times and places; which it does only by that consciousness which is inseparable from thinking, and, as it seems to me, essential to it...."[3]

But is this true? There are actually several serious problems with thinking of ourselves as being essentially persons:

1. *The Fetus Problem.* If what I am essentially is a person, a psychological being, then how can we make sense of the following common thought: "I was once a fetus"? Surely this is coherent. For instance, suppose your

---

1   Incidentally, for the sake of argument here, we are sharing in the assumption of most philosophers working on personal identity today that every concrete object that exists belongs most fundamentally to one and only one kind, a kind which provides the object's identity conditions across time. This isn't a universal assumption, though, and there are alternatives to it one should keep in mind. One alternative is the view that certain objects simply don't have a fundamental essence. Another alternative is the view that an object's essence doesn't provide its identity conditions, or at least the identity conditions that matter. Keep these alternatives in mind as we proceed.
2   A *person* is being thought of here as necessarily having a psychology, and not merely as a human organism, contrasted with other organisms. In this rather special technical use of the word, a live human organism lacking all higher brain functions and permanently unconscious, thus without any psychology, wouldn't be a *person*.
3   John Locke, "Of Identity and Diversity," in John Perry, ed., *Personal Identity* (Berkeley, CA: University of California Press, 1975), p. 39.

mother still has the photo from her sonogram, and as you see it, you say, "Wow, that was me?" To take another instance, suppose you had fetal alcohol syndrome, having certain psychological difficulties as a result of your mother's drinking while she was pregnant. Wouldn't it be correct to say that *you* had been damaged while in the womb, and that perhaps you are now owed some sort of compensation because you were harmed as a fetus? Nevertheless, if you are essentially a psychological being, and a fetus (especially prior to developing a brain) is not, then you simply could not have been a fetus. But this seems incorrect, given our natural and common way of talking. Just as it is clear that I existed prior to being an adult, so too it seems clear that I existed prior to being a person.

2. *The PVS Problem.* Suppose that you get into a terrible accident that destroys your brain's capacity for consciousness, while leaving the brain stem intact, resulting in your body's being in a permanent vegetative state (PVS) in the hospital, permanently unconscious but with the capacity for spontaneous breathing, a heartbeat, and other biological functioning. Isn't the correct description that *you* are the one in the PVS? Certainly this is what your devastated parents, spouse, and friends would think as they continued to visit that hospital room. Nevertheless, there seems no way to render this way of thinking coherent if you are essentially a person, for you could not be this individual in the PVS, given its lack of psychology: if the individual in the PVS isn't a psychological being, then this individual isn't a person, and if this individual isn't a person, then this individual can't be you. But again, this seems to be the wrong answer. Just as it is clear that I will continue to exist after retiring as a professor, so too it seems clear that I will continue to exist after going into a PVS.

3. *The Person/Animal Problem.* Suppose I'm essentially a person, a psychological being. When did I come into existence? Presumably, I appeared when my psychological motor started running, likely at the late fetus/early infant stage. What, then, happened to that pre-psychological organism, that human animal? Did it die? If so, what happened to its remains? Can there be death without any remains? Perhaps, then, that organism just disappeared. Nevertheless, this is quite unlikely; organisms don't just disappear, as far as we know. Perhaps, then, that organism (the human animal) still exists, its existence somehow overlapping with mine (the person). But then when

looking at my body you would see two distinct beings, the human animal and the person. Indeed, these would be two wholly distinct *substances*. This would be, at the least, quite odd.

A similar problem attaches to the other end of the life spectrum. If I am a person, when do I go *out of* existence? It would seem that when my consciousness ends, so do I. But then does the PVS patient *begin* to exist at my (the person's) death? This seems unlikely. After all, that patient is a biological organism, and biological organisms are typically brought into existence by some kind of birthing process, whereas there just is no such process here. Did it then simply *appear*? Again, that is quite unlikely: organisms neither simply appear nor disappear. Perhaps, then, it was in existence from the fetal stage, and thus overlapped with me over the course of my life. But then, once more, when looking at my body now you'd be seeing two distinct substances, the animal and the person, which would be very strange.

These are just some of the problems that have motivated the development of a very different thesis about our essence, and thus a very different thesis about our identity across time.

The Biological Criterion

The alternative view is that we are essentially *human animals,* specific types of biological organisms. While we are persons during much of our lives, we are not *essentially* persons. Instead, personhood is just one stage we animals live through, one in a series of non-basic kinds to which we temporarily belong. Other non-basic kinds include fetus, infant, toddler, adolescent, teenager, adult, senior citizen, and, perhaps the kinds of the senile, the demented, or the PVS. Further, if we are essentially animals—biological creatures—then this fact yields its own criterion of personal identity:

> **The Biological Criterion**: *If X is a person at t₁, and Y exists at any other time, then X=Y if and only if Y's biological organism is continuous with X's biological organism.*

There are some important features of this criterion worth discussing. First, you will no doubt have noticed a key difference between this formulation and our previous criteria, namely, this one is broader. In all of our previous formulations, the criterion of personal identity told us what makes X and Y the same *person*. The current criterion, however, purports to tell us what makes something that is a person at one time (X) the same *thing* as a Y that may or may not be a person at a different time. This is simply because advocates of the Biological Criterion believe that what I am essentially was not always, and may not always remain, a person, so in order to capture my identity conditions across time, we should not restrict the class of those things to which I might be identical only to the class of persons. I could, after all, be one and the same thing as my future PVS stage. Of course, no one likes to think of himself or herself as a *thing*, so many advocates of the Biological Criterion use the term *individual* instead, rendering an alternative formulation of the criterion as follows: X *(a person) at t1 is the same individual as Y at any other time if and only if Y's biological organism is continuous with X's biological organism.* I will use these two formulations interchangeably throughout the book.

The second thing to notice is that this criterion is tracking the *continuity* of organisms. What this means is fairly simple: one organism is continuous with another just in case the life-sustaining functions of the former organism are inherited by—they continue on in—the latter organism. Another way to think of the continuity involved here is that it just describes the relation that obtains when a biological organism is, in principle, uniquely traceable across space-time.

Third, while it may seem as if the Biological Criterion is just a version of the Body Criterion with more syllables, there is actually a subtle but important difference between the two. As Eric Olson has explained, while it seems perfectly clear what a biological organism is, it is actually surprisingly unclear just what a human body is. Indeed, what exactly is your body? There are two possibilities: either (a) your body is the material object that you can feel in some direct way and are able to move just by willing it, or (b) your body is just whatever it is that we're talking about when we attribute certain physical, spatial, or time-based (temporal) properties to you in our ordinary ways of speaking.

On the first possibility, whatever it is you can feel and move directly is your body. But there are all sorts of problems with this account. For one thing, those who are paralyzed cannot feel or move what are still certainly parts of their bodies. Relatedly, I cannot move various internal organs, like my liver, at will. Does that mean that my liver is not part of my body? In a different vein, I can move my right foot directly. Does that mean my right foot is my body? Or suppose I'm holding a pencil in my hand. When I write something down, don't I move the pencil directly? Does that mean it's my body, or perhaps just part of my body? Finally, what do we say about those with prosthetic limbs? Are those limbs included under the concept of "my body"?

On the second possibility, we carve out the concept of your body in terms of ordinary ascriptions of physical properties to you. So when we say, "You're tall," we're ascribing the property of tallness to you, and insofar as that's a physical property, whatever it is that bears that property *just is* your body. Similarly, when we ascribe certain spatio-temporal properties to you, for example, "I saw you at the gun show playing with the bazookas yesterday," then whatever it is that took up space at that particular time and place just is your body. Ultimately, then, whatever has *all* the physical and spatio-temporal traits we could ordinarily attribute to you is what counts as your body. The problem here is that this definition assumes exactly what is in question here—that I am my body—because it renders all physical and spatio-temporal properties attributable to *me* properties of my body. But there are some people who disagree, who think that I am distinct from my body. If they are right, then there would actually be *two* bearers of the attributed physical and spatio-temporal properties: my body and me. By insisting there's only one such bearer, however, this second attempt to provide a clear conception of "human body" also assumes what's at issue, and so fails as well.

What all this means, therefore, is that the concept of a "human body" is simply too unclear to do any real work for us as part of a criterion of personal identity. As it turns out, then, Weirob was relying on an unusable concept of who (or what) she was. The advocate of the Biological Criterion, however, has no such worries. This criterion provides meaningful persistence conditions for me across time in virtue of my being an *animal*, not a human body, and what counts for our purposes as an animal, as a living human organism, is easily conceptualized as falling under a commonsense biological category. (Although we will see in the chapters to come that the boundaries of what's included under the concept of a human organism are less clear-cut than the advocates of the Biological Criterion would have us believe.)

So much for the details of the Biological Criterion itself. Why should we believe it? There are several considerations in its favor, some of which we have already run across. We will sometimes put these in terms of its relation to its chief rival, the Psychological Criterion:

1. *The Biological Criterion seems to provide a more plausible story about our essence than the Psychological Criterion.* The Psychological Criterion, remember, seems to imply that we are essentially persons, but if that's the case then it's very difficult to make sense of perfectly ordinary ways of talking, like "I was a fetus," and "If I go into a PVS...," and it's also difficult to make sense more generally of the relation between persons and their animal organisms. The Biological Criterion, however, easily handles these worries, for it identifies us as essentially animals, in which case I— this individual that is now in its "person-phase"—was indeed a fetus, could eventually be in a PVS, and my animal organism and I are simply one and the same thing.

2. *The Biological Criterion allows there to be a tight and direct connection between the metaphysical criterion of identity and the epistemological criterion of identity (perhaps even more so than the Psychological Criterion).* Recall the distinction between these two types of criteria from the Introduction. A metaphysical criterion of identity will tell us what makes X and Y identical. An epistemological criterion of identity will tell us how we can identify whether or not X and Y are identical. Many people think, then, that it would be good to have a metaphysical criterion of identity that would make it easy to identify when that criterion has been met in the real world, and the

Biological Criterion seems tailor-made to provide just this. After all, how is it that we typically reidentify others, identifying whether or not the person we're dealing with now is the same person as the one we dealt with earlier? By recognizing their human organisms. True, we sometimes reidentify people without seeing or hearing them (via e-mail, say), but here it might be thought that what we're doing is reidentifying their organisms *indirectly*. The Psychological Criterion, on the other hand, might be thought to have more difficulty in this arena, for we cannot reidentify streams of psychology directly at all (I can't somehow *see* your psychology), nor does it seem as if we are even doing so indirectly sometimes: when I see your face across a crowded place, I know it's you, without making any further inferences about your psychology. In this respect, at least, the Psychological Criterion may be as irrelevant as the Soul Criterion.

3. *The Biological Criterion is broader and more inclusive than the Psychological Criterion, providing persistence conditions for human animals that are not, or won't be, persons.* Suppose an anencephalic[1] infant is born without a cerebrum, and this infant manages to live for a month. Surely the month-old anencephalic infant is the same individual as that just born anencephalic infant, even though neither possesses (or will ever possess) the capacity for consciousness. The Psychological Criterion must thus remain silent about the persistence conditions for these human infants, whereas the Biological Criterion includes them as *one of us*, human animals, whose persistence conditions are the same for members of that group with or without a psychology. Insofar as we are inclined to think that, at least with respect to identity, the cases of humans with and without the capacity for consciousness should be treated alike, the Biological Criterion has a distinct advantage over the Psychological Criterion.

There look to be some real advantages to the Biological Criterion. However, recall that the Psychological Criterion had its own set of advantages as well, so in order to engage in a fair comparison of the two views,

---

1   *Anencephaly* is lack of a major portion of the brain, skull, and scalp, resulting from improper fetal development. The lack of a forebrain means that the child will be permanently without any conscious functions.

we need to have before us some of the main *problems* associated with the Biological Criterion.

1. *The Conjoined Twins Case.* One of the real problems for the Body Criterion, recall, was the case of the Hensel twins, who seem to have one body but are clearly two persons. If what makes X and Y the same person is their having the same body, and Brittany and Abigail have the same body, then they would have to be the same person, according to the Body Criterion, which is obviously false. Wouldn't the same be true of the Biological Criterion, however? Wouldn't Brittany and Abigail be the same human organism, which would imply that they are identical with each other? Not necessarily. David DeGrazia endorses the possibility that theirs could be a rare case of two *overlapping* organisms. After all, they (mostly) have two distinct sets of organs above the waist, that is, they each have their own hearts, brains, stomachs, and so forth. And insofar as these organs are what typically provide the regulatory and sustaining aspects of living organisms, Brittany and Abigail can easily be thought of as two organisms that overlap to some extent.

This is too quick, however, for we might just as easily point to other features of the Hensel twins that strongly suggest that they are *one* organism. For example, they have a single skin, a single liver, a single urinary tract, a single blood stream, a single immune system, and a single reproductive system. Furthermore, even their distinct sets of organs function together in the integrated way distinctive of living organisms, such that if one sister's set of distinct organs were to fail, the other sister's organs would also fail immediately thereafter. But if we think of the death of organisms as consisting in the irreversible cessation of the integrated functioning of its organs, then there would be just one death here, the death of a single organism.

Obviously, the answer here depends on how we define "organism," and this is a matter of some controversy. Now there are some cases of conjoined twins where DeGrazia's interpretation is clearly correct. The original "Siamese" twins, Eng and Chang Bunker, were joined at the chest by a five-inch-wide band of flesh (and their livers, while individually complete, were also fused). In such a case, the thought that they were distinct organisms that very slightly overlapped is a natural one. But suppose there were a case at the opposite end of the conjoined spectrum, one in which there were two heads on one body, but even the heads were partially fused, having one brain stem, say, but having two distinct faces—two eyes, noses, and mouths—and two distinct centers and streams of consciousness (given distinct cerebrums). The interpretation of two distinct but overlapping organisms would become much harder to maintain in such a case. Individuating organisms by pointing to distinct cardiopulmonary regulatory systems, say, something that could work to render the Hensel twins distinct organisms, wouldn't work in this case, given that there would be only one heart and one set of lungs. And individuating the organisms in virtue of their autonomic control centers wouldn't work here either, given that these twins would share a single brain-stem. Indeed, it's difficult to think of any non-arbitrary way to individuate these (hypothetical) twins as distinct organisms.

When faced with such a case, DeGrazia (a defender of the Biological Criterion) holds out the possibility that this could be a case akin to Multiple Personality Disorder (MPD), in which there is indeed just one organism, but one with two distinct centers of consciousness. This seems too much of a stretch, however. For one thing, the centers of consciousness could be simultaneously engaged and each could be continually aware of the other, which is not the case for most of those with MPD. But aside from the analogy to MPD, DeGrazia's view would imply that here we would *not* have two individuals—he still maintains the one-to-one correlation between organisms and individuals—while in the Hensel twins case we *would* have two individuals (overlapping organisms). But surely what leads us to believe the Hensel twins are both distinct persons *and* distinct individuals—their communication, their disagreements, their conscious coordination, their insistence on individuality, their independent ways of thinking—all of these features could be present as well in the more extreme case. It is hard to believe, then, that if the Hensel twins would be distinct individuals, our imagined extreme conjoined twins would not be as well.

2. *The Corpse Problem.* When I die, I will leave behind a corpse. But what is that corpse's relation to me, the human animal? Upon my death,

there will still be a physical continuity between me and my dead body, but doesn't the Biological Criterion then imply that I will *be* that dead body, that it will be the same individual as me? What is the advocate of the view to say here?

There are generally three replies one might give. First, one could embrace the implication, and affirm that I will indeed be that corpse, that that's what *I* will be at some point in the future. But although some writers have embraced this implication, it seems wildly implausible: surely that corpse will not be *me*. Indeed, our ordinary practices strongly support the intuition that, upon our deaths, *we are no more*. Thus the grieving and mourning that takes place when our loved ones die. If we thought they still existed among us, such behavior would be odd, if not downright incoherent. To remain plausible, then, the Biological Criterion must accept that I go out of existence with the death of my biological organism. But if I am not my corpse, then it must be a numerically distinct object from me.

This fact leaves the advocate of the Biological Criterion with two ways of dealing with the issue: (a) when I—the human animal—cease to exist at death, my corpse—a distinct individual object—pops into existence; or (b) my corpse-to-be, a distinct individual object, has existed all along, coinciding in space-time with my living biological organism. The latter option is independently quite implausible, but even worse, it undermines one of the main motivations for the Biological Criterion in the first place, namely, to avoid the problematic implication of the Psychological Criterion that persons and human animals are both numerically distinct objects but also both wholly coincide. If option (b) were taken, though, the Biological Criterion would be in precisely the same jam, having to make sense of the bizarre fact that seated in my chair at this moment are two numerically distinct objects, me (a human animal) and my corpse-to-be (which would suddenly make things very creepy).

To avoid this implication, then, the best bet for the advocate of the Biological Criterion is to opt for (a), that when I cease to exist, my corpse then pops into existence. And at first glance, it does seem we are talking about very different sorts of objects: the animal I am is alive, its various organs are functionally integrated, it uses resources from its environment to maintain a stable regularity, thus preserving its form over time, and so on. My corpse, on the other hand, will have non-functioning organs, will make use of no environmental energy for self-sustenance, and will eventually lose its form more or less entirely over time. So why not think that the corpse comes into existence upon my exit?

One reason to be hesitant about such an answer, though, comes from the worry that we may not have a firm grip on what constitutes the death of an organism, and this uncertainty will carry over into uncertainty about *when* the corpse comes into existence. It would be rather odd, though, that we would have such trouble marking the difference between two such categorically, qualitatively, and numerically distinct objects. A further worry is that the definition of death might wind up being a matter of pure stipulation. But surely a matter of metaphysical reality—the coming-into-existence and going-out-of-existence of numerically distinct objects—couldn't depend on convention in this way.

3. *The Transplant Intuition.* Regardless of the considerations in favor of the Biological Criterion, our intuition in the *Who is Julia?* case, that Julia is the survivor in Mary Frances's old body, likely remains strong. This intuition cuts sharply against the Biological Criterion, however, for that criterion maintains, along with Weirob, that as long as Mary Frances's regulatory biological mechanisms remain in place in her original body the individual that is Mary Frances remains as well, even if that organism gets a new brain (or cerebrum, which is all that's needed to make the point). So the survivor is a deluded Mary Frances, someone who *thinks* she's Julia, but is sadly mistaken.

This implication is unlikely to sit well with many of us, though. After all, we typically identify with our psychologies, thinking that we are essentially psychological creatures, and if our brains underlie that psychology, then we go where our brains (or cerebrums) go. It is difficult to believe, then, that if our cerebrum were removed, and replaced with someone else's, that *we* would somehow remain, and remain permanently deluded. That individual, after all, would have no psychological connection to us whatsoever, and this worry leads us to our final problem with the Biological Criterion.

4. *The Prudential Concerns Problem*. Remember how we started all of this off: we wanted to know what the rational grounds for anticipation or special concern are. We have been assuming that personal identity is at the very least a necessary condition of rational anticipation and special concern: I can't rationally anticipate some future person's experiences or have that special sort of *self*-concern unless he will be me. But we might plausibly think that what we wanted to know assumed something even stronger, namely, that identity is a *sufficient* condition of both rational anticipation and self-concern, that is, my identity with some future person is what in fact provides me with sufficient reason both to anticipate his experiences and have special concern for his well-being.

If we go with this stronger assumption, though, the Biological Criterion fails, for it can't be solely in virtue of the fact that he is my biological continuer that I have a reason to anticipate, say, some future person's experiences. To see why, simply consider the case in which I fall into a PVS. Would I have any reason whatsoever—let alone a sufficient reason—to anticipate this biological continuer's experiences? Surely not, for the simple reason that he will be incapable of undergoing any experiences for me to anticipate! Similarly, we might hold that I have no reason to have any sort of special concern for the well-being of my PVS descendant, given that, because he would lack the capacity for conscious experiences, he would lack the capacity for well-being as well. The stronger sufficiency assumption, then, favors the Psychological Criterion, for it maintains that any future person who is me will at least be my psychological descendant, and so will at least be a conscious experiencer.

One reply here would simply be to deny the sufficiency assumption. Perhaps it's a mistake to assume that identity is sufficient for making anticipation rational. After all, it may not be rational for me to anticipate the experiences of my 90-year-old self (assuming I live that long!), insofar as he's likely to be *very* different psychologically from me, despite the fact that he'll still be psychologically continuous with me. Nevertheless, we can capture what seems important about the sufficiency assumption, without denying this claim about my 90-year-old self, by making a crucial distinction between what's rationally *required* and what's rationally *permissible*.

Surely one is not rationally required to anticipate the experiences of one's 90-year-old self; indeed, one may not be rationally required to anticipate the experiences of *any* of one's futures selves. But certainly it is rationally *permissible* to do so, that is, it is *not irrational* to do so. The sufficiency assumption, then, could simply be the claim that personal identity is what makes anticipation and special concern rationally permissible. And if this is the case, then the Biological Criterion still fails the test, for it can't be solely in virtue of some future individual's being biologically continuous with me that it is suddenly rationally permissible for me to anticipate his experiences. Something more is needed, and that something more must be psychological in nature.

Nevertheless, even if we were to deny the sufficiency assumption, we've still got the necessity assumption to deal with, namely, the claim that personal identity is *necessary* for rational anticipation and special concern. And with respect to even this assumption the Biological Criterion comes up short, in light of the transplant cases. Suppose Julia knew her cerebrum were going to be transplanted into Mary Frances's body, and that the resulting person would be exactly similar to Julia psychologically. Many of us would think it would be perfectly rational for Julia to anticipate the experiences of, and have special concern for, the survivor. If we persist in assuming personal identity is necessary for that activity, though, only the Psychological Criterion passes this test; the Biological Criterion has to maintain that the survivor is Mary Frances, and so it would not be rational for Julia to anticipate *anyone's* experiences, say, for she would be dead. But again, this will seem wrongheaded to many of us.

Summary

We are left, then, with several reasons for and against both of the main theories of personal identity, and these reasons are summarized in the following chart:

	THE PSYCHOLOGICAL CRITERION	THE BIOLOGICAL CRITERION
CONSIDERATIONS IN FAVOR	• Does well in "intuition pump" science fiction cases • Accounts for self-identification very well • Explains the rationality of anticipation	• Incorporates the most plausible account of our essence • Accounts for third-person reidentification very well • Includes a plausible story about the identity conditions of non-person humans (e.g., anencephalic infants, fetuses, PVS patients)
CONSIDERATIONS AGAINST	• The Method of Cases problem • The Essence Problem (which includes the Fetus Problem, the PVS Problem, and the Person/Animal Problem)	• The Conjoined Twins case • The Corpse Problem • Can't account very well for the Transplant Intuition • Can't account very well for rational anticipation

So which side wins? This is obviously not an easy call, for there are powerful considerations both in favor of, and against, each theory. And we must not make the mistake of thinking that, for example, because the Biological Criterion has more bullet points against it than the Psychological Criterion does, it is somehow worse off, for while these are indeed real problems for the theory, the Essence Problem is a far more serious, or weighty, worry for the Psychological Criterion than any of these. And while it may also seem as if its inability to account well for rational anticipation counts as a devastating blow to the Biological Criterion, we cannot forget that one might be interested in the issue of personal identity *independently* from its relation to our practical concerns—one might think of it solely as an interesting puzzle in metaphysics—and so from that perspective this so-called problem may be no problem at all (more on this point in the final chapter). But at any rate, as things stand it actually seems as if the *sets* of problems for each theory are roughly equal in seriousness.

It is quite unclear, then, just how one side might convince the other to join its ranks. But if we cannot determine which theory of personal identity is correct, how can we determine the right answer to our identity-related ethical questions? After all, if we apply the Psychological Criterion to the problem of abortion, say, we are likely to get a very different answer from what we'd get if we applied the Biological Criterion. So what shall we do?

There are three general options. First, we might devote much more energy than we have to explore possible defenses against the objections raised against one of these theories. This is the work that many advocates of each theory have recently undertaken. The idea is to show how the objections raised against the *other* side's theory are insurmountable, while the objections raised against *one's own* theory are, well, surmountable. Because both sides have extremely smart advocates, though, we might be warranted in a persisting skepticism that the standoff will end via this method anytime soon.

A second option is to gain additional data about the viability of each theory by seeing how plausible its implications are for all of our practical concerns, both prudential and moral. Up until now, we have been considering how the views account for only our prudential concerns, but it may be that once we understand their implications for our moral concerns—concerns having to do with abortion, advanced directives, moral responsibility, compensation, and so forth—we will come to see that one theory is clearly superior to the other (at least in the way it accounts for such concerns). This is the strategy we will employ in Part B of the book, in fact. Of course, there are some genuine problems with this approach as well—not the least of which is that the correct criterion of personal identity may not answer to our practical concerns at all!—but we will save discussion of these concerns for the final chapter.

A third option is to explore an entirely different path, to find a new alternative to both theories. This is to recognize the standoff and, in a way, to try to move beyond it, to show that there is still something important to say about how identity relates to our practical concerns that simply doesn't depend on the standard criteria. This is a rather radical approach to the issue, of course, but it may be the best way in which to proceed in light of our current standoff. At the very least, we need to consider whether or not it is possible to find such an alternative. This, then, is what we will attempt to do in our next chapter.

WORKS CITED OR REFERENCED IN THIS CHAPTER

DeGrazia, David. *Human Identity and Bioethics*. Cambridge: Cambridge University Press, 2005.

Johnston, Mark. "Human Beings." *Journal of Philosophy* 84 (1987): 59-83.

——. "Reasons and Reductionism." *The Philosophical Review* 101 (1992): 589-618.

Locke, John. "Of Identity and Diversity." In *Personal Identity*, ed. John Perry. Berkeley, CA: University of California Press, 1975, pp. 33-52.

Olson, Eric T. *The Human Animal*. Oxford: Oxford University Press, 1997.

Wilkes, Kathleen. *Real People*. Oxford: Oxford University Press, 1988.

Williams, Bernard. "The Self and the Future." In *Problems of the Self.* Cambridge: Cambridge University Press, 1973, pp. 46-63.

CHAPTER THREE

Alternative Approaches

In this chapter, we consider two fairly radical alternatives to the standard approach to articulating the relation between personal identity and our practical concerns explored in the last chapter. There we were left with a kind of standoff: both the Biological Criterion and the Psychological Criterion have serious advantages and serious disadvantages, and it's hard to know which one is more plausible (or if *either* is all that plausible) as a result. In light of this sort of standoff, various authors have been motivated to propose intriguing new possibilities for understanding the relation between identity and ethics. To this point, we have been assuming, along with the advocates of the standard approaches, that what matters to our practical concerns is some criterion of numerical identity. The first alternative we will discuss in this chapter, however, denies that *numerical* identity is what matters to our practical concerns, whereas the second alternative we will discuss denies that *identity* is what matters at all.

Narrative Identity

To this point we have been trying to come up with a workable criterion of numerical identity, an account of what makes a person at one time identical to some person or individual at some other time. This is because, quite simply, many advocates of the standard approaches have assumed that numerical identity is the only sort of identity relevant to our practical concerns. As it turns out, though, there is another sort of "identity" that may be what's actually important here, a more everyday sense of the term familiar from cases in which someone undergoes an "identity crisis." More generally, this alternative sort of identity has to do with what makes us *who we really are*. Marya Schechtman has been the most articulate in developing what has often been an unclearly-presented position, so in laying out the view we will (mostly) follow in her footsteps.

To understand the sense of identity in question, consider a few cases. Suppose Kyle has been out of college for a few years. He was an English major, but though he enjoyed it, he never considered going on to graduate school to study more of it. After graduation, he returned home to live with his parents, and he has since bounced around from low-paying job to low-paying job. He parties on the weekends, sleeps in late during the day, goes to his job (when he has one), and plays a little music occasionally on his guitar. His parents have grown very frustrated with him, and Kyle is feeling the pressure to "do something" with his life, but he just doesn't know what that "something" is or should be.

Consider next Jack, a cop for ten years. Over the past year, sparked by a new love interest, he's been studying Buddhism, and he has come to consider himself to be a fledgling Buddhist. More and more, though, he sees a conflict between his job and his new religious beliefs. Being a police officer may require him to shoot someone in the line of duty, whereas his Buddhism requires him to be a pacifist, never to react with violence to the deeds of others. He is growing more and more concerned over this conflict (and other conflicts, including those about the various attitudes he should take to other people), and he is coming to the realization that only one of these lives can be lived honestly and wholeheartedly. So which is he really, he wonders, a cop or a Buddhist?

Consider finally Sarah, for many years a miserable and pitiful person. She was an alcoholic and a misanthrope, getting fired repeatedly for her hateful comments or her absenteeism, spiraling ever deeper into debt and, for a little while, homelessness. One day she hit rock bottom, finding herself broke and alone in an alley, mysterious bruises on her arms and face, and a crushing hangover. "That's it," she thinks, "This can't be who I am." She contacts a relative, who agrees to take her in on the condition that she embark on a twelve-step program, which Sarah is more than willing to do. She thus starts a painful program of recovery, at the same time trying to work on her social skills, with the intention of being sober and the owner of a new life in ten years. After much hard work, she finds herself ten years down the line as a sober, industrious, and well-liked person. In a quiet moment one day she reflects back on her former life and thinks to herself with a kind of wonder, "Wow, I really did it!"

What we have seen here are three different arenas in which a non-numerical sense of identity is in play. Kyle simply doesn't know who he is. He feels, in a way, unformed as a person, without any real identity, and there simply seems to be no obvious direction for him to go to find one. Jack, on the other hand, also doesn't know who he is, but his bafflement isn't due to having no direction; instead, it's due to having too many directions. His commitments are in tension, pulling him down two different and exclusive paths, and as he stands at the point of their divergence, he's uncertain which way he'll go. Sarah, finally, was taking one horrific path with her life but managed to make the radical decision to leave it for another. She was miserable being who she was, and she finally became determined that she was not going to be the type of person living that kind of life, and so she embarked on a series of changes that would make her into the type of person she could eventually be happy being.

These scenarios bring out the sense of identity at issue, which responds to what is known as the *characterization* question. To understand this question, consider the question our previous theorists have been attempting to answer: "What makes X identical to Y?" This is what's known as the *reidentification* question: it asks about the conditions under which some X at one point in time is properly reidentified as Y at some other time. The answer, then, must be given in terms of numerical identity, which is about the relation something has only to itself. By contrast, the characterization question is about the relation one has to various experiences, actions, and psychological characteristics. In other words, 'the characterization question asks about what makes some psychological characteristic, say—a desire, care, commitment, belief, project, goal, and so forth—*mine*, a feature of the real me. So instead of asking about the conditions under which an individual at some other time is one and the same individual as me, it asks about the conditions under which various psychological characteristics, experiences, and actions are *properly attributable* to the real me.

According to Schechtman, the characterization question is more appropriate to finding a relation between identity and ethics than is the reidentification question. One reason we might think this stems from recognizing the difficulties our theories of numerical identity have repeatedly run into when applied to our practical concerns. But another is the seemingly natural fit between the characterization question and those practical concerns. In seeking to account for anticipation, we seem to be wondering, "What makes those expected future experiences *mine*?" In seeking to account for self-concern, we seem to be wondering, "What makes those future states I'm specially concerned about *mine*?" And similarly with questions of responsibility and compensation: "What makes those actions for which I'm responsible—or those burdens for which I'm to be compensated—*mine*?" Consequently, given that these aren't questions demanding any sort of reidentification, and given that they seem to be more naturally and closely connected to our person-related practical concerns, we may well have been asking the wrong question all along. What we should have been asking, it seems, was the characterization question.

What is it, then, that makes some actions, experiences, or psychological characteristics mine? Answering this question does not require an appeal to a criterion of numerical identity. Instead, according to advocates of this approach, what it requires is an appeal to the following:

The Narrative Identity Criterion: *what makes an action, experience, or psychological characteristic properly attributable to some person (and thus a proper part of his/her identity) is its correct incorporation into the self-told story of his/her life.*

This answer to the characterization question points to a process by which we *constitute* ourselves, and it involves telling ourselves a story about our lives, about where we've been and where we're going. It is via this narrative process that our identity is developed, maintained, shaped, and changed, and it involves several aspects worth discussing.

1. *Narrative identity is about what unifies a set of experiences into the life of a single person.* Instead of being about reidentification or the numerical identity relation, narrative identity is explicitly about the way in which the life of a subject of experiences becomes unified as the life of a genuine *person*, that is, it's about how the experience some five-year-old has of getting her first haircut becomes woven together with the experience an 80-year-old has of putting on a wig for the first time, such that both experiences *become* experiences that are part of the same person's life. Insofar as narrative identity is about persons, then, it privileges psychology over biology, that is, it renders the question of our essential nature—and thus the Biological Criterion—practically moot; this is explicitly a view about a certain sort of identity for a certain sort of creature, namely, *persons*. But insofar as it is also not about numerical identity, narrative identity is unconcerned with discovering the relation that makes a person at one time identical to a person at a later time at all, so it renders the Psychological Criterion practically moot as well.

2. *What renders certain experiences as unified into the life of a person is precisely the narrative that person constructs about those experiences that shapes them into that of one life.* This is a bit tricky, but the general idea is this. Experiences are not experiences *of a person* until and unless they have been incorporated into that person's life via some narrative structure, that is, until and unless they have been *appropriated* by the person as his or her own. This is, in part, because such experiences are simply meaningless unless viewed both in relation to other experiences and to the person having them. To take a simple example, suppose I have dinner with my wife. This experience is meaningless considered as some isolated event: try thinking of it as simply an image, a snapshot, of a table, food, and a woman on one side of the table. But that woman *means something* to me, as may the restaurant and the food, and what I do in thinking

back to that night is connect those events and people as one night in my life story: I remember driving to the restaurant, having a fight with my wife on the way, making up halfway through dinner (thus the explanation for that sideways smile on her face), enjoying the jambalaya so much I bought a Cajun cookbook later, and so forth and so on. The various events that made up that evening become intertwined with one another, and then with other strands of my life, via my act of narration. And something similar goes for future events: insofar as I anticipate experiencing some event, I weave it into the story of my life. If there's some party I'm looking forward to on Friday night, I "see myself" there—I may even rehearse in my head certain things I want to say to some people—and insofar as I do so I incorporate those future experiences into my life, that is, I claim them *as my own.*

3. *What constrains the incorporation of various experiences is whether they "fit together" into one's narrative, and whether they approximate reality.* First, the narrative of one's life has to be coherent; it has to make sense as a narrative. If one can't articulate some experiences or events as coherently part of one's life story, then they aren't any meaningful part of that story. Suppose, for instance, someone were to give you the following account of some past event: "I was a loving, compassionate husband, so I would hit my wife on a daily basis." This story simply makes no sense. The motives of such an individual would be unintelligible if what he says actually took place. Consequently, some aspect of the narrative must be revised: either the events in question never happened, or the person's description of who he was is just wrong.

Relatedly, one can't just make up any old story one would like to connect the various experiences that have occurred; instead, there must be some significant correspondence between the narrative one constructs and reality. It may somehow make sense for me, for example, to weave Napoleon's experiences into my own life. It may help to explain my current monomania, say, if I were to include as part of my life story that I had been the general of many victorious battles against various countries in Europe. But this simply won't be accurate or telling as part of a genuine life narrative—indeed, it is the kind of thing the mentally ill do.

Of course, these constraints will be met by degrees in actual practice: some narratives will simply be more coherent than others, some narratives will be more fractured than others. But (it's been argued) we should think of the ideal of perfect intelligibility as the aspect of our narratives to strive for, despite its probably being unattainable. What we want is that our life stories make as much sense as possible, and to that end we'll take what we can get. And the more the various elements of our lives fit together, the more defined we are as characters, and the more stable, sharp, and coherent are our narrative identities.

4. *Narrative identity presupposes numerical identity.* This is an important point. To adopt an account of narrative identity is not to suggest that there is no such thing as numerical identity, or that there is no point to investigating its nature, or that we as persons aren't also individuals with persisting numerical identities. Instead, narrative identity assumes the presence of numerical identity, and what its advocates maintain is just that narrative identity *accounts for our practical concerns* in a way numerical identity cannot. The real relation between identity and ethics, they claim, is that between *narrative* identity and ethics.

There are two points here. First, just as in fiction, a person's narrative is senseless unless it is the narrative of *one and the same* individual. So narrative identity is about what unifies the various actions and experiences of one and the same subject of experience into the life of a genuine person. But narrative identity is actually neutral between competing accounts of the numerical identity of that subject of experiences. In other words, the story we have told about narrative identity is perfectly compatible with the truth of either the Psychological Criterion or the Biological Criterion: what makes certain psychological elements mine, part of my ongoing biography as a person, may obtain regardless of whether or not what makes me the same individual across time is biological or psychological continuity.

The second point is that it is narrative identity, and not numerical identity, that purportedly does the real work in accounting for our practical concerns. Thus, while numerical identity is *necessary* for rational anticipation—I cannot rationally anticipate some future experiences unless I expect them to be the experiences of the individual who will be *me*—it is not sufficient. In other words, it is not enough that some future individual will be me for it to make sense for me to anticipate his experiences, for the simple reason that he may be in a permanent vegetative state. Instead, it makes sense for me to anticipate some future experiences only if those experiences will be *mine*, that is—according to this position—only if they will be the experiences of a *person* and they fit coherently and accurately into my own ongoing, self-told life story.

It is worth saying more here about the purported advantages of the narrative view over numerical identity views with respect to our practical concerns. And insofar as the Psychological Criterion looks to have a more plausible connection to our practical concerns than the Biological Criterion, we will focus on it. So according to the Psychological Criterion, what grounds my rational anticipation of some future experience is just that that future experiencer will be uniquely psychologically continuous with me. But one might well think that, just because there's some overlapping chain of direct psychological connections between me and some eighty-year-old person, that isn't sufficient to ground my rational anticipation of his experiences. Suppose, after all, that I live entirely in the moment, flitting about to do whatever is in accordance with my strongest desire at any particular time, and that I have no ongoing projects, plans, or goals and lack self-reflection altogether. It's very hard to think of me as any kind of genuine person, or agent, at all. Instead, I am what Harry Frankfurt has famously called a *wanton*, someone who doesn't care about how his life is going or what he is to make of it.[1] Now there will be between me and my future eighty-year-old self unique psychological continuity; he will indeed be me. But this fact of numerical identity doesn't seem to provide any sort of grounds for rational anticipation on my part; after all, *what is that eighty-year-old man to me?* In no real sense will his life be mine; indeed, it's hard to think of my having any sort of life *at all*. So what rational sense can be made for my looking forward to his experiences? The narrative identity view has a real advantage over the Psychological Criterion

---

1   See Harry Frankfurt, "Freedom of the Will and the Concept of a Person," in Harry Frankfurt, *The Importance of What We Care About* (Cambridge: Cambridge University Press, 1988). The adjective *wanton* means capricious, frivolous, unrestrained, arbitrary.

here, therefore, given that it can explain why unique psychological continuity isn't sufficient to ground rational anticipation; instead, rational anticipation requires the kind of personhood and psychological unity that only narrative identity delivers.

A similar account may be given for self-concern. What an application of the Psychological Criterion seems to warrant is a special sort of concern that I, a person at one point in time, may have for the person who will be me at some future point in time, such that what grounds this concern is that person's unique psychological continuity with me. So the Psychological Criterion localizes the target of self-concern to some future moment from the perspective of the localized present moment: I-now care about the well-being of I-later. On the narrative identity view, however, self-concern is a concern I, a narrative self, have for that very same narrative self—for *me*, narratively construed—and this isn't a localized kind of concern at either end; rather, it is *global*. To have self-concern is thus to care about the whole self whose life I am creating, and the Psychological Criterion cannot seem to capture this important aspect of it.

In addition, it is my self-concern that, in a way, *makes* that future mine. As Schechtman puts it, my concern for the future

> is an ongoing, active orientation that creates a kind of experience that is not present without it. The subject worrying about his future is a narrative self and not some particular moment of this self, so the effects of self-concern do not consist only in the fact that at one moment (or even at each moment) a particular *anticipated* future changes a person's present. Instead, the formation of a narrative brings into being a temporally extended subject who has this concern for her whole self. By the time someone is in the position to worry about the future he is already more than a momentary creature.[1]

Finally, even if an advocate of the Psychological Criterion were to try to adopt a more global vision of self-concern, it's unclear why one should

---

1 Marya Schechtman, *The Constitution of Selves* (Ithaca, NY: Cornell University Press, 1996), pp. 156–57; emphasis in original.

care about a self unified by unique psychological continuity; after all, many of those individual experiential moments may just be *irrelevant* to me and the way in which I conceive my life, so there would likely be a serious disconnect between the self I actually care about and the self the Psychological Criterion would provide me rational warrant to care about.

What all of this seems to suggest is that the kind of identity that matters for our practical concerns is narrative, not numerical, identity. If this is true, then we could move beyond the standoff reached in the last chapter by admitting that we were focusing on the wrong type of identity all along. Nevertheless, *is* this true?

Evaluation of the Narrative Identity Alternative

So what are we to make of this view? The most important advantage it has going for it is clearly practical: it provides what seems to be the best way thus far to account for the rich phenomena of anticipation and self-concern, and it does so while remaining neutral between any particular criterion of numerical identity, and so it avoids the metaphysical standoff we ran into in the last chapter. Remember, what Weirob wanted from the get-go was a criterion of personal identity that helped us make sense of these practical features of our lives, and narrative identity seems to do this very well.

Nevertheless, while it initially seems to have this significant practical advantage, there are still some real concerns we might have about the view as a whole, including:

1. *The Endpoints Problem.* Narrative identity is presented as being about the unification of various experiences, actions, and psychological characteristics into the life of a single individual, a unity that comes via the biography we construct for ourselves, constrained only by considerations of coherence and approximation to reality. It answers the question "Who am I?" by stating, as DeGrazia puts it, "*You are the individual who is realistically described in your self-narrative or inner*

story." But this construal actually allows that various non-experiential or non-psychological events, even pre- and post-personhood, could be included in one's narrative. For example, I may coherently and correctly say, "I was born prematurely," or "If I'm ever in a permanent vegetative state, you may turn off the machines keeping me alive." It seems, in other words, that narrative identity isn't necessarily about the identity of *persons* at all.

Now in itself this expansion of the enterprise does not constitute an insurmountable problem for the narrative identity view. Indeed, there are those, like DeGrazia himself, who seize on it as a way to show that narrative identity is quite compatible with, and actually presupposes, a Biological Criterion of numerical identity. A Psychological Criterion, by contrast, could not be presupposed by a narrative identity incorporating these pre- and post-psychological events.

But this way of putting it just reinforces our earlier point that, while the endpoints of one's narrative identity have to be constrained by the endpoints of one's *numerical* identity (according to narrative identity theorists), as it turns out this just isn't how self-narratives often work. A variety of events may be incorporated into my self-narrative, some of which will be contained within the arc of my biological life, but some of which won't. For example, while I will certainly want to include details of my being born into my narrative, I may also want to include details of what happened to me at various stages of fetal development. Now most Biological Criterion theorists have no problem with this, for they think that our biological lives begin around the two-week stage post-conception, at the time the possibility for twinning has passed. But why should my self-narrative start there? After all, were I to find out that during the first two weeks post-conception my embryo had indeed split and then fused back together (as may very well happen), that event would surely play a role in my self-narrative: I really could have been—and was, for a bit—a twin! And if events during that first two week period can play a key role in my narrative, why not events prior to that? Why isn't what happened to

---

1   David DeGrazia, *Human Identity and Bioethics* (Cambridge: Cambridge University Press, 2005), p. 83; emphasis in original.

my mother's ova, or my father's sperm, relevant? Indeed, if we are looking for *explanations* of my current identity, for what makes me who I truly am today, why aren't the events in my parents' lives (and their parents' lives) relevant to my narrative as well?

On the other end of the spectrum, while I may indeed incorporate events happening to my potential PVS-stage as part of my narrative identity, why can't I also incorporate events happening to my *corpse*-stage as part of that identity? Why can't I say, "When I die, I'd love to lie in state as did Lenin, to be viewed and adored by the masses for years on end"? Suppose, through some crazy series of events, that this in fact happens to me. Then suppose that someone comes through one day and spits on my corpse, fomenting a riot, and, ultimately, a political revolution. Surely these events are just as much a legitimate part of *my* narrative as anything else in my life. But there just is no plausible theory of numerical identity that incorporates one's years-old corpse as identical to oneself. So the endpoints of narrative identity are not in fact constrained by the endpoints of numerical identity. And this leads to the next problem.

2. *Prescriptive or Descriptive?* What precisely is the upshot of this theory about narrative identity? Is it a *descriptive* enterprise, describing the way we in fact do think of our lives, or is it a *prescriptive* enterprise, prescribing the way we in fact ought to think of our lives? As it turns out, there are problem with both interpretations. If it is a descriptive thesis, then it is false. As Galen Strawson has pointed out, there are certainly some people—"Episodics," he labels them—whose self-experience is clearly non-narrative, that is, they do not consider themselves as being selves who were there in the past or who will be there in the future. This is not to say these people are wantons either. They may be quite self-reflective, and they likely also have goals, projects, and plans. They just don't weave their various events into a single narrative arc, or claim to see meaning in some of their experiences only in relation to others. Now Strawson, who himself claims to be an Episodic, thinks such lives are perfectly normal and non-pathological, and while such a life may strike us as perhaps odd or shortsighted, it certainly cannot be ruled out as *nonexistent*.

Perhaps, then, the narrativity thesis is prescriptive, providing us with the formula for how we *ought* to view our lives. But why would this be the case? Why should we create these inner stories, tying together the various events of our lives into a coherent narrative? One natural thought might be that doing so provides us with a valuable kind of self-knowledge and so points us to the proper targets for our self-concern, anticipation, and the like. Viewing the various moments of our lives as part of a larger biography may also provide them with greater resonance: to see my victory in a race, say, as part of the biography of someone who overcame cancer and sacrificed a great deal to be there makes the victory so much more than the feeling of pleasure one might experience in the moment; it may also serve to *redeem* a significant portion of one's life. On the other hand, though, there may very well be serious drawbacks to this sort of biographical tracing. Sometimes, to discover fully who I am is to discover some ugly truths, ones that may very well cripple me and destroy any reason for self-concern. Some of us have hearts of darkness, and it may in fact be better for us (and for those around us!) simply to leave those hearts as they are. At the very least, though, more needs to be said in favor of narrative identity, if this is the proper interpretation of the thesis. More generally, it is simply unclear *what* the proper interpretation of the thesis is supposed to be.

3. *The Practical Concerns Problem.* Narrative identity's greatest strength is in its alleged ability to account for all of our various practical (ethical and prudential) concerns. We have seen how it might do so for anticipation and self-concern. But what of our other practical concerns? We will explore how it deals with moral responsibility and compensation later on (in Chapters Seven and Eight, respectively). These are the four person-related practical concerns for which Schechtman takes us to desire an account. But as it turns out, (a) there are other concerns for which narrative identity doesn't give a good account at all, and (b) it's not entirely clear that narrative identity gives the best account of even these four.

Start with (a). There are some person-related practical concerns for which narrative identity is in fact irrelevant. The most obvious has to do with reidentification. Suppose I haven't seen you, an old friend, in ten years and so we arrange to meet at a local restaurant to catch up. I arrive early and I'm waiting to see you come in. After ignoring several people as they walk by, I finally make a judgment about one of them and call out your name to that person. What justifies me in doing so? It can only be that I believe that person *to be you*. But this sort of reidentification is surely not a matter of narrative identity. That is, I am not making some sort of judgment about which experiences or psychological elements are truly yours or are part of the biography of your life. Instead, I'm making a judgment solely about numerical identity: I'm judging that the person I see before me now *is one and the same person as* the person I was friends with ten years ago. And something similar is true of *first-person* reidentification. When I see the photo on my mother's coffee table and say, "I was so cute back then!" I am justified in doing so solely in virtue of the fact that the photo is a picture of me, and not insofar as the experiences of that child are incorporated into my biography.

When it comes to legal—and even possibly moral—responsibility, we are likely relying on numerical identity as well. It may not matter, for instance, if some person incorporates his past criminal actions into his true life story; instead, all that may matter for the rest of us is that his DNA matches up to the criminal's, and so, for the purposes of the law, he is simply the same person as the criminal. And a similar story might be told for cases of (legal) compensation.

Now Schechtman admits as much, claiming that what a reidentification/numerical criterion can't capture are just the four practical concerns of anticipation of survival, self-concern, responsibility, and compensation. This may well be perfectly okay, but it does introduce a fracture into our formerly unified account. For we had been taking for granted that *all* of our practical concerns would bear a relation to the *same* criterion of identity, namely, the *true* one. But now it may be that there's one type of identity related to one set of concerns, and another type of identity related to a different set of concerns. As just remarked, this may not be problematic in itself, but it's worth noting now as one of the key methodological points we will consider explicitly in the final chapter.

Nevertheless, it's uncertain whether narrative identity is actually the best way of accounting for even the four practical concerns (point (b) above). While we will consider responsibility and compensation in Part B, for now we can at least discuss the main practical concerns of this first part of the book, anticipation and self-concern. As it turns out, they may well still be, at least in part, about numerical identity. Take first self-concern. While sometimes it is indeed appropriate to say I am concerned about the fulfillment of *my* desires and goals (making the issue about the characterization question and ultimately narrative identity), at other times it seems much more appropriate to say that I am concerned about the well-being of the *person* who is me (numerical identity), where this also isn't a concern for my robust narrative self. Indeed, one key difference between narrative identity and numerical identity is that the former (typically) derives from first-person, subjective considerations, whereas the latter (typically) derives from third-person, more objective considerations. So while it's certainly possible to view my life and care about it from the inside, as the narrative self living it, it's also possible to view my life from the outside, to judge its overall value and have concern for it purely with respect to its various moments of enjoyment, say (this is how a utilitarian might view the matter; see Chapter Eight). When I do so, I'm assessing the value of these various moments *in total*, perhaps independently of how they are weaved into my narrative arc, and so to do so I must have an account of *numerical* identity that makes the person to whom they belong one and the same across time.

As for anticipation, suppose that I am terribly ill, and I am wondering if I will survive the night. Now I may indeed be wondering if it makes sense for me to expect any future experiences in the morning to be mine—this would be a kind of anticipation that asks the characterization question and whose answer depends on narrative identity. But I may also simply be wondering if there will be someone waking up in the morning *who will be me*, and this would be a kind of anticipation depending on the sense of numerical identity.

Thus, while narrative identity may be relevant to *some* of our practical concerns *some* of the time, it may not provide the exclusive account of all of the practical concerns its advocates have alleged of it. Furthermore, the theory of narrative identity itself isn't nearly as clear as it needs to be to play the significant role it is supposed to play when applied to the world of ethics. For instance, what are the right endpoints of the narrative and what makes them so? And are we to take the theory as descriptive or prescriptive? These are difficult questions that go to the heart of the view. What are we to do, then? There is another, even more radical, alternative to explore here, one that is founded on a powerful objection to all of the various theories of identity (numerical and narrative) we have seen to this point.

Identity and What Matters

The objection stems from a series of thought experiments made famous by Derek Parfit.

> *Whole Brain Transplant Case*: I get into a terrible motorcycle accident. My body is a wreck and my heart will soon stop pumping, even though my brain is fine. As it turns out, my entire brain can be transplanted into the healthy cranium and body of my twin (whose own brain has just suffered a crippling aneurysm). The operation is a complete success, and the survivor wakes up fully psychologically continuous with me. What has happened to me?

This is obviously a version of the *Who is Julia?* case, and as we have recognized before, most people will want to say that I am the survivor here. Indeed, the only view we have run across that would unequivocally deny this conclusion is Weirob's Body Criterion. But this seems quite implausible, and as it turns out, even the advocates of the more sophisticated Biological Criterion would agree that I have survived, just as long as my brain stem—the regulator of my biological functioning—were transplanted as well. And it is not hard to see why most people would think I am the survivor here, for the resulting person would remember (or at least seem to remember) my life, carry out my intentions, persist in my beliefs and desires, have a character exactly like mine, and bear a close physical resemblance to me. Indeed, there would be no difference whatsoever, from the inside, between what things will be like for the post-transplant person and what things would have been like for me had I simply undergone any other sort of operation and awakened afterwards. There seems no compelling reason, then, to deny that, in this case, he is me.

> *The Single Hemisphere Transplant Case*: Suppose that I have severe epilepsy, and one hemisphere of my brain is, as a result, removed to end my epileptic seizures, an operation known as a hemispherectomy. Many people have actually undergone such an operation and become eventually able to function reasonably well (with their remaining hemisphere learning how to take over the tasks previously performed by their missing hemisphere). Surely those who underwent the surgery were themselves the survivors of it—to say otherwise would be to say that the doctors performing the surgery were killing their patients, which is absurd—so there should be no doubt that I would still be alive in this case. But now suppose that, as in the first case, I get into a motorcycle accident and my body is about to expire. This time, however, only one hemisphere of my brain continues to function, and so it alone is transplanted into the healthy body of my twin brother. The post-operation person will once more wake up being fully psychologically continuous with the pre-operation me. What, then, has happened to me?

Once more, it seems as if I would be the survivor. If I would be the survivor in the Whole Brain Transplant Case, and I would also survive the loss of one hemisphere of my brain, there would be nothing of any additional relevance missing in the Single Hemisphere Transplant Case that would suddenly make me no longer the survivor. But if we agree with this assessment in both of these first two cases, what happens when we combine the cases?

> *The Double Transplant (Fission) Case*: Suppose that I'm in a motorcycle accident, with the usual havoc having been wreaked on my body, but that I have two healthy brain hemispheres, each of which is essentially the duplicate of the other (that is, there are no real differences between their abilities). Now suppose my two *triplet* brothers suffer aneurysms.

One hemisphere of my brain is thus transplanted into one brother's body, whereas the other hemisphere is transplanted into my other brother's body. After the operation, two people—call the one with my right hemisphere Righty and the one with my left hemisphere Lefty—wake up and both of them are fully psychologically continuous with me.

This case should also sound familiar. It is a more down-to-earth version of the Divine Duplication case we discussed in Chapter One. Of course, one might think that fission is even more far-fetched. Indeed, why think we can learn anything of value at all from considering something like this, something which could never actually happen?

One reply is that, at least in terms of the most important aspect of the case, fission of a kind has already occurred. The two hemispheres of our brains are connected by a bundle of fibers known as the corpus callosum, a bundle that enables the two hemispheres to communicate with one another. Scientists have found that severing the corpus callosum in patients with severe epilepsy can significantly reduce their seizures. But they've also found something else in such patients, namely, what seem to be two separate streams of consciousness. This was revealed in specially designed psychological tests. Our right hemisphere controls the left half of our body, while our left hemisphere controls the right. Once the patients' corpus callosum had been severed, though, it was as if each hemisphere of their brains communicated independently of the other. So they would be presented with a wide screen, one half of which was blue, the other half of which was red, such that each hemisphere "saw" only one color via the halves of each eye it controlled.[1] On each half of the screen was the question, "What color do you see?" One of the patient's hands wrote "blue," and the other wrote "red." And there have been other fascinating experiments and anecdotes along these lines. One patient claimed that there were times in which, when he was hugging his wife, his left hand would push her away.

---

1   The right hemisphere is connected to the right halves of each retina, and the left hemisphere to the left halves. So if this divided screen is presented too quickly for this subject to move his eyes and expose the halves of the screen to both halves of each retina, the red stimulus goes only to one hemisphere, and the blue only to the other.

So what does this mean? There seems to be, in such patients, a division of consciousness into two streams, each of which is unaware of the other. But we can easily see how this real-life case is relevant to fission, for all we are supposing in this thought experiment is that the division of consciousness came via a permanent physical separation of the two hemispheres. Whether or not such fission is ever technically possible, then, should not be a concern, given that what might have been thought to be the deeply impossible aspect of the separation—the division of consciousness—seems already to have occurred.

Consider the case, then. The first question we have about fission is exactly the same as the question we had in the Divine Duplication case, namely, what has happened to me? There are four, and only four, options:

Option 1: I survive as both Righty and Lefty? This might seem the most appealing answer, at first. After all, I would survive the Whole Brain Transplant, and I would survive the Single Hemisphere Transplant, so why not think I'd survive, just twice over, in the Double Transplant? Unfortunately, this cannot be the case, given the simple and obvious fact that there are *two* people post-fission, and two does not equal one. In other words, we want to know what has happened to *me*, one person. If we say that I am *both* Righty and Lefty, and they are two distinct persons, then we'd be forced to say that *one* person equals *two* persons, or one equals two, which is just false.

Of course, you might simply deny that Righty and Lefty *are* two persons. Instead, you might say, I am one person with two bodies and a permanently divided stream of consciousness. But making this move would cause all sorts of other serious difficulties, especially with regard to our concept of personhood. Suppose Righty and Lefty go off and live on opposite ends of the earth, and have a variety of very different experiences. It would become very difficult to continue to think of them as one single person in that case. In addition, suppose they were to play poker against one another. Would it really be just a game of solitaire? What if one shot the other in a rage? Would it be murder or suicide? And suppose, through some very strange and incestuous turn of events, they make love to one another. Would it instead simply be a case of masturbation? Once we think about it, the negative implications of calling Righty and Lefty both me, a single person, are too overwhelming to bear.

Option 2: I survive as Righty? Here you might agree that I can at most be only one of the survivors (who are each individual persons), and then insist that I go where my right hemisphere goes. But why think this? Indeed, both hemispheres are essentially duplicates of the other, and both Righty and Lefty would be fully psychologically continuous with me, so what non-arbitrary reason is there to think that I would be Righty and not Lefty? Of course, if you adhere to the Biological Criterion, you might think that I go wherever my brain stem goes (which can't be divided), and if it goes with Righty, he would be me, but if goes with Lefty, then he would be me. But it would be quite odd to think that my entire identity would be preserved in that small bit of regulatory biology, especially when both Righty and Lefty would have their own brain stems doing precisely the same regulatory biological work as my original brain stem. Indeed, it would be almost as arbitrary to insist that my original brain stem must remain intact for *me* to remain intact as it would be to insist that either Righty or Lefty is me.

Option 3: I survive as Lefty? The same reasoning applies here: what non-arbitrary reason is there to think that I would survive as Lefty, and not Righty, given that they'd each be exactly similar to me (psychologically, at least)?

Option 4: I do not survive? As it turns out, this is our only other option, and it must be correct. I can't survive as both, and there's no reason to think I've survived as one and not the other, so I must not survive fission. (Of course, if my original brain stem went into neither Righty nor Lefty, the advocate of the Biological Criterion discussed above would agree that I do not survive as well, but for a different reason.) This is rather extraordinary, though. If I survived the Whole Brain and Single Hemisphere Transplant cases, why would a *double* success count as some sort of failure? The reason is simple: the numerical identity-relation is a one-one relation—it holds only between one thing and that same one thing—but the relation that holds between me and the post-fission people must be one-many, holding between one thing and more than one thing (if we accept that the survivors are two distinct individuals). So the relation that holds between me and the survivors cannot be the identity relation. *I do not survive fission.*

But now we need to ask the crucial follow-up question: *does this matter?* In other words, is the fact that the identity relation is missing between me and the fission survivors an important fact? And it is here where Parfit has famously said no: identity is in fact *not* what matters in this case. To see why, consider things from the internal perspective of each survivor. Start with Righty. He'll seem to remember my life, right up to the moment in which he went under anesthesia. He'll also have my intention to go out and party tonight, he'll believe that the surgery was the right thing to do— as did I—and he'll have precisely my level of love for poker, polka, and okra. But now consider things from Lefty's perspective. He'll be exactly psychologically similar to Righty, so he too will share my memories, intentions, beliefs, loves, and so forth, in exactly the same way Righty does.

For both fission-products, then, it will be precisely as if *I* had awakened from the surgery. So if we look at things from my pre-fission perspective, everything that matters to me about ordinary survival will be preserved in both of my fission products. The only difference between this and ordinary survival will be that, whereas I would bear the relevant intrinsic relation to only one person in the ordinary day-to-day case, here I bear that relation to *two* people. Now "survival" entails identity: for me to survive some surgery, the post-surgery person has to be identical to me. But since there is no identity between the post-fission persons and me—solely because identity can obtain only one-one—I don't survive fission. But because everything that *matters* to me about ordinary survival obtains—twice over!—then what occurs in fission is *just as good as* ordinary survival.

And what *is* the relation that obtains between me and the fission-products that preserves what ordinarily matters in survival? Now it's true that there is a bit of physical continuity between us: they each have a portion of my original brain (not quite half). But of course this is important only insofar as that brain portion supports *psychological continuity* between us. What matters in ordinary survival—what I look forward to in day-to-day survival—is that the person who wakes up in my bed, say, will remember my life, act on my intentions, see and approach the world as I would have, love and take care of the things I love and take care of, and so forth. And whether or not there is one person or there are two people who will do this is—at least to some extent—unimportant.[1] Identity, then, is not what matters; rather, what matters is psychological continuity. Call this view, therefore, the **Identity Doesn't Matter** (IDM) view.

If we accept a view like this, there will be a number of important implications for our practical concerns. We are currently focused on anticipation and self-concern, and this view does quite well in accounting for them. What we have realized is that some sort of psychological continuity relation does the best job of grounding these patterns of concern. The problem we kept running into, though, stemmed from the pairing of *identity* with psychological continuity. In the Divine Duplication case, for instance (our precursor to fission), we saw how the only way to avoid the violation of the transitivity of identity was to make up a seemingly arbitrary restriction: the relation between X and Y has to obtain *uniquely*. But this meant that, if God created only one version of me in heaven, I'd have reason on earth to anticipate survival, whereas if God created two copies of me, I'd have no reason *at all* to anticipate it, given that I couldn't survive.

We can see now, though, just how silly this attitude is, given that we have a very legitimate alternative: simply focus on psychological continuity *directly* and in so doing divorce our practical concerns from the identity relation itself when identity diverges from psychological continuity. It is thus not "that he will be me" that is my reason to anticipate someone's experiences or have a special concern for him; rather, it is "that he will be my psychological successor."

There are other, more radical, implications of the view, however. The most important stems from the fact that psychological continuity

---

1   There may indeed be some practical worries to think about were fission to take place. For instance, which one gets access to my bank account? Which one goes home to my wife? These are not minor problems! A more careful way to pitch the fission scenario, then, is just this: suppose the prospects of my fission-products would be just as good as my own (without fission). In *this* scenario, then, it should be clear that the loss of identity between me and the fission-products is not an important loss.

is made up of overlapping chains of psychological connectedness, and connectedness, unlike identity, comes in *degrees*. In other words, the relations that together constitute psychological connections—memory, intentions, beliefs, desires, cares, and character—obtain in stronger and weaker forms, relations that sometimes alter in strength from day to day. So my memories of yesterday are far stronger (and greater in number) than my memories of twenty years ago; my character now more closely resembles my character yesterday than the one I had as a child; most of my current beliefs, desires, and cares were held by my yesterday's self but not my childhood self, and so on. But now, given that many of these connections that themselves constitute psychological continuity are matters of degree, if our practical concerns are grounded in psychological continuity then it looks as if our practical concerns themselves ought to be matters of degree as well.

This could mean, for instance, that I might be rationally justified in caring less about my distant future selves, solely insofar as I expect them not to be very close psychological continuers of mine. That retirement-age self, I might think, will not care about the things I now care about, nor will he much remember my current experiences or carry out my current intentions. Why, then, should I care as much about, and sacrifice as much for, him as I do my tomorrow's self, who will be much more closely related to me psychologically? This approach might also go for the rationality of anticipation: I have more reason to anticipate the experiences of those selves I expect to be more closely psychologically related to me. And there will be, as we shall see, some very interesting implications of the view for more explicitly ethical concerns, such as moral responsibility, compensation, advanced directives, and ethical theory generally.

But the most radical implication, directly relevant to what started off our investigation in Chapter One, is that this view could allow for the rationality of anticipating the *afterlife*. Here's how: suppose God exists and has the will and ability to create, upon your death, a duplicate of you in Heaven. Now this is a very big supposition, but it at least seems logically possible. It is quite implausible, however, to say that this person in heaven will be *you*. For one thing, he or she will not be biologically continuous with you, so the Biological Criterion rules out your identity with this person. Furthermore, the Psychological Criterion, as we have already seen, has a very hard time accounting for this case, just given the possibility of Divine Duplication or the possibility that an impatient God creates your duplicate even before you die. And given that narrative identity presupposes numerical identity, and neither criterion of numerical identity can account for your surviving your death, it looks like none of our criteria of identity allow for the possibility of such survival, in which case, if rational anticipation attaches to identity, it can never be rational to anticipate surviving one's death.

But if rational anticipation attaches to *psychological continuity*, then it could be rational to anticipate the experiences of that heavenly duplicate after all. He or she will be just like you psychologically: he or she will seem to remember living your life, persist in your beliefs/goals/desires, have a character just like yours, and so on. So what would happen, were God to make a copy of you in heaven, would be *just as good as ordinary survival*. Would the survivor be you? Probably not, although that would, on the IDM view, be irrelevant. Rather, what matters is that he or she would be psychologically continuous with you, and in light of that possible relation, it could be perfectly rational to anticipate his or her experiences in Heaven. Why wouldn't this be good enough, then? Indeed, it is this sort of possibility to which Dave Cohen refers in his final mysterious remarks to Weirob.

Evaluation of the IDM View

Of course, we know by now that no theory regarding persons and personal identity is problem-free, and the IDM view is no exception. Perhaps the most significant objection launched against it comes from Mark Johnston, who says that, while the fission case may give us a reason to divorce our practical concerns from personal identity *in the fission case*, it doesn't at all give us a reason to divorce them in all our other ordinary cases. And let's face it: fission just never happens!¹ So yes, if it were to happen, we might want to *extend* our ethical and prudential practices to deal with it, and we might ground our practices at that point on something like psychological continuity, but until that day occurs (which is quite unlikely), our practical concerns remain grounded on identity. Indeed, something like self-concern is just that: *self*-concern. It is a special sort of concern for the person who is *myself*, not the person who will be psychologically continuous with me, and that self-concern is simply part of a coherent set of self-related concerns I have simply in virtue of being a normal human being. I care about *my* friends, *my* family, and yes, *my* self, and there's no reason to think that some thought experiment about a technologically improbable procedure should have any force in undermining that very natural pattern of concern.

This is an important point, not just for the view under consideration but also for our overall project. Even if we allow such crazy cases like fission into consideration, what is the precise lesson we should draw from them? Should we really radically revise our current practical concerns in light of them? Why not instead simply preserve our ordinary concerns as the default until we actually encounter such a bizarre scenario in real life? Indeed, should metaphysical considerations more generally play *any* revisionary role in our practical concerns? These are some of the difficult questions we will put off until the final chapter. For now, however, it may suffice to reply that the fission case specifically may not be meant to cause us to revise our practical concerns at all; instead, it might be meant simply to *reveal* to us what we're already committed to given our practical concerns as they stand, namely, that these concerns in fact track psychological continuity in our ordinary lives. In other words, what the fission case may reveal to us, in dramatic fashion, is not that we *ought* to extend our patterns of concern to our psychological continuers in just this peculiar sort of case, but that in thinking carefully about the case we may in fact

---

1　Well, maybe something like fission happens in the very rare cases of surgical detachment of the hemispheres; but it doesn't happen in the radical form imagined to produce Lefty and Righty: the brain transplantation necessary for it just isn't technologically possible.

find that we *do* (or would) extend these concerns to both psychological continuers, that they would be successors *already* caught in the net of our ordinary natural concern. Nevertheless, more would need to be said to defend the IDM view in this way from Johnston's powerful objection.

Conclusion

We have certainly discussed quite a lot of material in this first part of the book, but what exactly is it, if anything, that we have accomplished? To see where we find ourselves, it may be helpful to retrace our route in getting here. What motivated the enterprise was a question that nearly all of us probably have: is it rational for me to anticipate surviving the death of my body? To get an answer to this question, we had to find out whether or not it was possible for *me* to survive the death of my body, and in doing so we assumed that what makes anticipation rational is personal identity, that is, in order for it to make sense for me to anticipate some future person's experiences, that future person must be me.

In our first chapter, then, we tried out the suggestions of Weirob's dialogue partners—exploring both Soul and Memory Criteria—and found, along with Weirob, that they were either irrelevant or simply unable to do the job we wanted, which was to provide a criterion of personal identity that provided a logically possible mechanism getting us from here to the afterlife. It thus seemed as if survival of death was impossible. But as it turned out, even the other "non-immortality" theories of personal identity discussed in the dialogue—the Body Criterion and the Brain-Based Memory Criterion—seemed to stumble over significant obstacles as well on the road to plausibility.

We then turned in Chapter Two to a discussion of the two most sophisticated theories of personal identity on offer, the Psychological and Biological Criteria, in order to see what their relation might be to our day-to-day prudential concerns—anticipation and self-concern—independently from the vexed question of the afterlife. What is it, we wanted to know, that makes it rational to anticipate the experiences of, and have a special sort of concern for, that person who will be getting out of my bed tomorrow, going to my classes, fulfilling my role at work, and so forth? Once again, we assumed that the answer was, in its general form, one of personal identity: what makes it rational is that that person in the morning *will be me*. And so we set out to see which criterion of personal identity grounds this practical work. We first found that, while it did very well in accounting for our practical concerns, the Psychological Criterion ran into serious difficulties with respect to both its method (the Method of Cases) and its implications about our essence. But the theory that did fare well in *those* respects—the Biological Criterion—itself fared rather poorly in accounting for several of our key intuitions, as well as our practical concerns generally.

We turned, then, in the present chapter, to an exploration of a couple of radical possibilities. First, we considered abandoning numerical identity in favor of narrative identity, which focused on the question, "What makes me who I am?" rather than on the question, "What makes me the same person across time?" And while this move seemed to yield some fruit with respect to *some* of our practical concerns, it wasn't, at the end of the day, a very clear theory, nor did it seem distinctly relevant to other of our practical concerns.

The second radical possibility was simply to abandon the assumption that had been guiding us all along, namely, that it is personal identity that grounds rational anticipation and self-concern (and perhaps other of our practical concerns). This possibility was motivated by consideration of the famous fission case. By far the most plausible response to that case was to admit that I don't survive, but this admission, on the IDM view, wasn't supposed to bother us, given that I would still be fully psychologically continuous with both fission-products. Indeed, on this view, what matters is precisely this relation—psychological continuity—and this is the relation that does or ought to ground anticipation and self-concern, even though we had mistakenly assumed it was identity that was doing that trick. One of the IDM view's most important virtues, then, is the way in which it cuts right to the chase: we kept wanting to find a psychology-based account of anticipation and self-concern (for example, the Memory Criterion, the Psychological Criterion, and narrative identity), but we kept running into problems constructing a theory of personal identity around the relevant psychological relations. What the IDM view does is simply deny the identity part, while preserving the psychological relations, simplifying our search profoundly. It also provides the possibility of rationally anticipating the experiences of some heavenly person, despite the fact that he won't be me, which seems to be about the most we can legitimately ask for.

There are problems with the IDM view too, of course, one that we have already seen, and others that we will explore later. But it has certainly earned a place of consideration among our other prime contenders, the Psychological Criterion, the Biological Criterion, and narrative identity. But now what? Are all four views on equal footing, or are some more plausible than others? This is certainly something for you to consider, and there is another very important question for you to mull over as you do so: what role should our practical concerns play in our exploration of personal identity? In other words, we have set aside some views as just irrelevant to these concerns, and we have noted it as a problem when some view could not account for them very well. Were we right to do so, however? Or should we instead simply try to figure out the right criterion of personal identity, say, with no regard whatsoever for how it relates to our practical concerns until *after* we have somehow independently determined what the "right" criterion is? And how would we determine that, if we make no reference to our practical concerns?

These are hard questions, and we will take them up explicitly in the final chapter of the book. For now, though, we leave these matters open as we turn to a different set of issues. Up until now we have focused exclusively on the relation between personal identity and our self-regarding reasons and concerns, discussing the issues of anticipation, self-concern, and immortality. From here on out, however, we will turn away from the issue of how to deal with ourselves to concentrate on the issue of how to deal with other people: what is the relation between personal identity and morality, we will ask, specifically *other-regarding* morality? In exploring the upcoming moral issues, we will find out a variety of interesting ways in which identity may be relevant, and in so doing we may also find some ways to answer the hard questions posed above.

WORKS CITED OR REFERENCED IN THIS CHAPTER

DeGrazia, David. *Human Identity and Bioethics*. Cambridge: Cambridge University Press, 2005.

Frankfurt, Harry. "Freedom of the Will and the Concept of a Person." In *The Importance of What We Care About*, by Harry Frankfurt. Cambridge: Cambridge University Press, 1988.

Johnston, Mark. "Human Beings." *Journal of Philosophy* 84 (1987): 59-83.

———. "Human Concerns Without Superlative Selves." In *Reading Parfit*, edited by Jonathan Dancy. Oxford: Blackwell, 1997.

Nagel, Thomas. "Brain Bisection and the Unity of Consciousness." In *Personal Identity*, edited by John Perry. Berkeley, CA: University of California Press, 1976.

Parfit, Derek. *Reasons and Persons*. Oxford: Oxford University Press, 1984.

———. "The Unimportance of Identity." In *Identity*, edited by Henry Harris. Oxford: Oxford University Press, 1995.

Schechtman, Marya. *The Constitution of Selves*. Ithaca, NY: Cornell University Press, 1996.

Strawson, Galen. "Against Narrativity." *Ratio* XVII (December 2004): 428-52.

PART B

Personal Identity and Other-Regarding Ethics

CHAPTER FOUR

Moral Issues at the Beginning of Life, Part I: Killing

In this chapter we will conduct the first of a two-part exploration into the ways in which personal identity may be relevant to moral issues at the beginning of life. First up in this chapter are moral problems regarding killing new life, namely, the problems of abortion and stem cell research. Ordinarily, of course, killing a human being is immoral. But in these cases, it's entirely unclear whether or not the entity being killed—a fetus, in the case of abortion, or an embryo, in the case of stem cell research—is indeed a human being. This is primarily a puzzle about identity in the sense of *membership in a kind*: are these entities—fetuses and embryos—members of the kind "human being" or perhaps "person," and so subject to moral protection like the rest of us? But in addition to these moral problems being about this sort of membership-identity, considerations of straightforward numerical identity are also importantly relevant. After all, given that I now have a certain moral status—surely it's wrong to kill me, other things being equal—if it can be determined that I'm numerically identical to that early-stage fetus or embryo, perhaps my moral status will transfer to such entities as well.

In both cases, we will begin with a somewhat controversial stance: we will take as a default position that the activity in question is morally permissible unless there are compelling objections otherwise. What we will look for, then, will be identity-based objections to abortion and stem cell research, and if none of these objections is compelling, the likelihood that these activities are truly morally permissible will be higher than it otherwise might have been. In addition, as we proceed, think about the ways in which some theories of personal identity themselves might be made more or less plausible by how well (or poorly) they account for certain aspects of these moral issues.

ABORTION

Parminder is nineteen years old and six weeks pregnant. She knows how it happened too. One night she and her boyfriend had some quickie sex outside of a club, and because passions were running very high, they didn't bother with contraception. But she and her boyfriend broke up about three weeks ago, so she's now on her own. She's also just finishing up her sophomore year in college: her plan is to complete a degree in biology and then go on to get her masters so she can teach biology in high school. Having a baby now would utterly destroy those plans: she'd have to drop out of college for several years and work at least one low-paying job, and who knows when she'd make it back to college? On the other hand, she could carry the fetus to term and then give it up for adoption, but she knows herself very well, so she knows that she's likely to become very attached to her unborn fetus over that period of time, which would make giving it up quite devastating psychologically. Furthermore, carrying it to term would again require her to drop out of college, at least for the remainder of the year, which would put her behind in her program and also cost her this semester's tuition, which she can ill afford to lose. After much consideration, she finally decides to abort her fetus at the local women's clinic. And while this does cause her some depression afterwards, she also realizes that her psychological trauma was likely far less than it would have been with either of the other two options. Nevertheless, was what she did immoral?

Many of you likely have very strong opinions in answer to that question. For some, Parminder's action would be morally permissible no matter what her reasons were. For others, Parminder's action would be morally *impermissible* no matter what her reasons were. And for others, the morality of Parminder's abortion actually depends on her reasons for undergoing it. Abortion remains a terribly controversial issue, of course. Is there anything we can learn about it, though, from considerations of personal identity?

In one sense, the answer will always be no. Personal identity is about the way the world is—a descriptive enterprise—and our question about abortion here is about what we ought to do—a prescriptive enterprise— and an "ought" cannot be derived from an "is." The world's being one way or the other just has no direct implications, on its own, for what we ought to do in that world. So even if we could determine the correct conditions for my identity across time, that descriptive truth *alone* could imply nothing whatsoever about the morality of anything, let alone abortion.

Nevertheless, there are still important ways for metaphysical facts to be relevant to moral *arguments*. Here is how: in making the case for some moral conclusion, among one's premises will have to be both normative *and* descriptive assertions, and the truth of these descriptive assertions may well depend on metaphysical considerations. Consider the following simple moral argument:

1. It is wrong to cause pain to any creature capable of experiencing pain.
2. Rats are capable of experiencing pain.

3. Thus, it's wrong to cause pain to rats.

Notice, then, that while premise 1 is a normative assertion, premise 2 is not. Instead, it's a descriptive assertion that, if true, would facilitate the transition from the first general normative principle to the practical conclusion about what we ought to do regarding the specific case of rats. Furthermore, premise 2 is one for which certain metaphysical considerations may be appropriate: what is the nature of pain, for instance, and are rats truly capable of it? In a similar way, then, metaphysical considerations about personal identity could be very important to arguments about the morality of abortion. So let us examine a few such arguments.

Moral Status Arguments

Many people think that the morality of abortion rests on the moral status of the fetus: is it a morally protected entity with a right to life? If so, then abortion is wrong *prima facie*.[1] If not, then abortion is *prima facie* permissible. The trick is to figure just what the fetus *is*, such that it has the requisite moral status. One popular way to articulate this status goes as follows:

1. It's wrong to kill a person.
2. A fetus is a person.

3. Thus, it's wrong to kill a fetus.

Obviously, the role that metaphysics might play would be with respect to the second premise. Why, then, might we think that a fetus is a person?

This is obviously a question about identity as membership in a kind, specifically the kind "person," and so the answer will depend first and foremost on what we mean by the term. We seem to have two general choices: either we are deploying a psychological definition or we aren't. Start with the former. Following Locke, a person would be a creature with a stream of consciousness that is capable of self-reflection. On that definition, however, premise 2 is just false: fetuses have no such capacities. Alternatively, then, we might assert that persons are non-psychological creatures, but this view runs into all sorts of difficulties. First, departing from a psychological-based understanding of "person" departs from common usage in an objectionable way: sure, you might make the second premise true by stipulating your terms to mean certain things, but if the meanings of those terms don't match up in some close way to common usage, your argument will just be irrelevant. Why should I care if your argument is valid and sound when what you mean by your terms just isn't at all what I mean by those same terms? Second, if you do indeed depart from common usage, what precisely are the non-psychological features

---

1   *Prima facie* means *at first glance, on initial consideration.*

sufficient for personhood that a fetus has? Presumably they would be biological features, but what reason do we have (other than to save the argument) to link biology with personhood? Indeed, what would seem to be going on in this case is that one would simply be *asserting* that a fetus has moral protection, without argument, but that would be to assume precisely what's at issue (otherwise known as *begging the question*).

A more plausible way to defend a version of premise 2 would be to back off the personhood claim in favor of a metaphysical claim that seems much more likely to be true, as in the following argument:

1. It's wrong to kill a *human being*.
2. A fetus is a *human being*.

3. Thus, it's wrong to kill a fetus.

Once more, of course, we need to figure out what's meant by "human being." But here the task would seem to be simpler: whereas "person" is likely a psychological term, "human being" is likely a biological term, referring to some kind of biological or physiological structure that both fetuses and the rest of us have in common. If so, then insofar as it's wrong to kill us *creatures-with-this-biological-structure*, it will be wrong to kill *fetuses-with-this-biological-structure* as well.

What, though, is the biological structure in question? In other words, what is it that makes some entity a member of the kind "human being," the possessor of some property (or properties) shared by all and only human beings? This turns out to be an extremely difficult question, for almost anything one chooses (that both we and fetuses share) will exclude some clear-cut human beings and include some clear-cut *non*-human beings. For instance, any rationality-based or functioning brain-based criterion will exclude anencephalic infants from the realm of human beings, along with humans in PVS, perhaps, while likely including some higher primates and possible non-human aliens. On the other hand, building some kind of physiological profile—for instance, saying that human beings are those entities that have two arms, two legs, a brain, lungs, heart, stomach, and so forth—will exclude many humans who are missing arms, legs, or various internal organs, while once more including many other non-human animals or aliens.

What has seemed most plausible, then, is to articulate some kind of *genetic* criterion of identity for membership in the kind "human being," along the lines of the following criterion put forward by John Noonan: anything with a standard human genetic code—whatever the details of the human genome turn out to be—is a human being. Unfortunately, this won't work either. For one thing, because *every cell in the human body* has a standard genetic code, every cell in the human body would be a human being, on this account, which clearly includes too much. If we combined this claim with the first normative premise, then, we'd get the utterly absurd conclusion that killing cancer cells would be wrong! For another thing, because not every human being has a standard genetic code—those with Down syndrome have one extra chromosome, for instance—this criterion would exclude too much as well. Startlingly enough, then, providing the necessary and sufficient conditions for membership in the kind "human being" turns out to be, if not impossible, extraordinarily difficult. (And don't think that you can avoid the issue by saying that a human being is simply whatever is born to another human being, because that just moves the problem back a step: what makes the birthing creature *itself* a human being?)

Perhaps, then, we might actually get some help here by considering the motivation behind the Biological Criterion. This is a criterion of numerical identity across time, of course, not a criterion for membership in a kind, which is the sort of identity we're currently concerned with, but recall that the motivation for the Biological Criterion comes from considerations about our essence, which *is* relevant to kind membership. The question is what kind of thing am I essentially? And the answer is that I am a living human organism. The conditions for my identity across time, then, are determined by these conditions for kind membership: what preserves my identity across time is just the continued existence of the same living human organism that I am.

Given this background, we might draw from our fictional Carlos, in Case 2 of the Introduction, to offer the following argument:

1. It would be wrong to kill me.

2. I was a fetus, i.e., I am one and the same individual as some past fetus.

3. Thus, it would be wrong to have killed that past fetus.

What I essentially am, on this view, is a certain sort of biological organism, and what preserves my identity across time is just the continuity of this organism. This means that what I am today is one and the same thing as the fetus from which I grew. So if it would be wrong to kill me—and surely it is—then it would have been wrong to kill the fetus that was one and the same as me lo those many years ago.

Now the extension from here should be obvious: if it would have been wrong to kill me-as-a-fetus, it would also seem to be wrong to kill any human fetus that is expected to develop normally, not in virtue of its *potential* to become a being with moral status, say, but entirely in virtue of its already being one and the same individual as that eventual adult human being with obvious moral status. Just to hammer the point home: what the argument does is simply try to reveal to us the non-obvious moral status of fetuses by pointing out the *obvious* moral status of adult human beings in combination with the Biological Criterion of identity. On this view, then, aborting a fetus would be (at least prima facie) immoral.

This now looks like a much more plausible argument than those explored above, but there are a few questions one might ask about it. First, what is the scope of the argument? In other words, if successful, it would be wrong to kill anything that is me (or you, or an individual like us), but when do I begin to exist? What are the conditions under which some organism becomes a member of my kind? How far back in the development of my human organism, therefore, would moral protection extend? To the point at which a brain develops? A spinal cord? The moment of conception? Before? These are very hard questions, but pursuing them in any detail would take us far afield. For now, we can at least admit that, if the account of our essence on which advocates of the Biological Criterion depend is true, there is some significant stretch pre-birth when individuals like us exist, and so a significant arena in which abortion would be immoral.

The second general question one might ask is in virtue of *what* is the first premise true, that it's wrong to kill me (and individuals like me)? As it turns out, when I'm an adult, I am many things: an adult (obviously), a human being, a person, a husband, a parent, and so forth. Which of these is relevant for a determination of my moral status? If my moral status is allegedly in virtue of my being a *person*, say, then the first premise of the above argument is true but the second premise is false, for a fetus isn't a person. On the other hand, if my moral status is allegedly in virtue of my being a *human organism*, then the second premise could now be true, but why should we continue to think that the *first* premise is true? After all, if what I am essentially is a human organism, a biological creature, then it's *not* so clear that it's wrong to kill an individual like me.

Here Tanya's response to Carlos in the Introduction may bear fruit, for she makes an oft-heard analogy to acorns and oak trees: just as it could indeed be wrong to treat a full-grown oak tree in a way that it would be perfectly permissible to treat an acorn, so too it might be wrong to treat a normal adult human being—a person—in a way that it would be perfectly permissible to treat a fetus, even though both are just different stages of one and the same individual organism. What this reply does, then, is point out that one's actual moral status may depend on what *stage of development* one is in, and not on the persisting *essence* of one's various stages. In other words, it might be that only persons get a certain level of moral status (due to their robust psychological capacities, say), so that even though I'm the same individual as the fetus from which I grew, only I (in my person-stage) get serious moral consideration.

This seems a perfectly legitimate move to try and make, but once one has done that, one is no longer drawing from any considerations of personal identity. Instead, one is exploring a purely moral issue: what entities, precisely, get moral status? Of course, it seems like it would be tough to get very far with this tactic, for it is rather difficult to think of what reasons one might give to distinguish between persons and fetuses, in terms of moral status, that wouldn't just beg the very question at issue: why, for example, are certain psychological capacities relevant to getting certain moral rights, say? But this is not really our concern, for we are interested only in those approaches to the issue for which considerations of personal identity are still relevant.

In sum, then, the only anti-abortion "moral status" argument (in which considerations of personal identity are relevant) that seems even remotely plausible is the one stemming from the Biological Criterion, according to which the numerical identity obtaining between fetuses and persons establishes the wrongness of killing fetuses. But this view is subject to a strong moral objection: why think that it's in virtue of my *essence* that I have the moral status I have, that it's wrong to kill me? Indeed, the failure of these "moral status" arguments in every case actually yields a more fundamental question: what in fact *does* make it wrong to kill me? It is in trying to answer this question that we will get to see both a powerful anti-abortion argument as well as a powerful reply to it grounded explicitly in personal identity.

The Future-Like-Ours Argument

In one of the most famous philosophical articles ever written on the topic ("Why Abortion is Immoral"), Don Marquis in 1989 argued that the various sides in the abortion debate have found themselves in a symmetrical standoff, precisely because they haven't gone to the heart of the matter, which is simply about what makes it wrong to kill ordinary adult human beings like you and me. Marquis' guiding thought is that, if we can answer that question, we ought to be able to answer the abortion question once and for all. How so?

Suppose I see you reading this book while moving your lips. Suppose further that, as it so happens, people who do that disgust me, so I follow you outside, pull out my Uzi, and shoot you forty-seven times, killing you in the process. Clearly, what I've done is immoral. But why? After considering a couple of possibilities, Marquis settles on the following: what makes killing you wrong is its effect on *you*, the victim, namely that it deprives you of all of the value of your future. In killing you, I'm taking away all the things you now value, of course, but I'm also taking away all of the "activities, projects, experiences, and enjoyments which would otherwise have constituted [your] future personal life."[1]

Now this seems on its face to be an extremely plausible theory of what makes killing adult human beings (prima facie) seriously immoral. But Marquis also gives several buttressing considerations. First, it explains why death is typically so bad for us, especially an early death ("He had his whole life in front of him!" we'd say). Second, it explains why we think killing someone is such a heinous crime, for it deprives the victim of so much more than virtually anything else we could do to him. Third, it explains why we think killing certain *non-humans*—both animals and aliens like E.T.—would be seriously wrong as well, for they could have futures of value very much like we do. Fourth, it explains why we might think some forms of euthanasia might *not* be wrong. Marquis' account is supposed to be merely a sufficient condition of wrongness—if an entity has a valuable future-like-ours, then that's enough to ensure that it's wrong to kill it—but the account leaves open whether or not entities that *don't* have futures-of-value may permissibly be killed. So it's possible that, if you have a terminal illness and are in extreme pain, it might be permissible to kill you (as long as you agreed to it), given that you don't meet the condition that would guarantee you a right to life. And many of us would agree with this implication of the theory. Finally, Marquis' view explains our deeply-held intuition that it's immoral to kill infants and young children, even though they're not yet persons, say.

What, then, does this account imply about abortion? The argument at this point is very easy:

1. It is (prima facie) seriously immoral to kill anything with a valuable future like ours.

2. A fetus has a valuable future like ours.

3. Thus, it is (prima facie) seriously immoral to kill a fetus.

---

1   Don Marquis, "Why Abortion is Immoral," *Journal of Philosophy* LXXXVI (April 1989): 183-202, p. 189.

There are many more details that Marquis gives to fill in the account (including a deeper discussion of value and valuing, along with a rejection of possible alternative accounts), but what we have before us will suffice to get the discussion going. So what are we to say about this argument?

Many objections have been launched against Marquis over the years, but there is one in particular that is directly relevant to our discussion of personal identity. Specifically, it is an objection to the second premise, denying that a fetus in fact has a valuable future *like ours*.

Return to the scenario above, where I kill you for a ridiculously trivial reason. Suppose we agree with Marquis that what makes this wrong is that I'm robbing you of your valuable future. Now what makes this a valuable future *to you*, that is, what does *your* loss now amount to when I kill you? As Marquis says, I'm taking away those activities, experiences, projects, and pleasures that would otherwise have constituted your future life. After all, suppose I killed a stranger instead of you. I would not have wronged *you*, even though I would have taken away the activities, experiences, projects, and pleasures of *someone*. So what's key to the wrongness of killing you is that I'm taking away a future of experiences that would have been *yours*, and of course this is the point that brings personal identity into the discussion, for if I hadn't killed you, there would have been (presumably) a person who existed next year at this time, say, who would have been enjoying his or her activities and enjoyments and who would also have been *you*.

But of course Marquis says more than just that what makes killing some entity E seriously immoral is that it takes away E's future, for what if E is an elm tree or an eel? We don't think that killing such entities is seriously immoral—on a par with killing an adult human being—even though they certainly have futures. What matters instead is that E's future is valuable *in the way our futures are valuable to us*. So what makes my future valuable in this way? It's not just that I'll be alive, but that I'll get to experience that life and enjoy those experiences. This value, then, seems to stem entirely from my future *psychological* life. But there is also something else that makes my future psychological life valuable, namely, its relation to my *present* psychological life. For it's not enough that I will experience certain things in the future for that future to be valuable in the way our futures are ordinarily valuable; instead, those experiences must take their place within a *life* of experiences, part of an ongoing stream of consciousness. For example, suppose I am currently working hard on some important project, like a cure for cancer. Suppose further that, in twenty years, I will have found that cure. There will surely be lots of valuable experiences surrounding that success, including parties, speeches, lots of money, and so forth. But those experiences will not be valuable, or nearly as valuable, without their relation to my long years of sacrifice and hard work. Suppose that, after finding the cure I had a terrible accident and suffered global amnesia, remembering nothing of the past twenty years. I would likely still be feted and celebrated worldwide, but those experiences would simply be meaningless to me, devoid of value, or at least devoid of anything like the value I would have had without the amnesia.

What this suggests is that what makes one's future have the value it ordinarily has is, at least in part, its relation to one's past. And given that the values in question are psychological, and a relation of personal identity across time is necessary, what we need to account for what makes for a valuable future-like-ours would seem to be found in the Psychological Criterion of personal identity. But then (to complete the objection) if what makes my future stage a "valuable future like ours" is that I'm now related to it by psychological continuity, and a fetus lacks the brain capacities for developing or sustaining the relevant psychological connections constituting psychological continuity, then a fetus simply doesn't have a valuable future like ours, and Marquis' argument fails. A fetus, while certainly having a future, is more like an eel or an elm tree with respect to that future than an adult human being.

Now Marquis might very well respond as follows: "Look, the Psychological Criterion fails to get our essence right, for it does not allow that we were indeed fetuses. But if I—the 'I' that refers to my essence as a human organism—was a fetus (which I indeed was), then it seems the Biological Criterion is what's relevant here, in which case my current valuable present was in fact my fetus's valuable future. In general, then, fetuses do have valuable futures like ours—what other kind of futures could they possibly have?"

This would be an effective response were it not for the point about psychological relations made above: for a valuable future to be *like mine* (and not like, say, that of an eel or an elm), it has to bear a certain sort of psychological relation *to my present psychological life*. But given the Marquisian point about our essence and the fact that we indeed once were fetuses, we wind up with a real tension here. How can we have the essence point coexist with the psychological point?

One way is to draw from considerations of narrative identity, as follows: "While I am indeed identical to that fetus (given the Biological Criterion, say), nevertheless what makes for a valuable future like ours is, in part, that one's future experiences can be incorporated *alongside one's current experiences* into a coherent life narrative. So what makes some future experiences *mine*—in the sense of narrative identity—is their relation to my current (and other life) experiences." On this hybrid view, then, while I am numerically identical to the fetus from which I developed, that fetus did not have a "future like ours," given that its psychological incapacities rendered it unable to be incorporated into a coherent life narrative. This move would thus admit the Marquisian response above, while nevertheless still denying the second premise of his argument.

Unfortunately, we have seen that there is no good reason to exclude the lives of fetuses from one's narrative; indeed, there will often be good reasons to *include* them. But if that's the case, and being incorporated into a narrative identity is the way in which one gets a valuable future like ours, then we might have reason after all to think that (many) fetuses do in fact have valuable futures like ours.

Nevertheless, there is a deeper problem here. What raised the need for, and produced the subsequent tension between, the various criteria of identity we have just discussed was the thought that, in order for some valuable future to be mine, I must be identical to the person who lives out that future. But this may not be true. Consider once more a case of Physical Fission, in which I am sliced down the middle and each side is given a fleshing-out shot, so that it grows back the missing body half. Suppose, though, that you are the one who slices me down the middle, and then you administer the fleshing-out shot to each half. On all plausible accounts of identity (biological, psychological, and narrative), I cease to exist in this case, even though there are two people in existence who are just like me in every respect. Of course, if only one of them had survived, I would still be alive; it's only in virtue of there being *two* of them that I cease to exist, given that the identity relation must hold 1-1.

Now consider my relation pre-slice to the post-slice people. It seems that everything that matters has been preserved, such that even though neither future is *my* valuable future—given that neither will be me—their futures are *just as valuable to me* as my own future would have been. To drive this point home, suppose that, instead of slicing me in half, you kill me with a flamethrower, completely destroying my body and rendering it beyond saving with the fleshing-out shot. Compare, then, my being burned to death with my being sliced in half and getting the fleshing-out shots. In both scenarios, I cease to exist at the same moment, and so am deprived of my valuable future, but in the latter scenario there would be two people in existence exactly like me, living as I would have, experiencing the things I would have, and enjoying how I would have. Surely, then, we would think that the torched-to-death scenario is far worse *for me* than the sliced-in-half scenario, despite my being deprived of my valuable future in both.

What this must mean, then, is that Marquis' analysis of the wrongness of killing is mistaken. Depriving someone of the future of value he or she would otherwise have had can't be *the* wrong-making feature of killing, because if it were, then both of the above scenarios ought to be equally wrong. But they're just not: the loss to me in the burned-to-death scenario is far greater than the loss to me (if any) in the sliced-in-half scenario. Sure, slicing me in half without my permission is most definitely wrong! It violates my autonomy, for one thing. But given the existence of my fission products, the wrongness isn't nearly so bad as when you prevent the existence of any such survivors, even though you equally deprive me of *my* future in both cases.

What, then, is the source of wrongness? Why is the burned-to-death scenario much worse? It could only be because burning me to death cuts off the relation of psychological continuity: it deprives me of the valuable future of someone who will be psychologically continuous with me. But of course there is such a person (two of them, in fact) in the sliced-in-half case, so what happens to me isn't nearly as bad as it is in the flamethrower case. What I want, in looking forward to my future, is that there will be someone who remembers my life (from the inside), someone who will experience and enjoy life—and certain elements of life—in the way that I do, someone who cares about what I care about, and so on. Whether or not he is *me* is less important than whether or not he will be related to me in the right psychological way.

These remarks are directly relevant to Marquis' argument. Depriving me of my valuable future isn't what makes killing me wrong. Instead, what makes it wrong is that it deprives me of a future psychological continuer (whose own present, it is assumed, will be valuable). But fetuses *have* no psychological continuers, given their lack of certain basic psychological capacities, and so they lack the feature of adult human beings that makes killing us wrong. As a result, a fetus doesn't have a valuable future *like ours*, and the argument fails.

What we have found here points to a general lesson: ceasing to exist may not be equivalent to dying. After all, there may be a couple of different ways to cease to exist, one of which (fission) involves no organismic death. And so, while there are a couple of different ways for me to deprive you of your valuable future, only one of them—via flamethrower—is wrong *for that reason*. But in any case, identity in and of itself may not have the value attached to it we might have thought it did. It remains to be seen just what role identity will play in our other ethical issues to follow.

HUMAN EMBRYONIC STEM CELL RESEARCH

It is worth exploring whether or not there is any relevant identity-related difference between abortion and stem cell research, and that's what we'll do in this section. First, though, it is important to be clear on the biological details of human embryonic stem cell (hESC) research. For the first five days after conception, the cells of the zygote remain entirely undifferentiated, but at about the five day mark certain cells at the outer layer separate off to form what's known as the trophectoderm, a ring of protective cells that will eventually form part of the placenta. The remaining cells form what's known as the inner cell mass (ICM). At this stage in development, this entity (both trophectoderm and ICM) is technically called the blastocyst, and when it is implanted in the uterine wall, the ICM cells soon become differentiated.

Stem cells come from the ICM cells of a *pre-implantation* blastocyst. To get them, one separates the ICM cells out and cultures them, and then the cells ultimately derived from those cultured cells are themselves stem cells, cells able to replicate indefinitely while remaining entirely undifferentiated, capable of developing into a variety of cell types. Indeed, after several months of culture, they can develop into anything from blood to nerve to muscle cells, which makes their potential enormously significant. For instance, they could provide an unlimited bank of transplantable cell types for the treatment of everything from heart disease to leukemia to Parkinson's and Alzheimer's diseases. But insofar as separating the ICM from the trophectoderm dissolves the embryo from which they came, hESC research has become a hot-button moral issue. After all, goes the reasoning, if the embryo is a human being, and human beings have full moral status, then hESC research destroys a human being, which is prima facie seriously morally wrong.

On its face, it might seem as if the debate over hESC research is just a subset of the larger debate over abortion, producing the same moral verdicts in both arenas, so that if, say, it turns out to be morally permissible to kill a fetus, it will then also be morally permissible to kill an embryo. After all, a fetus is more developed, and would thus seem to be a more morally significant entity, than an embryo. Furthermore, the good produced by an abortion—a benefit to the mother and perhaps a small circle of her intimates—is very small compared to the good produced by the destruction of an embryo for the sake of hESC research, namely, the potential to save countless lives. Nevertheless, there are reasons to view the permissibility of hESC research as a separate matter from the morality of abortion, for reasons similar to those just mentioned. First, there could be strong considerations in favor of viewing the fetus and the embryo as having a different moral status from each other, which might end up meaning that the exact same treatment to each (killing, for example) could be permissible with respect to one and impermissible with respect to the other. Second, the potential good effects of hESC research are far greater than the potential good effects of abortion, so on a moral theory in which we're to maximize good consequences, abortion could be immoral while hESC research was not.

We will briefly explore just the first set of considerations, given their possible link to identity, at least in the sense of membership in a kind. Why think, then, that a fetus and an embryo might each have a different moral status? One obvious answer will be that one is an individual like us, whereas the other is not. Perhaps, then, being an individual like us is sufficient for having a minimal right to life, whereas not being an individual like us isn't, so fetuses have a minimal right to life and embryos don't (at least insofar as they're not individuals like us).

This is too vague, though, for there are many respects in which fetuses are *not* like us: at early stages they have gills, tails, and lack brains (or many organs at all). And of course none of them are *persons* like us, as was pointed out in the previous section on abortion. So more needs to be said about just what it means to be an individual *like us* to get this argument off the ground.

Most advocates of the Biological Criterion will want to distinguish the fetus from the embryo in terms of which one is an *individuated human organism*. Now as alluded to in the previous section, there is genuine debate over the point at which we come into existence, but there is little debate over the point at which we are *individuated*. That is generally around two weeks after conception, when the primitive streak that will develop into the spinal cord is formed, preventing the organism from being able to split off into twins (or triplets...) any more. Once this possibility has been cut off, there is definitely only one organism in existence, and most advocates of the Biological Criterion will point to this entity as the beginning of the thing *I* once was.

One might say, then, that since only those entities that have developed beyond the two-week point are fetuses, and that is the point beyond which they can no longer divide, of the two types of developing entities (embryos and fetuses) only fetuses are individuated human organisms, and so for that reason fetuses might have a different moral status from embryos.[1] Now there will be legitimate questions here about why being an individuated human organism gets one moral status, but that is beyond the scope of our current inquiry.

Is there a way to grant, though, that fetuses are individuated organisms, while embryos are not, and yet still maintain that the moral status of both is equivalent, in virtue of some *other* property (or properties) they have in common? After all, many people, including President George W. Bush, agree with the following statement from Do No Harm: The Coalition of Americans for Research Ethics:

> Human embryos are not mere biological tissues or clusters of cells; they are the tiniest of human beings. Thus, we have a moral responsibility not to deliberately harm them....[2]

As a result, these folks must think that embryos are just like fetuses, and just like the rest of us, in virtue of our all sharing *something* in common, despite the fact that embryos may not be individuated human organisms (and fetuses aren't persons, etc.). Indeed, they do. So what is that something? The soul.

We set aside the Soul Criterion in Chapter One given that it seemed quite irrelevant to the question of personal identity. But there we were concerned with the question of identity across time and the possibility of immortality, and for *those* issues the soul—given its immaterial nature—does seem irrelevant. That is, given that our questions were about the identity of the *same* soul *across* time, the inability to reidentify souls was a crippling blow to the account. Here, however, we are not concerned about entities that may or may not have the same soul across time; rather, we are concerned about entities that may or may

---

1   One might also, of course, claim that *both* lack moral status, or at least the kind of moral status rendering abortion or hESC prima facie morally impermissible.

2   Quoted in Ted Peters, "Embryonic Stem Cells and the Theology of Dignity," in Suzanne Holland, Karen Lebacqz, and Laurie Zoloth, eds., *The Human Embryonic Stem Cell Debate: Science, Ethics, and Public Policy* (Cambridge, MA: The MIT Press, 2001), p. 129.

not have *a* soul at a *particular* time. And the thought held by many, and forcefully expressed by the Catholic Church, is that souls are what provide an entity with moral status, and they enter the body at the moment of conception.

Of course, the "true" moment of ensoulment has been the source of much controversy and alteration over the years. It used to be, for instance, that leading theologians of the Catholic Church (ultimately following Aristotle) thought that the souls of male fetuses entered their bodies forty days after conception, while the souls of female fetuses entered their bodies eighty days after conception. But let's take the most recent statement of the Catholic Church here as our guide: "From the moment of conception, the life of every human being is to be respected in an absolute way because man is the only creature on earth that God has 'wished for himself' and the spiritual soul of each man is 'immediately created' by God; his whole being bears the image of the Creator."[1] As a result:

> [T]he fruit of human generation, from the first moment of its existence, that is to say from the moment the zygote has formed, demands the unconditional respect that is morally due to the human being in his bodily and spiritual totality. The human being is to be respected and treated as a person from the moment of conception; and therefore from that same moment his rights as a person must be recognized, among which in the first place is the inviolable right of every innocent human being to life.[2]

What can we say about such a view?

To begin with, simply allowing that the thing to which the soul attaches—the embryo—isn't yet an individual human organism won't get one off the hook when it comes to the possibility of twinning and fusion. Suppose, for instance, that we have a five-day old embryo, and that it indeed has a soul, and then suppose it divides into twins. What happened to the original soul? Either (a) it divided too, (b) it went along with one

---

1   From *Instruction on Respect for Human Life in its Origin and on the Dignity of Procreation: Replies to Certain Questions of the Day*, Introduction, Section 5, on the web at http://www. vatican.va/roman_curia/congregations/cfaith/documents/rc_con_cfaith_doc_19870222_ respect-for-human-life_en.html.
2   Ibid.

of the twins while the other got a new soul, or (c) it went out of existence, replaced in the twins with two new souls. Every one of these options yields real trouble for the view, however.

First, on virtually every theological account of souls, they cannot divide. Instead, souls are widely thought to be "simple" entities, without extension or composite parts, indivisible and incorruptible. This would seem to eliminate option (a), then, as plausible theologically. But on either of options (b) or (c), the view that embryos are human beings—because they have souls—from the moment of conception is false, for both options involve *some* embryos—either one twin or both—getting their souls, and thus their moral statuses, several days *after* conception.

Furthermore, there are independent problems with each of options (b) and (c). On option (b), for instance, the soul goes with one of the twins but not the other. But which one? And why? Indeed, given that neither twin has any distinguishing features at this point, what non-arbitrary reason could the assigner of the souls—God, presumably—have for keeping it with one twin over the other? God would not do *everything* for a reason, then, given such a case.

On option (c), according to which the original soul just popped out of existence, alongside the "death" of the original embryo, then it looks like we would have reason to mourn such an event. After all, if the original embryo had full moral status in virtue of its soul, but it, along with its soul, ceased to exist at the point of twinning, then shouldn't that be as tragic an event as when a full-fledged person ceases to exist? But that's clearly absurd. Surely no one thinks the formation of twins is a *bad* thing, somehow involving the sacrifice of one human being for the sake of two others, an event we should mourn.

Now one might object here that, while the original embryo ceased to exist, this sort of event isn't mourn-worthy given that the original embryo's incorruptible *soul* lives on. What made it a human being, one might say, could still be in existence. So perhaps God brings that original soul to heaven, to live out its immortal life there, or perhaps that soul is then implanted into another embryo later (the source of reincarnation, say). So given that the soul could easily live on, there's no cause for mourning in the twinning case.

But this sort of response is seriously problematic as well, for why should we then think that hESC research is morally problematic, or that human deaths *at any stage* are tragic, or to be mourned, at all? After all, if one's soul will just survive one's physical death, what's so bad about death?

We can get a bit clearer on these worries by figuring out the precise relationship between my soul and me. Is an immaterial soul something I *am* or something I *have*? In other words, is the soul my essence, so that to remove my soul is to remove me, or is the soul not my essence, so that to remove my soul is to leave me, my essence, intact? If the former, and if the soul is eternal, incorruptible, and so forth, then it's impossible for me to die! I cannot be killed or, really, harmed in any serious way, given that my soul cannot be killed or harmed. Now one might reply that one's physical body is one's property—the house for one's soul—and so to destroy my body is actually to harm me in a very serious way. But if this is the case, then most of us have been viewing and assessing cases of "killing" in a completely wrongheaded way, for we have thought that to kill someone was to cause him to *cease to exist*, and that was the source of killing's serious wrongness. But on the soul-based view under discussion, killing someone isn't wrong in virtue of its causing someone to cease to exist; rather, it's wrong in virtue of rendering someone *homeless*. But then all of the rhetoric surrounding the condemnation of stem cell research—that it sacrifices and destroys one human being for the sake of others—is simply false. And once we recognize that the tradeoff actually involves simply making someone homeless versus saving many other lives, it becomes much more difficult to register a strong objection to the wide-ranging life-saving research in question.

On the other hand, suppose I am *not* my soul; suppose, rather, that it is some attribute I get at conception. Now setting aside the deep worry that I—an individuated entity—don't yet exist at conception, suppose we allow that the embryo that will *become* me (ignoring the possibility of twinning and fusion) gets its soul at conception, and it is in virtue of that soul that the embryo has the same moral status as a human being like you and me. One might wonder, of course, why such a view wouldn't just beg the question. In other words, how is the positing of this invisible, immaterial thing that somehow grants a physical entity a certain moral status any different from simply asserting that the physical entity in question just *has* moral status? But at any rate, were this the way things worked, then again, we would have much more mourning to do, for many zygotes and embryos—around 25%—are spontaneously aborted (miscarried), often without the mothers even realizing they were pregnant. What does this mean, though? Millions (perhaps billions) of "human beings" are dying all around us every day, often without our knowing it, a slaughter of massive proportions. Why, then, do we not mourn these deaths equally with the deaths of infant or adult human beings? Indeed, why do we not mourn these deaths *at all*? And if God is ensouling these entities, granting them moral status, what could the point possibly be? It would be as if God were granting them moral status just so they could spontaneously be destroyed *as human beings*, which should make their deaths much more tragic than they would otherwise be. But this way of viewing the matter makes God look less than good: after all, if you had a choice between granting human moral status to a creature that was going to die soon or letting the organism die without having any such human moral status, which would *you* choose? It seems obvious the less cruel way to go would be to refrain from granting human status to the doomed creature. Nevertheless, the implication of an arbitrary, even immoral, God is hard to shake if souls are what get us moral status from the moment of conception.

There might be one last attempt to retain the view, though, for one might hold that God in fact ensouls *only* those human organisms that He knows will make it to a certain well-developed point in pregnancy. If God is omniscient, after all, then He'll know which organisms will make it and which ones won't, and so to avoid the absurd "spontaneous abortions tragedy" just discussed, perhaps He grants moral status only to those that will survive. But of course this won't help out the person who objects to hESC research (and abortion) either, for the moral permissibility of those practices would now be *guaranteed* insofar as the practices themselves would ensure that the organisms in question wouldn't survive, and given that God would know this, they wouldn't be granted souls, or have human moral status, to begin with.

We are left, then, with little reason to object to hESC research. Given that only pre-individuation embryos would be destroyed, identity-based grounds for objection are absent, given that, on our main theories of identity, an individual like us has yet to come into existence, and so killing the embryo would not be akin to killing one of us. It seems instead that the only ground for granting regular human moral status to an embryo comes from something like the Catholic Church's doctrine that zygotes and embryos are ensouled. But as we have just seen, it is very hard to get a clear handle on such a doctrine, and even when we can articulate the various possible versions of the view, a host of other problems, both logical and theological, quickly ensue. It seems much more likely, then, that just as there didn't seem to be any good identity-related objections to abortion, so too there may be no good identity-related objections to hESC research.

WORKS CITED OR REFERENCED IN THIS CHAPTER

DeGrazia, David. *Human Identity and Bioethics.* Cambridge: Cambridge University Press, 2005.

Holland, Suzanne; Lebacqz, Karen; and Zoloth, Laurie, eds. *The Human Embryonic Stem Cell Debate: Science, Ethics, and Public Policy.* Cambridge, MA: The MIT Press, 2001.

Instruction on Respect for Human Life in its Origin and on the Dignity of Procreation: Replies to Certain Questions of the Day. Available on the web at http://www.vatican.va/roman_curia/congregations/cfaith/documents/rc_con_cfaith_doc_19870222_respect-for-human-life_en.html.

Marquis, Don. "Why Abortion is Immoral." *Journal of Philosophy* LXXXVI (April 1989): 183-202.

McMahan, Jeff. *The Ethics of Killing.* Oxford: Oxford University Press, 2002.

Noonan, John T. "An Almost Absolute Value in History." In *The Morality of Abortion: Legal and Historical Perspectives.* Cambridge, MA: Harvard University Press, 1970.

Parfit, Derek. *Reasons and Persons.* Oxford: Oxford University Press, 1984.

Peters, Ted. "Embryonic Stem Cells and the Theology of Dignity." In Holland, et al.

Shoemaker, David. "Embryos, Souls, and the Fourth Dimension." *Social Theory and Practice* 31 (2005): 51-75.

Thomson, James A. "Human Embryonic Stem Cells." In Holland, et al.

CHAPTER FIVE

Moral Issues at the Beginning of Life, Part II: Creation

In Part I of this two-part discussion of issues at the beginning of life, we examined relations between identity and the morality of ending the existence of new life via abortion or embryonic research. We turn now to identity-related moral issues surrounding bringing new life into existence. Specifically, we will discuss the morality of cloning, moral limits on pre- and post-natal genetic interference, and worries about the ways in which our current family and policy choices may determine just what sorts of people will be brought into existence in the future (known as "population ethics"). And once again we will explore whether or not considerations of identity can provide any objections or support to the practices in question.

CLONING

In exploring the topic of abortion in the previous chapter, we found that one might cease to exist in a few different ways. But just as there might be multiple ways to go out of existence, there also might be multiple ways to come into existence. One of the most controversial would be via cloning. Despite the fact that there have yet to be any human clones (that we know of), the technology does seem to be at a point where it would certainly be possible, if it's not already, within the next few years. But would it be immoral to bring someone into existence via this method? More to the point for our purposes, are there are any identity-related considerations either for or against it?

There is just one objection to cloning that is relevant to personal identity, but before we explore it, we should take a moment just to get clear on precisely what the biology of cloning consists in. The controversy all started with Dolly, the adult sheep produced via the "nuclear cell transfer" cloning technique developed by Ian Wilmut's Roslin Institute in Scotland. What Wilmut's group did was to take some mammary cells from an adult ewe and then render them dormant (to stop cell division, for one thing). Then they extracted some unfertilized egg cells from another ewe, removed those cells' nuclei and DNA, and mixed these genetically empty cells with the mammary cells. Stimulation with a mild electric current fused the genetic material from the mammary cells with the egg cells and began embryonic development of the fusion. The resulting embryos were, finally, implanted in the uteruses of yet other ewes. Eventually, these ewes gave birth to five live lambs, each of which was a genetic twin of the original mammary cell donor. Only one of these lambs, however, survived into adulthood, and that was the famous Dolly. Dolly has since been put to death, after contracting a lung infection in 2003, but it is unlikely that her illness was related to her being a clone. Since Dolly, several other animals have been successfully cloned using the nuclear cell transfer technology, including cows, goats, pigs, rabbits, cats, and mice. The thought is that it will only be a matter of time until the procedure would work with humans, even though it would be much more complicated. Would it be *morally* permissible, however, to do so, even if we perfected the technology?

There have been several objections advanced against human cloning—that it would conflict with our moral image of the family, that it would soil or undermine human dignity, and that it would use people as means and not ends, to name just three—but the one that matters for our purposes is the one articulated in the Introduction by Howard, in his disagreement with Annie: cloning you, say, would rob your clone of a unique identity. Insofar as he or she would be *genetically* identical to you, he or she would lack the uniqueness necessary for a *personal* identity. And insofar as the loss of one's personal identity is a very bad thing, we have reason to prevent that loss by preventing human cloning.

This sort of argument clearly struck a chord with many people. Consider some illustrations (compiled by Patrick Hopkins). After the announcement of the Dolly success, *Time* magazine had a picture of exactly similar sheep over a background of thirty small copies of that picture with the headline, "Will There Ever Be Another You?" At a protest around this same time, people held up signs saying "I like just one of me." On *Nightline*, one person against the technology noted that "this is taking somebody's identity and giving it, at the genetic level, to somebody else." In *U.S. News & World Report*, we were told that "Making copies [cloning] pales next to the wonder of creating a unique human being the old-fashioned way." Even President Clinton joined in: "My own view is that human cloning would have to raise deep concerns given our most cherished concepts of faith and humanity. Each human life is unique, born of a miracle that reaches beyond laboratory science. I believe we must respect this profound gift and resist the temptation to replicate ourselves."

On its face, though, this is just a bizarre argument. For one thing, it assumes that personal identity is a matter of genetic identity, but no plausible theory of personal identity takes that line. Indeed, any theory that did so would be seriously problematic: identical twins are genetically identical, but no one believes that they lack a unique personal identity thereby. In fact, one clear way to think of the clone would be as just the *delayed* identical twin of the donor. If we thus think of the clone in this way, it becomes very difficult to think of it as losing any uniqueness whatsoever. After all, if simultaneous identical twins lack no significant uniqueness—they have different experiences, memories, beliefs, desires, and even physiognomies—then we would have even less reason to think that delayed identical twins would lack uniqueness, given the additional differences between them of time and place of development.

Both of our leading theories of numerical identity would agree. The Psychological Criterion clearly implies that the uniqueness of identity across time consists in the uniqueness of psychological continuity. But the clone's and donor's psychological streams will just not be continuous with one another. The Biological Criterion, on the other hand, may seem more closely aligned with the objection, but it is actually in lockstep with the Psychological Criterion on this point: the clone and donor are quite obviously two distinct organisms, neither is biologically continuous with the other, and so they both have a unique personal identity.

Perhaps, then, the objection gets some traction, not from considerations of numerical identity, but from considerations of *narrative* identity. After all, if I were just a "copy" of my father/brother, I might have a hard time figuring out just what my unique place in this world could be. After all, what would make the various experiences and psychological features that occurred *mine*, in the unique sense desired? Wouldn't these traits have already been someone else's? And a loss of uniqueness might conceivably be felt on the part of the donor: where once these various traits were mine, he might think, in sharing them with my clone I will lose my grip on what makes me my own unique self. And it's possible these worries could lead to the kind of "identity crisis" and fragmented self that we strongly wish to avoid.

Nevertheless, it is once again difficult to make sense of such a worry. Surely the story of a clone's life could be just as unique, coherent, and unified as anyone else's life, including that of the donor. Narrative identity is simply about the way in which one organizes and connects various experiences and psychological characteristics into a unified storyline, and given that genetic identity does nothing to determine one's experiences and at most only partially determines one's psychological characteristics, there is no reason to think that any of our narrators—be they clones or donors—will tell anything like the same story; indeed, how *could* they? Sure, the narrative of a clone will be heavily *influenced* by the fact that he is a clone, but why should we think that when it comes to the arc of that person's life that fact will be any more influential than typical facts about one's origins are in non-cloning cases? And even if the facts of one's cloning origins *were* more influential than regular facts about origins, wouldn't this be yet another way in which one's narrative identity would be *unique*?

All in all, then, it looks like there is just no good argument against cloning from considerations of personal identity. Of course, this doesn't mean that there are no good arguments against cloning; it just means those arguments won't come from the world of personal identity, and that is our focus here.

One final note, related to our discussion of abortion in the previous chapter. Suppose cloning were more or less perfected, such that we could take any living cell from virtually any part of my body and ultimately produce a healthy fetus genetically identical to me. If this were possible, it would pose yet another serious problem for Marquis' anti-abortion argument. According to him, remember, it's wrong to deprive any entity of a valuable future-like-ours. But on our supposition, virtually any cell in my body could be turned into a clone of me, with a clear-cut future-like-ours. So the implication of Marquis' view is that it would be wrong to deprive *any of those cells* of a future-like-ours, that is, we would be morally obligated to clone every one of those available cells (and ultimately every one of my clone's available cells, and of course every one of *everyone's* available cells). But surely that is absurd. So here we have yet another reason to believe that Marquis' argument is seriously problematic.

If personal identity considerations do not provide any good argument against cloning, it does not follow, of course, that cloning is ethically acceptable. A lot of other arguments have been raised against it, from other directions, but we won't go into these here.

GENETIC INTERVENTION

Let us turn now to explore a very different sort of ethical problem related to origins. Suppose you carried the gene for Huntington's disease (HD), but that you were also married and wanted to have a child. There is a 50/50 chance that any child of yours would inherit the HD gene. It is a terribly debilitating disease, and if one has the gene one will eventually get the disease. You certainly don't want your child, therefore, to inherit it. As it turns out, a new scientific treatment will allow you to prevent your child from carrying the gene. The treatment is gene therapy, and it comes in two options. The first option is to alter the genetic structure (the genome) of your gametes (sperm or egg), such that any zygote produced will be absent the HD gene. The second option is to wait until after both fertilization and individuation have occurred (roughly two weeks after conception), and then alter the genome of that fetus, such that it will be absent the HD gene. Should you permit such genetic intervention? If not, why not, and if so, which one?

We are concerned in this part of the book to explore the identity-related considerations in various moral arenas, and in this particular arena such considerations seem to be front and center. Some of these considerations will be trivial, or have very little moral relevance, but others will definitely be more central to the issues at stake. And, as we will see, some of the issues in prenatal genetic intervention have implications for both postnatal genetic intervention and very serious issues in population ethics, so there is much of importance to discuss.

Prenatal Genetic Therapy: Pre-Conception Cases

Consider first, then, the case just given. I imagine that most of us would be inclined towards permitting the gene therapy. But why? And which option should one take? Initially, it seems as if this is a win-win situation: a disease-free child you will love and care for will be brought into the world. What could be wrong about that? But what is the precise identity of this post-therapy child? And if its identity is different from the child that *would have* been brought into the world without such therapy, might there not be a wrong committed in the prevention of that other child's existence?

To sort some of these issues out, we need to begin with Saul Kripke's famous point about origins in his book *Naming and Necessity*. The question he considers is about whether or not one person could have been someone else. So, for example, does it make sense to say that you could have been Julia Roberts? Kripke's answer is an unequivocal No. As he puts it, "How could a person originating from different parents, from a totally different sperm and egg, be *this very woman?*"[1] How, in other words, could you—the particular individual that you are—have been any *other* individual, given that what makes you the particular individual you are would have been absent in the imagined alternative scenario. Unless the particular sperm and egg that combined to produce you in fact combined to produce you, you would not have existed.

Now this point is most certainly one with which advocates of the Biological Criterion might be inclined to agree. After all, if my essence is that of an individual organism, then it's quite true that this particular organism could not have existed as the product of any other combination of gametes. But might there be reason to qualify Kripke's point on some other criterion? One might think, for instance, that an advocate of the Psychological Criterion who focused solely on identity conditions for *persons* (without necessarily thinking that personhood is our essence) could deny Kripke's point. After all, what makes one any particular person may not necessarily depend on one's biological origins; it could be, for instance, that my particular set of self-conscious psychological characteristics and capacities could have been instantiated in a variety of biological organisms. So even if I, the particular person I am, in fact originated from the particular parents I had, it seems to remain *possible*, anyway, that I could also have originated from different parents, or that Julia Roberts might have originated from my parents. In other words, I could have been her, if by "I" we are referring to this particular Shoemaker-person, and by "her" we are referring to that particular Roberts-organism.[2]

Nevertheless, it's reasonable to believe that Kripke was making a point about our *essence*, in which case the move made by the Psychological Criterion theorist will likely not hold: if one's essence is that of a human animal or organism, then surely *that* particular individual could not have

---

1 Saul Kripke, *Naming and Necessity*, 2nd ed. (Cambridge, MA: Harvard University Press, 1980), p. 112.

2 Another way Kripke's view might be false is if what I am essentially is a *featureless* soul, that is, a substance that has neither physical nor psychological properties of any kind. If so, then that soul could have been attached to Julia Roberts' body and psychology instead of mine, such that I (my current featureless soul) could have been someone else (the featureless soul of the person we think of as Julia Roberts). Nevertheless, this view is deeply problematic, for reasons we won't go into here, and we may safely ignore it.

originated from any other combination of sperm and egg. So if we stick with this understanding of the idea, I could not have been Julia Roberts (nor she me). What, then, does this have to do with prenatal genetic therapy (PGT)?

Some have thought that Kripke's point implies that any child resulting from a combination of sperm and egg, each of which had undergone genetic therapy, would be a different child from one resulting from a combination of sperm and egg absent such therapy. The thought, then, must be that genetic therapy to an egg, say, yields *a different egg*. But why should we think this? Surely if we can remain the same individual through quite remarkable amounts of change (from early-stage fetus to infant to exuberant child to sullen teenager and so on, all the way through to senior citizen), a gamete could remain the same gamete through some genetic change. Of course, how much change is compatible with preservation of the same gamete could be a difficult question to answer, but it seems clear that qualitative change, in and of itself, implies nothing whatsoever about quantitative change, and this dictum ought to apply equally well to both humans and gametes.

It could very well be, then, that PGT on gametes wouldn't in fact change the identity of any resulting child. On this construal, it would be just as if we'd taken the existing child and simply removed her HD gene, and there would surely be nothing immoral about that. What, though, if PGT on pre-conception gametes did in fact alter them significantly enough for us to agree that the gametes that *would have* produced the child are no longer the gametes that *in fact* produce the child? This might happen in one of two ways: either we determine that the gene therapy in question would produce such significant qualitative change to the gamete that it could no longer seriously be construed as identical to the original, or the therapy might require some time, a genetic therapy *to me* (the parent), such that some gametes I will produce in the future will be altered sufficiently to ensure that any child produced will lack the HD gene. On this latter possibility, the pre-therapy gametes that would have contributed to the production of a child with the HD gene are no longer in existence at the post-therapy point of combination. Either way, though, the child that would have come into existence pre-therapy is not identical to the child that actually does come into existence post-therapy.

Here we've got a clear case of identity loss. But does this matter morally? It seems that the only way in which it could is if we thought we had an obligation to bring about the existence of all potential individuals. But this is surely absurd. After all, it's one thing to lose the identity of an already-existing individual, but it's another thing altogether to lose the identity of a *never*-existing individual, a purely possible creature. It's very difficult, then, to generate a moral problem with this sort of pre-conception PGT. Nevertheless, there is a fascinating collection of problems suggested by cases like this—that of wrongful life and population ethics—and we will explore them in the final section of this chapter.

Prenatal Genetic Therapy: Post-Conception Cases

Turn now to cases of post-conception therapy. For most advocates of the Biological Criterion, remember, conception doesn't mark the relevant spot of individual origins. Instead, they maintain, that point does not occur until twinning and fusion are no longer possible, once the primitive streak has formed at around fourteen days post-conception. For them, then, PGT as applied to pre-conception gametes is fundamentally no different from PGT as applied to pre-individuation zygotes, at least with respect to identity-affecting considerations. Given that the therapy surpasses a certain threshold of qualitative change to the entity in question—whether a gamete or a zygote—it will yield a different individual than would have existed without the therapy. But further, given that we do no moral wrongs by not bringing someone into existence, and we also ought to do what we can to ensure that those brought into existence have a decent quality of life, it would seem as if we do no moral wrong in engaging in pre-individuation genetic therapy, and indeed it might be wrong *not* to do so.

What, though, of post-conception, post-*individuation* fetuses? Suppose we were able to provide fetuses that carried the HD gene with PGT to eliminate it? Would this be morally problematic on identity-affecting grounds? On the Biological Criterion, that fetus is already an individual, with a unique (biological) identity. But given that individual organisms can undergo quite a bit of change without losing their identity, so too it would seem a fetus could undergo PGT without losing its identity. In this case, then, PGT would have a conceptually pure *therapeutic* effect, benefiting the very same individual who underwent the procedure. And given that there seem to be no significant identity-related moral objections to doing so to adult human beings like us (it's standard medical procedure, after all), there ought to be no such objections either for doing so to fetuses.

Are there any plausible objections to PGT from the other criteria of identity? It does not really seem so, for similar reasons. On the Psychological Criterion, where the identity in question is the identity of *persons*, if PGT takes place early in the pregnancy, prior to the fetus' development of certain minimal psychological capacities, then the therapy could indeed be identity-affecting, for it might have an effect on the psychological characteristics the eventual person would have, and so determine which person comes into existence. But again, it is hard to object to a treatment that keeps some potential person from coming into existence while providing a benefit to another person that does come into existence. On the other hand, if the therapy that takes place occurs to an already-existing person (perhaps a late-stage fetus, with certain developed psychological capacities), then it will not be identity-affecting, and so will not be morally objectionable on those grounds.

One might wonder, though, about a case in which PGT produces psychological discontinuity. Granting that the late stage fetus could indeed be a person, with the capacities necessary for psychological continuity (a stretch, to say the least), a genetic therapy that yielded psychological discontinuity—although it is hard to imagine just what this might consist in—could perhaps be morally problematic. After all, if the therapy actually caused an existing person to cease to exist (rather than preventing a potential person from coming into existence), that would seem to constitute a serious prima facie moral wrong, wrong on a moral status account, wrong on Marquis' "future-like-ours" account, and likely wrong on any other account. But as already mentioned, it is difficult to think of a *genetic* therapy that would have this effect, and even if it did, the case advocating the possibility of *prenatal* persons is a very hard one to maintain.

For similar reasons, it would be unlikely for there to be serious objections to PGT coming from advocates of narrative identity. Insofar as there might be prenatal experiences that the later adult may want to weave into her narrative, there would be no reason to think that the experiences of the pre- and post-therapy fetus couldn't be incorporated into one life story. After all, if narrative identity presupposes numerical identity, and numerical identity may be preserved across such qualitative changes, as previously discussed, then genetic therapy shouldn't undermine narrative identity either. And even if narrative identity normally presupposes a Psychological Criterion of numerical identity, and we grant that there could be prenatal persons whose psychological continuity could be cut off by PGT, it is hard to believe that a narrative incorporating both pre- and post-therapy stages of the organism could seriously be interrupted. After all, the kinds of experiences had by fetuses could hardly play a serious role in the storyline of a life, so even if the pre- and post-therapy fetus were to turn out to be different persons, there could easily be a narrative told later that unites them. In other words, it's unclear that narrative identity would have to presuppose the numerical identity of the Psychological Criterion at all. Finally, even if we admit there to be *two* narratives here, a pre-therapy story and a post-therapy story, would PGT be morally wrong? It's not at all clear that it would be, simply because we don't know what the moral value and status of a narratively unified life is supposed to be. Sure, *our* lives are valuable and have the requisite moral status, and this *might* be in virtue of their being subject to a certain sort of narrative treatment, but why couldn't it also be the case that the narrative must be of some duration, or must include being born, or must involve some other restriction distinguishing us from early-stage fetuses? We just don't know, and until the relation between narrative identity and moral status is spelled out more clearly, it's difficult to know what to say about such a case.

Of course, part of the problem yet again is the difficulty of thinking about fetuses as persons, or as significant stages in a narrative. But what if we consider cases of genetic therapy to clear-cut persons? At this point, things might get more complicated.

Postnatal Genetic Therapy

It might be thought that postnatal genetic therapy might be morally objectionable in a way that prenatal therapy is not, but as it turns out the same arguments from above mostly apply. If we accept the Biological Criterion, then genetic therapy at any point in the life of an individuated organism would be unlikely to change its identity, given that, on such an account, preservation of identity is compatible with a whole host of physical, and even genetic, changes. Of course, if genetic interference somehow transmogrified the human organism into a pig, then we'd surely want to say that such a treatment was identity-affecting. But given the current and foreseeable functions of genetic *therapy*, it is simply hard to imagine the motivation for, or development of, any such treatment (more on this in a moment, however). And if the therapy would not be identity-affecting, it would not be objectionable on those grounds.

Similarly, if we accept the Psychological Criterion or the moral relevance of narrative identity (which consists primarily in a kind of self-created psychological unity), it is hard to think of any genetic therapies as being identity-affecting. While undergoing genetic therapy itself may turn out to change one's life, it will nevertheless be an event that changes *one life*. It may alter the direction of the path of one's life, perhaps, but not the fact that there is but one path. A change in my genetic structure, once again, is unlikely to have any significant effect on my stream of consciousness, or the way in which my various psychological stages are related. Genetic therapy, on these views, will (hopefully) be genuinely therapeutic, providing one with a benefit, without affecting one's identity in any significant respects. Thus, insofar as we think of therapy generally as morally permissible, it is hard to think of a reason not to include genetic therapy—of both the prenatal and postnatal varieties—as morally permissible as well.

Nevertheless, as hinted at a moment ago, there do remain some more exotic cases worth exploring.

Other Sorts of Genetic and Biological Interference

Consider first genetic *enhancement*. While few people register objections to genetic therapy, many do with regard to genetic enhancement. What, though, is the difference? In general, therapy (genetic and otherwise) aims at correction, whereas enhancement (genetic and otherwise) aims at improvement. Think, then, of a baseline of health and human functioning, the point at which most of us typically reside: our organs function more or less as they are supposed to, our quality of life is decent, and so forth. Genetic therapy typically aims at correcting conditions below this baseline, whereas enhancement technology aims at taking people at or above the baseline and moving them up from there. So while therapy is an attempt to correct some disease or impairment, enhancement is an attempt to produce certain superior traits, such as height, athleticism, memory, and so on. And genetic enhancement (GE) would aim to bring about these traits through an alteration of the genetic structure of gametes, zygotes, or individual organisms.

So why are there more objections to genetic enhancement than genetic therapy? With respect to genetic enhancement, after all, wouldn't the points made above still obtain? Pre-individuation genetic interference would determine what individual was brought into existence, but it would not cause any particular individual to cease to exist, whereas post-individuation genetic interference would not be identity-affecting at all, given that an individual identity can easily be preserved through (most) genetic change. So once I have become an individuated organism or psychological being, it is hard to imagine enhanced physical or psychological traits undermining either my biological or psychological continuity. Plausible objections to enhancement, then, would have to come from outside the world of identity.

And so they do. For instance, some object that genetic enhancement, especially at the prenatal stage, involves far greater risks to the health of the post-therapy individual than genetic therapy. Indeed, we know very little about just what the risks *are*, which puts us in an even more precarious situation. And while there are certainly risks attached to genetic *therapy*, its benefits are far greater, we want to say, than the benefits of having a certain eye color or height. Furthermore, there are serious concerns about genetic enhancement and justice. It is obvious, after all, who will take advantage of possible genetic enhancements for their children: the rich, who will have far easier access to such technology than most other people. But if they were the only ones able to take advantage of the technology, then their children would likely have even greater advantages in life than they already do. To the extent that this sort of unearned advantage is unfair, then, it provides a strong moral objection to genetic enhancement generally, as David DeGrazia has pointed out.

But of course neither of these is an identity-related objection, so it is beyond the scope of our discussion to pursue them further here. Nevertheless, might there be some cases in which identity is more directly relevant to the moral discussion? Indeed there are, but not in terms of numerical identity. Instead, objections to the possibility of certain forms of enhancement make most sense with respect to *narrative* identity. So consider some of the potential applications of genetic enhancement technology in the foreseeable future: (a) production of additional muscle tissue, enhancing athletic ability (steroids without the rage, perhaps); (b) enhancement of memory, enabling one to retain a far greater amount than typical humans; (c) dampening of appetite, such that one has the need and desire to eat less (while maintaining one's regular energy levels); (d) elimination of male pattern baldness; (e) decreasing of one's need to sleep as much, enabling one to make use of many more hours in the day; and (f) alteration of skin pigmentation, enabling one to look as if one were of another race. What identity-related moral considerations might be relevant here?

It is worth reiterating that there would be no effects, in any of these cases, on one's numerical identity. The post-enhancement person would remain the same person or individual as the pre-enhancement person, given that none of these procedures would interrupt either biological or psychological continuity. Indeed, many of the outcomes foreseen through internal genetic enhancement are already possible via external means—there are pills for baldness and diet, steroids for increased muscle mass, caffeine and methamphetamines for less sleep, and surgery for pigmentation alteration—and we don't think in any of these cases that there's a new person or individual produced thereby (while we may nevertheless have moral objections on other grounds). Of course, one might think that the genetic enhancements altering one's psychological features, like the memory enhancer, could be a problem for numerical identity on the Psychological Criterion, but surely such an interference would not interrupt psychological continuity; indeed, it would *enhance* it.

Narrative identity, however, may be another matter. Could it be, for instance, that such enhancement would cause one narrative subject's life to end and another's to begin? This is hardly likely, and two points will serve as rebuttal. For one thing, the enhancements in question are surely too trivial in many cases to warrant the end of a narrative arc or the beginning of a new one. Imagine the absurdity of someone who said, "That balding person you knew in the past no longer exists; the hairy-headed person before you is someone else!" Now it's true, we occasionally hear people talk in this way—"I'm a new man because of Rogaine!"—but notice the locution: *I'm* a new man; *I* have become someone else. Nevertheless, either this way of talking is incoherent or it is merely exaggeration. Surely it is the latter, which leads to the second point of rebuttal. To say that I'm a new man is simply to say that something has happened to me that reinvigorated me, or that has changed my life. But a life-changing event isn't an identity-changing event; indeed, we can't understand it *as* life-changing unless we view the event as part of a single narrative unity. My joy at seeing my hairy head in the mirror today simply makes no sense unless it's part of the same life story as my depression at seeing my pasty pate in the mirror a year ago. The two experiences are both clearly *mine*, woven together in my unified life story.

The foreseeable developments in genetic enhancement, therefore, will not be identity-affecting in a way that could yield any serious moral objections (although again, there may be plenty of non-identity-related moral objections to launch). But what of the possibility of more radical developments? In addition, what if we widen the scope of possible enhancements to include non-genetic sources? After all, there are plenty of non-genetic enhancements available now—cosmetic surgery, Prozac, steroids, etc.—that could also develop in unforeseen ways to make certain radical enhancements viable options in the distant (or even not-so-distant) future. What shall we say of them? Let's consider a few possibilities, some of which may fall into the gray area between therapy and enhancement.

To start, suppose a person born deaf were, through surgery, genetic interference, or radically advanced cochlear implant,[1] rendered able to hear. This would be a case that might be considered enhancement for some, therapy for others. Now once again, such an alteration would have no effect whatsoever on the person's numerical identity, on either the Biological or Psychological criteria. But what of this person's narrative identity? For some deaf people, being deaf is a core part of their identity, in the same way being black or gay is embraced by some as central to their identities. To lose this crucial aspect, then, would be to lose a significant part of one's (narrative) identity, to lose, in effect, the *narrator* of the story. For that reason, then, there might be, and in fact have been, identity-related moral objections to trying to get some deaf children to get the cochlear implant (which, as the technology currently stands, isn't a hearing aid, and doesn't provide "normal" hearing, but does provide a kind of auditory understanding of the environment).

There may be something to this particular sort of worry. Consider a partial analogy. Suppose a black child were able to "pass" as white, and his parents had the option of continuing to raise him "as black," or sending him off to live with his white grandmother permanently, where he would be raised "as white" and interact only with other white kids. Given socioeconomic reality, he would have certain opportunities and potential benefits in the latter arrangement that he wouldn't have in the former, so if that were the only consideration, there would be good reason for his parents to send him off to his grandmother (given their concern for his well-being). But there is another powerful consideration here, namely, the loss of a certain sort of cultural and communal touchstone

---

1   This "bionic ear" involves an electrical device behind the ear, which picks up sound and processes it into electrical impulses which it feeds into the cochlea, the organ inside the ear where auditory nerves leading to the brain are stimulated. It has provided "hearing" for over 100,000 people worldwide.

that may represent a central part of who he is. Indeed, we use the term "identification" to convey the idea here, as in "He *identifies* with the black community," or "He self-identifies as black," where this is taken to mean that he considers the cultural aspects, world views, and ways of life associated with the black community as being *his own*, as being deeply attached to (and perhaps the source of) many of his most central beliefs, desires, goals, memories, and intentions. A move that would threaten these central psychological features and attitudes, then, could seriously be taken as a threat to his (narrative) identity, and so may be taken to constitute a significant moral reason against doing so. Similarly, then, future enhancements/therapies enabling deaf people to "hear normally" might be objectionable on the same sort of grounds (as might enhancements/therapies enabling gay people to "become straight").

It is unclear just what to say here, precisely because the idea of narrative identity is so amorphous (as discussed in Chapter Three). On the one hand, there's a sense in which being suddenly raised in a very different sort of way and community could certainly disrupt one's "sense of oneself," but is this reason to think that the *narrative of one's life* has been significantly disrupted? It actually seems more likely, as was suggested above, to think of what occurs in such cases as constituting a significant alteration to the ongoing story of one's life, but that presupposes that it is just *one* ongoing story.

On the other hand, there does seem to be a very interesting connection between identification and identity that the narrative identity view may (at least partially) capture well, and that can explain the sense of loss occurring in such cases. Those features of my psychology with which I identify—whatever that turns out to mean, precisely—could well count as my core features, those without which I am not *me*, in some important sense. Taking these features away, therefore, could well be morally objectionable on such grounds. This relation between identification and identity is something we will explore in more detail in Chapter Seven, however.

Nevertheless, consider now a few more radical cases of enhancement (or, again, therapy, depending on your view of what the relevant baseline is). These cases, while not currently possible, could nevertheless occur in the not-so-distant future, and they are genuinely puzzling in certain respects. Start with a case famous in fiction, written about in the novel *Flowers for Algernon*, written by Daniel Keyes (eventually made into the movie *Charly*, for which Cliff Robertson earned an Academy Award for Best Actor). Charly Gordon is a mentally challenged janitor who volunteers for an experimental intelligence-enhancing treatment. Charly notes his own progress—or "progris," as he puts it—as he passes through the "normal" range into super genius territory fairly quickly. During this latter period, he reflects on his earlier life and realizes that much of what he believed was false, that the people he thought were his friends viewed him merely as entertainment (and now view him with resentment for his superior abilities). But he also gains sexual and emotional maturity, realizing the possibility of a deep emotional connection with his former teacher. Eventually, though, given the merely temporary nature of the neural enhancement, the intelligence fades, until Charly returns to his former intellectual level, having forgotten what it was like to be the genius, once again content with his lot in life.

Suppose, then, that a *permanent* neural enhancement like this were possible. Would there be any identity-based moral objections to doing so? The one view that provides an immediately straightforward answer here is the Biological Criterion: because the biological organism of the post-treatment subject would be continuous with the biological organism of the pre-treatment subject, there would be no loss of numerical identity here, and so no identity-based grounds for objection. But this answer once again reveals some of the cruder limits of the Biological Criterion, for surely, we want to say, there is something about the janitor-Charly (JC) and the genius-Charly (GC) that is profoundly different, different in a way that seems to warrant treating them as very different moral agents, even though they are both fully-grown human organisms.

Does the Psychological Criterion answer any differently? One might think this criterion treats the case as less cut and dry, in a way that may better comport with our intuitions. Compare JC and GC, after all. Even if there is no real difference in terms of their biological organisms, there is a profound difference in their psychologies: their beliefs are different, as are their desires, intentions, and general character. Even memory has been affected: when GC "remembers" the experiences of JC, they are remembrances of events that have a very different interpretation for GC than they do for JC, even insofar as a determination of "what in fact happened" will be different for both (given GC's knowledge that JC's co-workers were simply being cruel to JC, rather than engaging with him). All of these psychological differences could well suggest a different person has emerged along with the neural enhancement.

Nevertheless, the Psychological Criterion does not go this far, for given that each gradual Charly-stage along the way was strongly psychologically connected to the immediately previous Charly-stage, then JC and GC are in fact uniquely psychologically continuous, and thus the same person. So at the end of the day, the Psychological Criterion yields the same answer as the Biological Criterion: the subject of neural enhancement would preserve his identity throughout the process, and so this criterion would provide no identity-based objections to the procedure.

Does switching to consideration of narrative identity produce a different answer? It *might*. Because the pre- and post-treatment subjects would likely have radical differences in the way they view the world and their various experiences in it, and because they would each also be likely to identify with a very different set of core psychological components, one might easily see two distinct narratives here. So JC might constitute one narrative ego and GC might constitute another. This fact could provide an identity-based objection to such treatment, for it would cause the "death" of JC, an abrupt conclusion to his narrative.

Nevertheless, the argument might also go in the other direction, with GC recognizing the experiences of JC as *his own* as well, as being necessary to make sense of his current predicament and experiences. The narrative arc of this person's life may well then have to include the events pre- and post-treatment in order for it to be at all coherent. On this view, there would be just one narrative ego, incorporating the events of both JC's and GC's limited "lives." If this were the case, then the narrative identity theorist as well should have no objections to such treatment on identity-based grounds.

So which is the right way for the narrative identity theorist to reply? The point is that *both* are possible, and plausible, replies. Note that one's narrative identity is the identity one constructs *from the subjective point of view* via a self-told story about one's life. That said, the actual narratives that are constructed depend on the existence of actual narrators and the ways they go about weaving the events of their lives together. So while we may speculate about ways in which various hypothetical narrative egos may embark on this process, in the end the only thing that matters is how actual narrators in fact do so. This may be frustrating from the perspective of those of us on the outside trying to get determinate moral verdicts for these cases, but it's an implication of their view that narrative theorists may find refreshing: how can we know what to do in such cases, they might ask, unless we know what effects our actions will have on an actual person's life *as lived from the inside*? Indeed, this is a question worth keeping in mind.

Suppose, nevertheless, that we go ahead and grant that identity obtains between the pre- and post-treatment subjects, and yet we deny that identity is *what matters* in survival. Instead, in accord with the IDM view discussed in Chapter Three, we might insist that what matters will just be the various psychological relations involved. In addition, we might refine the IDM view to emphasize one of those relations—psychological connectedness—over psychological continuity, as being what *really* matters in survival. Now we might apply this view here on behalf of the pre-treatment subject. He is, we are assuming, mentally disabled, but he may be perfectly content with his life regardless. After he is given the neural enhancer, however, he will be radically different psychologically, that is, the post-treatment subject won't be psychologically *connected* with the pre-treatment subject. If connectedness is what matters for rational anticipation and self-concern, the pre-treatment subject may simply have no reason to look forward to, or care about, the experiences of the post-treatment subject: after all, the earlier stage will simply have no understanding whatsoever of what that later stage's life and experiences will be like; it would be like him trying to imagine the life and experiences of a stranger. But if his own way of viewing the world is to be lost forever, he might have good reasons to object to such a treatment, and so we may have good moral reasons to object to it on his behalf.

This is a way of viewing our identity-related moral issues in a way we haven't explored before, but as we will see, it may provide a plausible answer in a number of cases. What it does, again, is prize apart the question of our identity from the question of our prudential and moral concerns, attaching those concerns instead to certain psychological relations. As we have already seen and will see again, this IDM view is not without its problems, but it is worth keeping in the mix.

The Charly case is one in which enhancement involves radical psychological alteration. Our next and final case is one in which enhancement involves radical *biological* alteration. A little background is in order, however. First, it is already possible to create chimeras in the animal community. Various goat genes can be inserted into a sheep zygote, for example, and the animal produced will have genes of both species, a creature with short goat hair intermixed with tufts of sheep wool, called a "geep." Second, there are already, in laboratories around the country, breeding programs for "transgenic" animals, those with very small amounts of human genes. The point is to breed animals that will have organs suitably transplantable, without rejection, into humans. So, for example, when one human gene is inserted into the fertilized egg of a pig, the zygotes occasionally develop into fetuses and ultimately newborn piglets that carry a human gene in every one of their cells.[1] It is hoped that their mature livers, say, or hearts, will be more suitable for transplantation into humans than previous animal organs. Finally, human embryonic stem cells have been injected into the brains of fetal mice, producing adult mice with approximately 1% human brain cells (no "humanlike" activity was detected, however).

Given this background, then, it is not hard to imagine some radical future possibilities. For instance, why not mice with 100% human brain cells (Stuart Little?)? Or creatures with the shape and external form of humans and most of the internal organs of pigs? Or creatures with 50% human parts and 50% chimpanzee parts? Now none of these is currently possible, and it is quite likely that most governments around the world would ban even the attempts to create such creatures. But practical likelihoods and

---

1   See, for example, Jeff McMahan, *The Ethics of Killing* (Oxford: Oxford University Press, 2002), pp. 212-13.

political considerations are not our business here; instead, we are concerned to articulate what our views of identity might suggest about morality and moral status generally. What, then, are we to say about the status of such possible chimeras and the morality of such genetic interference?

As the technology currently stands, these creatures would be products of genetic interference at the prenatal stage (either on gametes or on embryos). As such, the moral status of the adult products would depend on an account of moral status that was independent of considerations of personal identity: pre-individuation genetic interference, we have already seen, does not *change* the identity of an individual (on the most plausible versions of our theories of identity), so the question of what moral status the new individual created by the interference would have wouldn't be an identity-related question. It *would* be an identity-related question, however, if we added one further science fiction twist: suppose we could alter an *adult* human being's genome in one of these ways, such that some or all of its parts quickly developed into the parts of another animal, say. We would thus begin with a creature that all would agree has full moral status. Would its identity change with such genetic alterations, and would such change in identity alter its moral status or give us moral reasons for or against the interference?

Again, as we focused primarily on radical psychological change earlier, let us now focus on radical biological change. So consider someone who, as the product of genetic interference, transmogrified into a chimpanzee. Both the Biological and Psychological Criteria would imply that the adult human being—and the person he was—has ceased to exist, given that such a radical change would surely involve severe biological and psychological discontinuities. The resulting animal would be neither biologically nor psychologically "one of us" any more, and insofar as there are prima facie moral reasons against causing "one of us" to go out of existence, there would be prima facie moral reasons against such interference. This conclusion, though, opens up the door to a very serious problem, one adapted from a case Derek Parfit calls the Combined Spectrum. (And while this is a problem for both of the main criteria of numerical identity, we will focus here solely on the Biological Criteria; it should nevertheless be easy enough to see how the problem can be extrapolated to the Psychological Criterion.)

Suppose I underwent genetic interference that yielded a creature with a combination of 99% of my original genome and 1% of a chimpanzee genome (perhaps the resulting creature would look just like me except for having a few more hairs on his back). Who would this creature be? There is little doubt that this creature would still be me, according to the Biological Criterion: surely the preservation of a human organism is compatible with some minor biological change, even if that change involves the integration of some small amount of non-human features. After all, if I were to receive a pig heart, my identity would certainly be preserved.

But if we allow that 1% change would not alter my identity, whereas 100% change would (the human to chimpanzee case above), then we can introduce a spectrum of possible alterations that forces the Biological Criterion into a real conundrum. Suppose scientists could introduce any percentage of genetic material from a chimpanzee into my body, producing a percentage of physiological change in accordance with the percentage of genetic change. Suppose further that they want to go right to the limit of what's (prima facie) morally acceptable here, so while they certainly don't want to cause me to cease to exist, they at least want to go as far as they can morally go (and suppose I also agree to be the subject of such an experiment).

The issue, then, is this: since I survive at the 1% mark, but don't survive at the 100% mark, there must be some percentage point on the spectrum, before which I survive and after which I don't. But where precisely is that percentage point? As long as the advocate of the Biological Criterion believes there to be a determinate point, he's in trouble. Suppose he picks the 50% mark. This would mean that, if the scientists introduce 49% of chimpanzee genes into my genome, the resulting creature would still be me, whereas if they were to introduce 50% chimpanzee genes, the survivor would not be me (it would be either a chimpanzee or, more likely, a different "manimal" altogether). But this would be very hard to believe, for several reasons.

First, how could the difference between my living and my ceasing to exist consist in a 1% difference in my genome? This makes my identity depend, implausibly, on a very tiny biological change. This answer is further complicated by the fact that we had already agreed that a 1% change (from 100% human genome to 99% human genome) would not change my identity. But now we are saying that a 1% change (from 51% human genome to 50% human genome) *would* change my identity! Now perhaps 1% somehow *matters more* to my identity in the middle range of the spectrum, but we would at least need some argument for why the tiny genome change occurring there would somehow be more important than the tiny genome change at the near end of the spectrum.

Second, what possible reason could there be for why my identity would be lost at *this* point of the spectrum and not at any other point? In other words, why would the 50% mark be *the* percentage point of change, as opposed to the 49% or the 51% mark? There could, indeed, be no evidence whatsoever for one spot being the right spot. Suppose the scientists ran the experiment at 50% and then asked the resulting creature who he was. Now he may or may not be able to respond. Suppose he were to respond by saying, "I'm Shoemaker!" Would we have any reason to trust this response? Probably not. After all, people have believed they were Napoleon, but we would have no reason to trust *their* self-reports, so why think this creature's self-report would be any more trustworthy? And what if the creature couldn't respond? Would that give us any reason to believe that he *wasn't* me? Of course not, given the possibility that I could have a stroke, which might make it impossible for me to reply but certainly wouldn't undermine my identity.

Such considerations have led some theorists to conclude that our numerical identity can actually be *indeterminate*. What gets us into trouble in the above case is precisely our assumption that there *is* some percentage point on the spectrum, before which I survive and after which I don't. But given the very implausible implications of that assumption, we might be better off simply abandoning it. Doing so would allow us to say that, in the middle range of the genetic spectrum, the identity of the creature is just indeterminate. This is a stronger claim than simply the worry that we may not *know* the answer to the question of identity here; it is instead the claim that *there is no answer* to this question. Indeed, what facts are we missing here? We know that, in the middle range, there will exist a creature that will have half of my genome and half that of a chimpanzee, resulting in a creature that will be, biologically, half-man and half-monkey. What information are we missing that could thus enable us to render a verdict on whether or not this creature will, in addition, be me? It actually seems as if we know all the facts there are to know about this case, so if we don't know the identity of the creature in the middle range, there is simply no fact of the matter *to* know.

This is a rather startling conclusion to draw, especially if we want to attach moral considerations to facts about identity. After all, if it's prima facie immoral to cause someone to cease to exist, but there's just no fact of the matter about whether or not I would cease to exist in the middle range of the spectrum, then what would that mean for the morality of the experiment? Is there thus no moral fact of the matter as well? That would also be a startling conclusion to draw. But perhaps the most startling implication of all would have to do with my own *prudential* reasons in the case. For I would want to know what self-regarding reasons there might be to undergo the experiment, based, one would think, on considerations of self-concern, but if it would be indeterminate whether or not I would be the survivor, and self-concern tracks identity, then it would have to be indeterminate whether or not I would or should care about that creature, and so indeterminate whether or not I should undergo the procedure. But if there's just no answer in such a case about what I should do, or about what the scientists should do, then we'd all be prudentially and morally frozen in a way that threatens to undermine the practical role of prudence and morality.

One solution, then, is to go along with the IDM view and divorce these prudential and moral concerns from numerical identity, attaching them instead simply to some other physical or psychological relation like psychological connectedness. Because connectedness comes in degrees, this move would allow for the indeterminacy of identity as such, yet it would still leave us with something to say about the prudential and moral reasons in such a case. For instance, suppose we believe that the relation that matters in ordinary survival is psychological connectedness, and that at the 50% mark of the spectrum there will be a creature there who bears to me only 50% of the psychological connections that would ordinarily obtain between me and my tomorrow's self. If my moral and prudential concerns properly track such relations, then I could be warranted in caring only half as much for that creature as I would for my tomorrow's self, and others could be warranted in being quite concerned about what's happening to me, albeit only half as much as they would were I to cease to exist altogether. And these more nuanced concerns could lead to more nuanced prudential and moral reasons about what to do in this sort of case.

Of course, no one thinks that prudential and moral concerns are controllable or expressible with such precision. The point, though, is simply that such concerns most definitely do come in *degrees*—I may care more or less about some object—and if identity does not come in degrees (you either are or are not identical to that individual who got out of your bed this morning), then it may make more sense to attach these person-related concerns directly to the metaphysical relations that do. This yields a more fine-grained account of our prudential and moral reasons that might better enable us to handle the more radical "enhancement" cases we have discussed.

WRONGFUL LIFE AND POPULATION ETHICS

Earlier we considered a case in which I undergo genetic therapy in order to alter my future gametes, ultimately allowing me to produce a child guaranteed to be without the HD gene. However, what if I had the therapy available to me and chose not to undergo it? In other words, consider the following two cases side by side:

> *Case 1*: I decide to undergo genetic therapy, and so ultimately produce
> an infant guaranteed not to have the HD gene.

> *Case 2*: I decide not to undergo genetic therapy, and ultimately produce
> an infant with a 50% chance of having the HD gene.

Now the gametes producing the infants in both cases are different—in *Case* 1 they'd be post-therapy gametes, whereas in *Case* 2 they'd be non-therapy gametes—so on the Kripkean view the two infants produced would be two distinct individuals. Suppose, then, that the infant in *Case* 2 does indeed get HD when she grows up. Does she have a moral complaint against me for not having gotten genetic therapy when I had a chance? In other words, did I morally wrong her with my decision not to get therapy?

This, it turns out, is a hard case. Our intuition is clearly that, other things being equal, I ought to have undergone gene therapy, that it was in fact immoral not to. But ordinarily when we think there is a moral wrong being done, we think of it as a wrong *to* someone. But whom have I wronged here? Have I wronged my existing daughter? *But she would not have existed* had I undergone genetic therapy; instead, another distinct individual would have existed. Presumably, if I have wronged someone, then I should not have performed the wronging action. But if I had not performed the wronging action in this case, the person I allegedly wronged would not even have existed! Alternatively, it seems equally clear that I have not wronged the infant I would have had if I had undergone genetic therapy, for then we'd be forced to allow that it's morally wrong for fertile couples not to be having sex constantly in order to bring into existence as many individuals as possible. I can wrong only existing creatures, not creatures that might possibly exist. Yet another consideration here is that, if I indeed could wrong my child by bringing her into existence in *Case* 2, I would have *benefited* the other child by bringing her into existence in *Case* 1, but this is just as strange a thing to say. How can causing someone to exist benefit her?

It's very difficult, then, to isolate the target of wrongness in my action, and this has turned out to be a significant philosophical problem. Nevertheless, people continue to bring forward "wrongful life" lawsuits that are directly related to, and infected with, this philosophical conundrum. Typically what happens in such cases is that the parents of a child with severe disabilities or birth defects sue their doctor or a medical company for negligence, on behalf of their child, often claiming that the doctor failed to inform the mother of an illness she had, undermining her ability to opt for an abortion instead of giving birth to a severely disabled child, a child who will never have a life worth living. The U.S. courts, however, have been quite reluctant to let such lawsuits go forward, for two reasons. First, it is very difficult to reconcile our deeply ingrained view about the high value of life with allowing someone to recover *damages* for being alive. Second, and more relevant to our purposes, the general thought behind compensatory damages in the tort system is that the plaintiff is to be returned, as near as is possible, to the state he was in prior to the harm for which the defendant is found liable. But in wrongful life cases, the plaintiff *would not have existed* were it not for the negligence in question, so there could in principle be no damages to recover. Instead, it seems, the only way to mete justice would be to prevent the plaintiff from having been born, but that's obviously impossible.

Nevertheless, one might say that we could at least get close to resolving the complaint here by allowing the plaintiff to die. After all, the baseline of comparison to the plaintiff's horrible life is non-existence, and where this is perhaps—*perhaps*—a sensible comparison for us to make, one could conceivably be "returned" to such a state by ceasing to exist. Of course, even though no court would ever rule in such a way (given the first reason above), it might still be a plausible philosophical solution. Nevertheless, we can concoct a case in which the children in both cases have lives worth living, but where one's life is better than another, and we get the same worries.

> *Case* 3: A 14-year-old girl chooses to have a child, which gives the child she has a poor start in life. Nevertheless, the child eventually winds up with a decent life.

> *Case* 4: That same 14-year-old girl chooses to wait to have a child until she's 30. That child winds up having a much better life as a result.

Once more, the children produced in both cases are distinct individuals. Now what is our moral assessment of the cases? Clearly, it seems that *Case* 4 is better than *Case* 3, that it would be better for the 14-year-old to wait to have the child. But better *for whom*? Suppose the mother's welfare is the same in both cases: she'll have to make the same amount of sacrifice and get the same amount of joy no matter what decision she makes. We might think, then, that it would better *for the child* if the mother were to wait until she were 30. But as we have seen, this can't be right either, for the child she has at 30 will just be *different* from the child she would have had at 14. And, correspondingly, if she had had the child at 14 it wouldn't have been worse for that child, given that that child wouldn't have existed otherwise, and that child's life is a life worth living, that is, it's (by stipulation) better for that child to have lived that life than not to have existed.

How, then, can we defend our intuition that it would have been better for the mother in *Case 3* to have waited to have her child, that indeed it was *wrong* for her not to have waited? If she hasn't wronged either herself or her child in either case, then how can our view about wrongness be plausibly maintained? This is the heart of what Derek Parfit calls *The Non-Identity Problem,* and it is extraordinarily difficult to come up with a plausible solution.

There are yet wider implications of these philosophical worries. To see what they are, consider two more cases:

> *Case 5*: As the threat of global warming continues to grow, governments around the world ignore the problem until it is too late. As a result of a variety of weather-related catastrophes, the lives of the people living between 2200 and 2500 are barely worth living.

> *Case 6*: As the threat of global warming continues to grow, governments around the world cooperate to enact a series of regulatory measures that slow down the warming trend to render it a non-threat. Because of the stringency of the regulations, the lives of people living between 2010 and 2200 are of a lower quality than they would have been in *Case 5*, but the lives of those living between 2200 and 2500 are much better than they would have been in *Case 5*.

This is a version of the Non-Identity Problem on the grand scale, and it should be obvious just how relevant and important the problem is when put in these terms. As in the child cases above, the identities of the individuals in *Case 5* and *Case 6* would, for the most part, be different. Far-reaching regulatory policies would likely play a critical role in determining the ways and timing in which people got together, so it would be quite unlikely that the identities of the two populations would have any overlap once we got to the year 2200. But this then means that no one is made worse off in either case, for which population is brought into existence will depend on which policy is chosen, and we cannot plausibly be said to harm anyone by bringing him or her into existence. Our question, then, is similar to that in the earlier child case: given that our choice of what to do will not be worse for anyone, is there any moral reason we can give for our intuition that the decision in *Case 6* is the right one?

The standard objection to the decision in *Case 5* is that it will lower the well-being of the future people who will have to live through the weather-related catastrophes. As many people put it, we are mortgaging our children's, and our children's children's, future. But now we can see that in one important sense this is false. No one is made worse off than they would have been if we had done otherwise given that they wouldn't have *existed* if we had done otherwise. The identities of our children depend, at least in part, on the policies we enact. Nevertheless, there is surely something wrong being done in *Case 5*. But what is it?

Once again, there have been a variety of replies given to this problem, but none has been terribly satisfactory. Exploring them, however, would take us too far afield, for we are concerned about the relation between identity and ethics, and the relevance of identity here is with respect to the creation of the *problem*, not the solution. Indeed, the proposed solutions, while fascinating, are squarely within the realm of moral philosophy, and have nothing to do with metaphysics. Nevertheless, the problems created for moral philosophy by these metaphysical considerations of identity and non-identity are terribly significant, problems that many smart contemporary moral philosophers are trying desperately to resolve.

Conclusion

We have not come to any definitive and sweeping conclusions in these two chapters on moral issues at the beginning of life, but we have perhaps gained some insight into how better to *approach* them. For example, one theme that keeps popping up is that we might get more traction in applying metaphysics to morality if we perhaps focused less on identity *per se* and more on the direct psychological and physical relations in which identity might partially consist. The relations that matter in identity and everyday survival come in degrees, and so they might be better suited than identity in some cases to ground our person-related moral concerns.

With respect to the specific moral issues discussed in these chapters, we reached the tentative finding that there do not seem to be any compelling identity-based moral objections to abortion, hESC research, cloning, or genetic interference. If we take the view that these activities are morally permissible in lieu of compelling objections otherwise, then this is progress of a sort, for we have cleared the path of a certain class of objections here. Of course, there may be plenty of compelling objections to the activities in question from outside the world of personal identity, but those are beyond the scope of our inquiry. It may also be that some of the objections discussed in this chapter may be buttressed in more sophisticated ways than we have been able to explore, in which case our tentative conclusion that the activities in question can withstand the class of identity-related objections may be too quick. But this is just the way in which philosophy proceeds, and for now we may be satisfied with our modicum of progress.

WORKS CITED OR REFERENCED IN THIS CHAPTER

DeGrazia, David. *Human Identity and Bioethics*. Cambridge: Cambridge University Press, 2005.

Hopkins, Patrick D. "Bad Copies: How Popular Media Represent Cloning." In *Ethical Issues in Human Cloning*, edited by Michael C. Brannigan. New York: Seven Bridges Press, 2001.

Keyes, Daniel. *Flowers for Algernon*. New York: Harcourt Brace Jovanovich, Inc., 1966.

Kripke, Saul. *Naming and Necessity*. 2nd ed. Cambridge, MA: Harvard University Press, 1980.

McMahan, Jeff. *The Ethics of Killing*. Oxford: Oxford University Press, 2002.

Parfit, Derek. *Reasons and Persons*. Oxford: Oxford University Press, 1984.

CHAPTER SIX

Moral Issues at the End of Life

In the previous two chapters we explored the relation between personal identity and applied moral issues at the beginning of life. In this chapter we turn to an investigation of the ways in which personal identity might be relevant to some moral issues at the other end of life. Specifically, we will examine two topics: the moral authority of advance directives, and the proper approach to "curing" multiple personality disorder. Personal identity directly impinges on these issues and procedures insofar as they are about the (moral relevance of the) relation that may or may not obtain between some pre-existing person and his or her descendant person-stage after some intervening procedure or significant change has occurred. So the general question we'll be asking here is precisely how much change to a person is compatible with a preservation of that person's identity, both numerical and narrative, and where identity (of either sort) is lost, what are the related moral implications? Let us start, then, with advance directives.

Advance Directives

Recall *Case 3* from our Introduction. After being diagnosed with early-stage Alzheimer's disease, fifty-five-year-old Meredith has signed an advance directive instructing her doctors not to use any extraordinary means to keep her alive if she gets very ill after having become demented.

When her sixty-five-year-old demented descendant contracts pneumonia, however, she is content and, when asked, expresses a preference to stay alive. Our question, then, was whose wishes have moral authority here, younger-Meredith (YM) or older-Meredith (OM)?

Most of us likely believe, some of us quite strongly, that YM's preference is authoritative. Indeed, we will take this intuition as the prime data to be accounted for in this section. How might we justify this stance, however, in light of the following seriously problematic dilemma, stemming directly from considerations of personal identity? Either YM is identical to OM or she is not. If so, then why think that YM's preference is authoritative, given that we normally think that one's *current*, or most recent, preferences are what ought to be taken more seriously? On the other hand, if YM is *not* identical to OM, then why think she should have any say *at all* over the life of OM, someone who has her own set of preferences on the matter?

To explain both horns of the dilemma, consider first a case in which different preferences are expressed at different times within the course of a single person's life. So suppose that, when I was a twenty-year-old college student, I preferred that all my excess money be given to environmental causes, whereas now that I'm sixty, say, I prefer that all my excess money be given to anti-environmental causes. Suppose, then, that you are my money manager, and the instructions you have been given are that you are to distribute my excess money "according to my expressed preferences." You are aware that, when I was twenty, I had expressed a very different preference than the one I now express. How ought you distribute my money? It seems clear that you ought to do so according to my *current* preferences; indeed, it is unlikely that many, if any, people would think that the twenty-year-old's preferences provide *any* reason whatsoever in favor of giving the money to environmental causes. How could they be binding in the least respect? But now the problem should be obvious: if the preferences of the twenty-year-old aren't binding, then why think the preferences of YM are binding in the advance directive case?

The second horn of the dilemma yields the same conclusion, given the way we normally think of other seemingly similar cases. Suppose I were in the bed next to you in the hospital, and I expressed the preference that, since you have pneumonia, you be allowed to die, whereas you express the preference that you remain alive. Surely none of us would think that my preferences are even relevant here, let alone binding. Of course, you might think that, if you and I are strangers, that's disanalogous from the original case, for in that case YM is at least more closely related to OM than any other person. But it's unclear that even a close relative's preference ought to be binding with respect to the life of someone who has clearly expressed the opposite preference.

Perhaps, then, the dementia is doing some serious work on our intuitions. So if YM *is* identical to OM, we might say, then YM's preferences ought to be binding, insofar as we should respect one's most recent *competent* preferences, and OM is just not competent at the time she expresses her preferences. Respecting one's earlier, competent preferences when one is currently incompetent is called respect for one's **precedent autonomy**. On the other hand, if YM is *not* identical to OM, then YM is at least like her closest relative, and insofar as we think the closest relative of an incompetent patient ought to make the decisions about that patient's future, we would think YM ought to do the same for OM. Where these decisions are based on what the patient would have wanted (which is of course tricky to determine), they are accepted as **substituted judgment**.

Nevertheless, there are still some problems here. Regarding the former issue, why think that YM's precedent autonomy should be respected here? For someone to have made an autonomous decision about some future event, we must presume she was reasonably well informed about all the relevant circumstances of that event. But given that there will be massive psychological changes taking place between YM and OM, how could YM be even remotely informed about what life will actually be like for OM? OM will be irreversibly *demented*, and how can any of us know what it's like to be demented in this way? It could just as easily be the case that, were YM somehow to fully appreciate what things would be like for OM, she wouldn't sign the advance directive after all. OM's contentment could actually turn out to be an overwhelmingly positive thing for her. Of course, the main point is that YM *would have no way of knowing* what OM's life and circumstances would be like *for OM*, so no document she signs directing certain actions on behalf of OM could count as well enough informed to be binding.

Regarding the issue of substituted judgment, there's an important disanalogy here. While we might think a close relative's decision about the life of a demented loved one would be binding at the time of her dementia, we would not, I suspect, think a close relative's decision about the life of a possible demented loved one *ten years before* her dementia would be binding. But that is what we'd be saying in this case. If YM is really a different individual or person from OM, but she's nevertheless like OM's closest relative, then we are saying the decision of OM's relative ten years prior to her dementia is binding here, more binding than OM's own stated preference! But given that we would be unlikely to accept this reasoning for a standard case of a relative and a demented patient, we ought to be suspicious of such reasoning in the case of YM and OM.

So what shall we say here? No doubt most of us still believe that YM's directive ought to be binding. But how can we reason our way to this conclusion, given the difficulties just cited? While up until now we have merely posited what would follow in the cases in which YM and OM both are, and are not, identical, what we need to do is look more closely at just what the details of the identity at issue would actually consist in.

Start with the Psychological Criterion. Would YM be identical to OM, on this view? Because this criterion is about the identity of *persons*, it's important to determine first of all whether or not OM would be a person. There is, in fact, reason to believe she might not be. For while she is indeed conscious, she may not be *self*-conscious, aware of herself as herself, in a way that many people (following Locke) think is necessary for personhood. Those with dementia suffer from a significant decrease in mental functioning, whose symptoms include disorientation and the loss of memories and language. Once such capacities are gone, then, it's highly likely that the capacity for self-consciousness is gone as well.

Of course, what the advocate of the Psychological Criterion needs is just that the various stages united by its identity relation are capable of *psychological continuity*, and this may not require full-blown Lockean personhood. Instead, it may simply require some minimally sufficient degree of memory, intentions, beliefs, desires, goals, and character. While it is often assumed that demented patients cannot meet this standard, many actually can, at least until the late stages. So depending on what precise stage of dementia OM is in, she might still bear sufficient psychological continuity to YM to be considered the same person.

Nevertheless, let's make the case as hard as possible and suppose from here on out that OM is in the late stages of dementia. We will suppose that most of her memories are gone by that point, as is her capacity for intention-formation, the ability to set goals, and the existence of much of a character. While late-stage dementia patients certainly have desires, they are very limited in scope—they are mostly about immediate biological needs—as are their associated beliefs. It does not seem, then, that OM, in this late stage, would have sufficient capacities for psychological continuity. According to the Psychological Criterion, then, OM is not the same person as YM.

What does this mean, though? If YM is a person, and OM is not, or if YM is just not psychologically continuous with OM (because OM lacks the capacities for psychological continuity), then YM would not be the same person as OM, in which case it would be hard to believe that YM's advance directive could be authoritative over OM's currently expressed preferences. This conclusion seems to cut against the Psychological Criterion, then, given our fairly strong intuitions otherwise.

What of the Biological Criterion? On this view, personhood is not our essence; instead, what I am essentially is an individual human organism, so whether or not OM is a person is actually irrelevant. Instead, what matters is that she is biologically continuous with YM—and she is—so YM is the same *individual* as OM. This might seem to establish a prima facie reason why YM's preferences about OM ought to be authoritative, then, for she may say, "When it comes to determining what's to happen to *me* when I'm no longer competent, it's my preferences now that ought to be authoritative."

One of the ongoing problems with the Biological Criterion, though, has been that it doesn't seem to offer the right explanation for our patterns of practical concern. What seems to matter in justifying my anticipation or concern for my future is not that the future individual in question will be my biological successor; instead, what matters is that he will be my psychological successor. Now certainly biological continuity is, given our current technology, necessary for psychological continuity—how could some future person be psychologically continuous with me without having my brain?—but that's not to say that biological continuity is doing any of the real work in tracking our patterns of practical concerns. One might rightly wonder, then, how the Biological Criterion could really justify precedent autonomy in the case under discussion. In other words, why think that YM's preferences should be authoritative solely in virtue of the fact that OM's biological organism is continuous with hers?

One reply, of course, is that we think such precedent autonomy is perfectly appropriate in other cases, for instance, when we recognize someone's wishes in how his corpse is to be disposed of, whether he is to be buried or cremated upon his death. What matters are the preferences of the corpse's living, competent predecessor. Nevertheless, there is a clear disanalogy between the two cases, for nearly all advocates of the Biological Criterion insist that, while I am indeed numerically identical with my demented descendant, I am *not* numerically identical with my corpse. Indeed, that corpse isn't an individual like me—a living human organism—at all. Instead, my determination of what I want done with my corpse after my death is just like my determination of what I want done with my house after my death: it's just a specification of how my *property* is to be distributed. So it cannot be identity that does the justifying work in the corpse case; one wonders, then, if identity would be doing any such work in the dementia case as well.

Let us turn away, then, from numerical identity to see what the advocate of narrative identity would say about the case. Narrative identity is a kind of psychological unity, wherein various experiences occurring at different times are unified as part of the same narrative when they can be woven together into a coherent, connected self-told story, such that the narrative ego at any given time identifies with all the experiences, correctly able to call them all "mine." The connection to practical concerns, then, is supposed to be rather obvious: narrative identity is what grounds my patterns of concern, so that the scope of any particular concern is defined and delimited by the range of my narrative identity. What, then, is the implication of this view for the case in question?

One might think that the narrative identity view could justify our basic intuition that YM's preferences in the advance directive are authoritative insofar as YM and OM are part of one and the same narrative, and YM's voice just is OM's *real* voice, autonomously formed. OM is, after all, much like a child, capable of having and expressing preferences based only on immediate desires, but incapable of having or considering long-range— what we think of as prudential—interests or desires, or reflecting upon and/or endorsing the desires that move her to action. She seems to lack autonomy, in other words. So even if YM and OM are part of the same narrative, YM's preferences may count as authoritative over OM's in virtue of their being the product of reflective, informed, autonomous consent, a kind of justified paternalism over her unreflective, uninformed, non-autonomous narrative descendant.

One immediate problem with this view is that, precisely due to her general lack of autonomy, OM may not be a person-stage *capable* of narrative identity. If what matters is the possession of certain robust psychological capacities, which themselves enable one to construct a single narrative out of various sets of experiences, then OM lacks the relevant capacities. She is a human being, sure enough, but she is not one with which YM could identify, nor is she herself capable of identification with YM or any other of her past or future stages. She may not be, in other words, a narrative ego. If the scope of precedent autonomy, then, is delimited by the scope of the stages with which one is narratively unified, then YM's preferences are simply not authoritative over OM's.

One might, then, attempt to offer a more watered down version of narrative identity to avoid this problem. Perhaps it doesn't matter if one of the stages incorporated into a single narrative is incapable of constructing a narrative herself; instead, perhaps all that matters is that some earlier stage is capable of projecting her self-narrative into that future stage. In other words, maybe all one needs to do to include a later stage into one's lifelong narrative is to make *plans* for it, to incorporate it as one's own when deliberating about prudential matters. This move would then allow us to (a) preserve a grounding relation between narrative identity and (prudential) patterns of concern, (b) establish narrative identity between YM and OM, and so (c) support the intuition that YM's advance directive is indeed authoritative over the wishes of her demented narrative descendant.

Is this watered-down version of narrative identity plausible, though? It cannot work as it stands, given that I'm able to make plans for all sorts of future stages, very few of which could conceivably count as part of my narrative identity. For instance, I make plans for the future stages of my children, saving money in a college fund, say, or networking with people who might help them get jobs. But in no way could my children be part of *my* narrative identity. In the same way, I could make plans for my corpse, but most narrative theorists don't want to allow our corpses to be part of our narrative identities. Indeed, this is one reason why they may insist that narrative identity presupposes numerical identity. Insofar as I am numerically identical with neither my children nor my corpse (because it isn't alive), neither of them could be part of my narrative identity.

So far so good. But now notice another implication of the view. If I may count as part of my narrative identity future stages of my (numerically identical) self simply by deliberating about and planning for them, then this would mean any future stages of myself that fell into PVS could be incorporated into my narrative identity as well. After all, I can surely create advance directives for what I'd like done with my future comatose self in the same way I can create advance directives for what I'd like done with my future demented self. But this implication of the view ought to be worrisome for advocates of the narrative identity view, for it would mean narrative identity is no longer about the incorporation of *sets of experiences* into a coherent storyline, which was the original purpose of the view. My future PVS stage will undergo no experiences whatsoever, so in what sense could he be part of my (psychological) narrative? The only answer that makes sense is that that future PVS stage is still part of my *life* story— whether or not he experiences anything—insofar as he's alive and he's me. But this answer would render the narrative identity view indistinguishable from the Biological Criterion of numerical identity: it would ground prudential concern, for example, in biological continuity, not psychological unity, so there would no longer be any reason to talk about narrative identity at all. Furthermore, we'd be right back to the worry about the Biological Criterion discussed above, that it actually doesn't do so well at tracking many of our various patterns of concern, which seem to depend on psychological relations of some sort.   ? circular

So what we might need to do is appeal once more to the Identity Doesn't Matter (IDM) view. What would it imply about the case of advanced directives? On this view, neither numerical nor narrative identity is what grounds our patterns of concern; instead, it is psychological connectedness or continuity, such that the degrees of our egoistic concern for some future stage (ought to?) correspond to the degrees of the psychological relations that obtain between us. Now as we've already seen, YM and OM will be very weakly psychologically connected; indeed, there will be a great deal of psychological *disunity* between them. And it may be precisely for this reason that YM wants to allow OM to die, even though she is a stage in *her* life, for the longer OM's stage exists, the more it will undermine the coherent meaning and unity of her life as a whole.

To explain, suppose YM had been striving her entire life for a variety of intellectual accomplishments, the most general being to gain as much knowledge as she could about the world around her. She thus deeply values the life of the mind, and in particular the life of *her* mind. It thus terrifies and deeply disturbs her to learn that she has Alzheimer's disease. What has made her life meaningful were her intellectual pursuits, and those will be completely lost at the end stages of the disease. For her to be demented will be a cruel and tragic denouement to her life, and she thus wants that ending to be as brief as possible, else it will make a mockery of all her previous efforts in life. It will, to her, make her life a tragic joke, rather than the meaningful life of the mind she has always wanted. She thus signs an advance directive in order to make her later demented period as short as she can, so it won't detract from the larger lived life.

As a result of considerations like this, Jeff McMahan has argued that decisions like YM's are about what is best for her life as a whole, and where there are lives of some psychological disunity, the *longest* unified stretches within them will count as being closest to the life as a whole, so the wishes of that longest unity will count as determining the prudential good of the whole. Insofar as YM's wishes are expressed from within her longest prudential unit—she is strongly psychologically unified at that point with most of the stages throughout her earlier life—those are the wishes that ought to count as articulating the good of the life as a whole. This means, then, that OM's good doesn't represent the good of the whole, and so ought to be sacrificed for the sake of that larger good, which is precisely what is articulated in YM's advance directive.

While this may seem a promising option, it is not without problems. For one thing, if we have abandoned identity as what matters in both survival and our practical concerns, it's unclear why what's best for the "life as a whole" should continue to matter as well. Instead, it would seem to make much more sense to focus solely on the various smaller, more tightly unified, stretches within one's life, so instead of something's being "good for my life as a whole," there would be things that were "good for this period in my life" and nothing more. This would mean, though, that the wishes of one period, or unity, would have no authority over any other, at least with respect to the good of the *whole*, given that the good of the whole would be unimportant. And this would mean, finally, that by the time of OM's existence, YM's period of life would simply be over, in which case it would be hard to see how OM's dementia could undermine YM's "life," and so further unclear why YM's wishes should any longer be authoritative over OM's.

We are thus led into a kind of thorny thicket here. None of our theories of personal identity seem to give a very good account of our deep-seated intuition that YM's advance directive ought to be authoritative over OM's current wishes. Those theories suggesting YM will be identical to OM run into difficulty explaining the relation between my prudential concerns and the identity in question: why does YM's mere biological continuity with OM, say, give her an egoistic reason to care about her? They also have difficulty explaining why this person's current preferences are to be discounted in this case, but not in other cases. On the other hand, those theories suggesting YM is either not identical to OM or that the identity relation between them just doesn't matter have difficulty explaining just why YM's preferences regarding OM's treatment are relevant at all: if YM is psychologically discontinuous with OM, why should YM have any say over what's to happen to OM? This was essentially the dilemma posed at the beginning of this section, and we haven't made a great deal of progress in resolving it. Of course, we shouldn't expect our theories of identity alone to resolve what is essentially a moral worry. What they can do (and have done), however, is render the problem in stark terms and clarify the issues at stake. If we want to preserve our intuition that YM's preferences are authoritative over OM, and if we think such authority derives from identity (of some sort) with the self whose treatment one is to determine, then there are various ways to establish that identity, some (the Biological Criterion) more successful than others (the Psychological Criterion, narrative identity). But at any rate, there remain serious problems about grounding authority in an earlier self's preferences, regardless of whether identity obtains or not.

One way out of the thicket, then, might simply be to *abandon* the deep intuition about YM's preferences being authoritative over OM's. This is indeed the solution urged by Agnieszka Jaworska, Rebecca Dresser, and others. On Jaworska's view, for example, those in OM's condition are actually still "capable of autonomy to a significant degree," and many of these sorts of demented patients "may still have authority concerning their well-being."[1] This obviously can't be a kind of autonomy that depends on robust deliberative and decision-making capacities; instead, it involves a capacity to *value* (where well-being is related to one's ability to live in conformity with those values), which Jaworska thinks demented patients may still possess (it doesn't, for instance, require being able to construct or survey the narrative arc of one's whole life). But at any rate, if this is what autonomy consists in, then to the extent a demented patient is capable of it, we should respect *her* wishes over the decisions of her earlier self, despite our intuitions otherwise.

This is an interesting and potentially promising account, but even Jaworska herself admits that *end-stage* dementia patients certainly lack

---

1   Agnieszka Jaworska, "Respecting the Margins of Agency: Alzheimer's Patients and the Capacity to Value," *Philosophy and Public Affairs* 28 (Spring 1999): 105-38, p. 109.

even a minimal capacity to value, which reintroduces us to the dilemma: as long as the end-stage patient is able to express a preference at odds with her earlier self (even though it's not dependent on any current values), our puzzle about identity and authority remains. Surely in this sort of case YM's preferences are authoritative. But if she's not identical to OM, then there's little motivation to grant her this authority, and if she is identical to OM, why doesn't OM get the last word? As mentioned earlier, this thicket is very thorny, and there's no clear way out of it.

The Death of Multiple Personalities

The moral problem we will discuss in this section is one that has been quite underappreciated. Nearly everyone who has written about the philosophical conundrums posed by Dissociative Identity Disorder (DID) (which used to be called Multiple Personality Disorder (MPD)) has focused solely on the "How Many Persons?" problem, that is, the problem of figuring out whether or not the number of different personalities of an MPD patient corresponds to the number of persons existing in that body. While this is an interesting and difficult metaphysical problem, it is actually the precursor to an even more difficult *moral* problem about the implications of the standard therapeutic approach to DID, and that will be our focus in this section.

Let us begin, though, with a brief discussion of the "How Many Persons?" problem, and the best way to do so is by considering the first famous case of DID. In 1906, Morton Prince published an account of a woman named Christine Beauchamp, who presented a number of different personalities to him in therapy. The original patient—nervous, conscientious, shy, and deeply religious—Prince called B1, and he took to hypnotizing her regularly as part of his treatment of her insomnia, headaches, and depression. One day under hypnosis, the patient referred to B1 not as "I," but as "she," and as Prince asked about this occurrence, he discovered "Sally," a personality seemingly different from B1's, and a personality who hated B1, calling her "stupid," and complaining that "she does not know half the time what she is about."[1] As it turned out, Sally professed to know all of B1's thoughts and actions—even B1's dreams—but denied they were her own. B1, for her part, had no knowledge of even the existence of Sally. For the periods when Sally was in control of the body, B1 lost that time, waking up having no idea what had happened. Sally was the near opposite of B1: flirtatious, assertive, loud, and completely irresponsible. She also did what she could to undermine B1's life and plans, ripping up letters, hiding money, tearing B1's clothes, sending her letters containing spiders, and so forth. She even wanted to kill B1 at one point, until she was reminded just what that would mean for herself.

Later on, another alternate personality ("alter") was revealed, a woman Prince called B4, and who Sally dubbed "the idiot." B4 was hot-tempered and prickly, and she knew nothing of B1 or Sally. Eventually, Prince discovered that, when deeply hypnotized, B4 and B1 were the same personality, what he called B2, and this was someone Prince judged to be the "real" Christine Beauchamp. Nevertheless, when he tried to get B2 to rise to the surface post-hypnosis, he always failed. Finally, Sally admitted that she had been preventing this from occurring—she herself was terrified of having to retreat to being a prisoner in her own body, someone aware of the thoughts and actions of the agent of that body without being able to have any effect whatsoever on what it did or thought. But after writing her last will and testament, Sally allowed B2 to wake up post-hypnosis as the person Prince thought was Christine Beauchamp.

So how many people were involved prior to this "self-sacrifice" of Sally? Here is how Prince himself describes the case:

> Miss Christine L. Beauchamp ... is a person in whom several personalities have become developed; that is to say, she may change her personality from time to time, often from hour to hour, and with each change her character becomes transformed and her memories altered. In addition to the real, original or normal self, the self that was born and which she was intended by nature to be, she may be any one of three

---

1   Morton Prince, *The Dissociation of a Personality* (London: Longmans, Green, 1906), reprinted in 1968 in New York: Johnson Reprint Corporation. Quotes are from p. 28 of the reprinted version.

different persons. I say three different, because, although making use of the same body, each, nevertheless, has a distinctly different character; a difference manifested by different trains of thought, by different views, beliefs, ideals and temperament, and by different acquisitions, tastes, habits, experiences and memories. Each varies in these respects from the other two, and from the original Miss Beauchamp. Two of these personalities have no knowledge of each other or of the third, expecting such information as may be obtained by inference or second hand, so that in the memory of each of these two there are blanks which correspond to the times when the others are in the flesh. ... The personalities come and go in kaleidoscopic succession, many changes often being made in the course of twenty-four hours. And so it happens that Miss Beauchamp, if I may use the name to designate several distinct people, at one moment says and does and plans and arranges something to which a short time before she most strongly objected, indulges tastes which a moment before would have been abhorrent to her ideals, and undoes or destroys what she had just laboriously planned and arranged.[1]

Prince thus makes clear that he thinks there were three people in one body. His reasons for believing this are that there were three different characters or personalities, two of the three personalities had no memory of the actions or thoughts of the others, and the personalities would switch very quickly and completely. Of course, each of these reasons individually is not very persuasive. First, most of us think (and all of our theories allow) that personal identity is compatible with (even significant) personality change, that one person can undergo profound alterations in character. Someone may be irresponsible and irrepressible as a teenager, dour and bitter as a middle-ager, and twinkly and wise as an old-timer, and we wouldn't think to call those three personalities different *persons*. Second, as we saw when considering the original Lockean Memory Criterion, identity is also compatible with memory loss. Just because one has forgotten some past experience, thought, or action, that doesn't at all mean that one is a different person from that past experiencer, thinker, or agent. Finally, just because one's personality changes quickly and completely,

---

1   Ibid. Quoted from the 1906 version, pp. 1-2.

that too doesn't mean that one is a different person thereby. Just watch the shy and quiet wallflower in the bar turn into the loud and crazy table dancer immediately after several shots of tequila.

But even if each of these conditions individually is not sufficient to establish distinct personhood, perhaps jointly they are. And once these conditions are combined, it does indeed become more plausible to think that we have three persons on our hands: when the personalities do change quickly, when one personality deliberately tries to undermine the others, when the non-remembering personalities exist so very closely in time to the personalities whose experiences they don't remember—in short, when the personalities are so proximate, distinct, and unrelated—we might be more inclined to think of them as different and individually complete persons. Nevertheless, this is still a bit unclear. Is there a more precise way to approach the issue?

Perhaps we have jumped into the deep end too quickly. For while we have been trying to determine whether or not the personalities are *distinct* persons, we haven't yet figured out whether or not the alters themselves are even *persons*. Kathleen Wilkes attempts to do so, borrowing from Daniel Dennett a number of more precise conditions for personhood and then applying these directly to the Beauchamp case. First, though, she considers the possibility that Beauchamp was one and only one person because she had one and only one body. Now as we have already seen in the case of the conjoined Hensel sisters (Chapter One), the one body/one person correlation is quite suspect. In fact, one might almost take the DID case as just an extreme version of the conjoined twins case. But what's interesting about many DID cases generally is that there is often disagreement among the alters about what their body actually is like! In some cases one alter will think of herself as being a brunette, while another will think of herself as blonde, one will think of herself as having brown eyes, another will think of herself as having blue eyes (and these differences are part of what causes the alters to dress in different ways). More dramatically, alters think of themselves as having differently-aged bodies from one another, ranging from childhood to old age. And in the famous case of Sybil (documented as having 16 different personalities) two alters were *male*, and so thought of themselves as having male bodies. Nevertheless, despite what all the various alters *think* about their bodies, the fact remains that they have only one body forced upon them, and for some this will constitute default evidence that there is just one person involved. So what might we say against this view?

We can start by thinking of what the necessary conditions of personhood might be. This is what Dennett does, and his list of qualifications seems quite plausible. According to him, to be a person is to be (a) a rational being; (b) a being to which certain conscious, intentional predicates (for example, beliefs, desires, emotions) are ascribed; (c) a being to which others adopt a certain sort of attitude or stance (for example, a being we treat with a certain kind of moral respect); (d) a being capable of *reciprocating* the stance in (c); (e) a being capable of verbal communication; and (f) a being capable of a kind of *self*-consciousness (for example, the capacity to be aware of, and have attitudes about, one's own thoughts, beliefs, and desires). Suppose, then, we take meeting these conditions to be necessary for personhood. Could Beauchamp's alters do so? It seems clear they could easily meet four of them. They were certainly rational, obviously had beliefs and so forth, had language, and were self-conscious. What, though, of conditions (c) and (d)?

Here is where things get a bit tricky, for these two conditions bring in the *moral* dimensions of the case precisely at issue. Start with (d), the condition that the being be capable of a kind of moral agency, able to reciprocate to the moral (or immoral) treatment of others. This was certainly true of Beauchamp's alters. While Sally sometimes treated the other alters cruelly, she occasionally expressed remorse for her actions and at the end engaged in a grand act of self-sacrifice. The other alters were clearly moral agents as well, treating Prince with respect, kindness, and so forth.

What, then, about condition (c)? The one person who dealt with all of the alters—Prince—did so in an inconsistent way. On the one hand, he stressed that he was treating just one person, the "real" Christine Beauchamp, and he took it to be his task to find out which one she was. In so doing, he thought at first that B4 was the real person, so when she appeared, he tried to eliminate B1 and Sally. Once he discovered B2, however, he thought *she* was the real person, so he then tried to eliminate B4 as well. Of course, we may well ask him: "*Who* were you treating prior to the revelation of B2?" After all, how could he want to cure the patient before him, when he hadn't even met B2 yet? On the other hand, he often seemed to treat all four personalities as moral agents, as individual objects of concern. He worried about how Sally's spitefulness towards B1 would affect B1; he engaged with Sally and became amused, even entranced, by her on occasion; he also genuinely sympathized with B4 when he told her he was going to eliminate her. This kind of treatment cuts strongly in favor of the view that he took up the moral stance to each of the various personalities.

So it looks as if all of Beauchamp's alters could (arguably) meet all of Dennett's conditions of personhood. In addition to this consideration, Wilkes cites several others, some of which overlap with Prince's. For example, they each had quite developed (and distinct) characters, self-images, and streams of consciousness. They also could each control the body on their own for long periods of time. Further, it was unclear who the "winner" of all this would turn out to be, certainly not to Prince, nor to the reader of Prince's book; indeed, he might have gotten it wrong in the end that B2 was the "real" person! Finally, think about what things must have been like "from the inside" for each of the personalities. With the exception of Sally, each one truly believed she was the "real" person, the *only* person, with Beauchamp's body, the one being treated by Prince. They would each affirm "That's not me!" when referring to the other personalities, and surely we should take this affirmation seriously.

It looks, then, as if B1, Sally, and B4 were all persons. Were they, though, *different* persons? If they were, then we have a very serious moral issue on our hands, for if it's prima facie wrong to kill a person, then it was prima facie wrong for Prince—or any psychologist or psychiatrist treating DID patients in the same way—to "kill off" B1, Sally, and B4. Elimination of multiple personalities would seem to make one a multiple murderer.

Can this be right? It seems as if there would have to be a very strong prima facie moral case against elimination of alters if they were both persons and distinct persons. But we have yet to settle the issue of whether or not they *are* distinct persons. It's possible, after all, that each of B1, Sally, and B4 was simply a different "side" of one and the same person, namely, Christine Beauchamp. So what reason(s) do we have for a judgment either way?

Consulting our theories of personal identity yields no straightforward answer. According to the Psychological Criterion, if B1, Sally, and B4 are indeed persons, they are also *different* persons, insofar as they are not psychologically continuous with one another. Instead, their chains of direct psychological connections are distinct: later-stage B1 remembers only those experiences of earlier-stage B1, carries out the intentions of only earlier-stage B1, and so forth. The same is true of B4 as well. Now one might think that Sally, being privy to the thoughts of both B1 and B4, was also psychologically continuous with them. But this was not true. While Sally reported being aware of the thoughts and actions of both B1 and B4, she never considered them *her own* thoughts and actions, but instead suggested she was listening in on those thoughts and spying on those actions, just as she would with another person. Further, she never carried out the intentions of B1 or B4 herself, nor did she share their desires, beliefs, or general character. So it's safe to conclude, on the Psychological Criterion, that the three alters were indeed different people.

This view is also suggested by considerations of narrative identity. Given the individual streams of consciousness for each alter—providing psychological unity within each alter and psychological disunity across them—it would be extraordinarily difficult for them to construct a coherent narrative incorporating the actions and experiences of the others. Instead, it is much more plausible to think of them as living out three distinct narratives, as having three distinct lives.

On the Biological Criterion, the answer is equally simple but points in the opposite direction: B1, Sally, and B4 were different personalities of one and the same biological organism. Now notice that this way of putting it is perfectly compatible with those different personalities actually being different *persons*. The Biological Criterion simply specifies that, even if they were different persons, they were the same essential human animal.

The question, then, is what is the right target of moral protection, persons or human animals? If it is human animals, then Prince's actions may have been morally permissible, for he never killed a biological organism; if it is persons, then Prince's elimination of the alters would seem to have been immoral.

Now oddly enough, Prince himself stated that his *aim* was to kill off the "non-real" personalities. For instance, he allowed that the elimination of B_1 would be something that, from her own perspective, B_1 would consider "annihilation" and "psychical murder." And once B_2 appeared in deep hypnosis, he intentionally set out to "kill" B_4 as well. But surely he didn't think of himself as an actual murderer! And neither, I suspect, do many of the rest of us. Indeed, this is one reason—the fact that we don't think he did anything at all immoral—that some theorists have maintained that the alters could *not* have been persons.

But how much should we let our actual normative practices determine the boundaries of our metaphysical concepts? That is, why think that how we treat some being has any relevance for what that being is? A quick stroll through the darker chapters of human history reveals plenty of cases in which this would have been (and was) precisely the wrong method to embrace. For example, should we have said of African and African-American slaves that they weren't humans or persons because they weren't treated as such? Or that Jews weren't humans or persons during the Nazi era? Or that women weren't humans or persons throughout much of our patriarchal history? Certainly not. Our normative practices alone shouldn't fix the boundaries of our metaphysical concepts, simply because many or all of us might be *wrong* in such treatment. Indeed, these are cases in which we want to say (in hindsight) that it should have been *obvious* that the slaves, Jews, and women were human persons, *and therefore* that they ought to have been treated as such.

The normative stance we take to the alters of DID patients, then, could well be wrong, despite our deep intuitions to the contrary. (Many otherwise good people had the deep intuition that slaves were less than human—such an intuition was codified in the U.S. constitution, after all.) Instead, if we believe these alters are distinct persons (distinct both from one another and from the so-called "real" self), and we also believe it's seriously prima facie immoral to kill persons, then we ought to extend moral protection to these alters and reject our deep intuitions on the matter as simply wrongheaded.

Now the only view on which one might plausibly defend the moral legitimacy of Prince's actions is the Biological Criterion, where one incorporates the caveat that it is human animals that are the relevant targets of moral protection and Beauchamp's alters just weren't distinct biological organisms (even if they were "persons" in some sense). On this view, Prince was indeed treating just one human animal the entire time, and what he did was in fact admirable insofar as he was enabling that individual to live her life much more efficiently and normally. She was, the advocate of the Biological Criterion might say, one (moral) individual with a fractured psychology, someone just like us (in all relevant metaphysical respects) but with a profound mental disorder.

This is indeed an initially plausible account of the case, one that would allow us to preserve our deep intuitions about the moral permissibility (or admirability) of Prince's actions, while even allowing us to preserve our belief that the different alters were different persons. But the account raises further questions. It is surely another deep intuition we share that it is in fact *persons* who are the relevant targets of moral protection. At the very least, being a person is *sufficient* for moral protection. But if the alters were in fact (distinct) persons, then that fact alone should have been enough to generate moral protection for them and render Prince's actions (prima facie) wrong. Of course, one may insist that the alters weren't persons-*like-us*, but this is nowhere near an uncontroversial claim—when they were in charge of the body, each alter was indistinguishable from any other normal person—and anyway it is unclear why we should privilege the "like us" part of the formulation when it comes to moral protection. After all, if we ran across an alien species that met Dennett's conditions of personhood, but in ways that were very different from the ways we do, or they were physical (or even non-physical) specimens that were very different from us, it's unclear that those differences would be at all relevant to determining the moral treatment such creatures would deserve in virtue of their personhood alone.

Relatedly, David DeGrazia suggests that even if the alters in a DID case are different persons, as long as the DID patient isn't a single human organism containing more than *one of our kind*, then DID cases don't pose any worries for the Biological Criterion. And he is not convinced that we are forced to say there are two (or more) of us in such cases. But surely if we were to ask the individual alters what they think of their upcoming "elimination," they would respond (and have responded) with great fear and anxiety, much as we would if asked the same question. If part of what makes a creature "one of our kind" is its ability to reflect on its own existence and have a variety of rich prudential attitudes regarding its future (and be able to plead for its own life), then it becomes very difficult to think of the various alters in such cases as not being one of us.

Of course, the alters could well be mistaken: they simply may not be distinct individuals, despite what they think. If they are actually part of the same individual, and if prudential concern tracks (biological) identity, then in pleading to remain alive they may well be expressing grave *imprudence*. They just don't know, one might say, what's in their own best interest. But again and again we keep returning to a variation of the following point: isn't it *appropriate* for someone to fear the extinguishing of her particular stream of consciousness? There will, after all, be no one in the future who will remember "her" experiences, no one who will carry out her intentions, no one who will have the special sort of concern for "herself" she now has. Here is where the IDM view may once more play a role, for even if no identity has been lost with the elimination of alters, they nevertheless seem to have undergone a serious loss indeed. Is it as bad as death? For many, it might well be. If so, then Prince's actions were at the least morally questionable.

Thus far we have been considering a case in which the alters of a DID patient were altogether eliminated (at least this was the stated intention). But most therapists now agree that the goal of therapy with such patients is *integration*, not elimination. As one therapist puts it:

Cured is total integration which remains stable for 3 years. It's all the alters together—into one being. *No one* is lost, they are just all there in a different way, they don't have to share time anymore, everyone is up front all the time but in an organized, calm way.[1]

Integration is a gradual, complicated process. The idea at the start is to get the alters to a state of cooperation and then co-consciousness with one another. At this point (and after memory of the initial split-causing trauma has been accessed), they are ready for full integration. The borders between their initially distinct streams of consciousness become grayed, and then eliminated, so that the eventually integrated person will remember the thoughts and experiences of the lives of previous alters to which the others had had no access. It also means, theoretically, that the integrated person will have full access to the previous alters' intentions, beliefs, desires, and so on. As a result, many therapists now believe that, upon integration of the various personalities, those personalities do not die (although the personalities often fear that death is imminent) but instead *fuse. E pluribus unum* ("out of many, one") could well be the successfully integrated patient's motto.

This procedure may well ease our minds about the morality of DID treatment, but should it? That is, is fusion truly morally preferable to elimination? Is it *metaphysically* distinct from elimination? Suppose, after all, that there were two pre-integration alters that were distinct persons (as seems plausible)—call them Adam and Brian—and then they were fused into one—call him Carl. As it turns out, this procedure yields a kind of reverse fission problem. To see the worry, we can simply ask the question, "What happened to Adam and Brian?" There are four options: (a) only Adam survived as Carl; (b) only Brian survived as Carl; (c) both Adam and Brian survived as Carl; or (d) neither Adam nor Brian survived, and Carl is a new and different person. Options (a) and (b) are implausible, assuming the fusion brought together the whole of Adam's and Brian's personalities. After all, what non-arbitrary reason would we

---

1   Paula McHugh, from an online conference on Dissociative Identity Disorder, Multiple Personality Disorder: to Integrate Personalities or Not to Integrate. See the transcript at http://www.healthyplace.com/communities/personality_disorders/site/Transcripts/DID_MPD.htm. Emphasis in original.

have for thinking it was just Adam, or just Brian, that survived? Option (c) is what the therapists who engage in this treatment might have us believe, but this too is tough to swallow, for why should we think Carl's now-perfectly-unified psychology and stream of consciousness is that of *two* persons? All sorts of difficult questions emerge on this option. If Carl were to take a deliberate overdose, would the death be a suicide or a double murder? Were he to get married, would it be illegal, insofar as it would be bigamy? Should he get twice the salary of everyone else at his job? If he were to do something extraordinary, would he be *Time* magazine's *men* of the year? This would surely wreak havoc on our concept of a person, and so is fairly implausible. What we seem to be left with, then, is option (d), according to which Adam and Brian cannot survive fusion, in which case it looks as if fusion may not be metaphysically distinct from death, insofar as both involve the elimination of a person. And if eliminating persons is immoral, then fusion is immoral.

Nevertheless, there might be a rejoinder here if we appeal to the IDM view. Remember, on this view, identity is not what matters for survival (or for prudence and morality); instead, what matters are the various psychological relations that obtain. Thus, even if there is no identity relation between Carl and his two predecessors, as long as there is full psychological continuity between Adam and Carl and between Brian and Carl then the relation between Carl and those predecessors contains everything that matters. So even though neither Adam nor Brian actually survives fusion, for each of them what occurs will be *just as good as* ordinary survival. We just can't call it "identity" because the relation between them and Carl doesn't obtain uniquely. This means that, while fusion may not be metaphysically distinct from death, it could very well be *prudentially and morally* distinct from death. So where our prudential and moral concerns track these sorts of psychological relations, neither Adam nor Brian should be worried about their impending fusion, and the therapist who brings them together would not be doing anything immoral.

There is one final scenario to consider here before we throw a monkey wrench into the whole works. We have considered a case in which the alters were presumably eliminated during therapy in favor of the "real" self, and we have also considered a case in which the alters were fused together while preserving full psychological continuity. What, though, of a case in the middle, one in which two alters—distinct persons, let us say—are so very different psychologically that many of their various desires, beliefs, intentions, and character traits simply couldn't survive alongside each other. So suppose that one alter hates the president and the other loves him, one loves to travel and the other is a homebody, one is a gambler and the other a miser. If they were fused, the survivor would be worse off, it seems, than before, for while the unaware alters could pursue their individual desires and intentions when controlling the body, now the fused person would be at constant war with himself, in a way that could easily threaten another fracture. (Imagine both hating and loving the very same object for its very same features—it would be extremely difficult, if not psychologically impossible, to do so.)

Surely, then, these psychological features would have to be rendered compatible, and there might be two ways to do so. On the one hand, the therapist might try to eliminate one of the conflicting desire-pairs. So, for example, one might attempt to get rid of one alter's hatred of the president, his love for travel, and his gambling ways (or one might alternate the elimination, getting rid of one alter's hatred of the president and then the other alter's miserly ways, say). At this point, though, we might be heading back into a morally troublesome area, for what if the eliminated desires or projects are central to this alter's identity? That is, what if he defines himself as a president hater, or a gambler, or a free spirited traveler? This is obviously a question of narrative identity, and it may be that were these features of him removed involuntarily, it could well count as a wrongful violation of psychological unity and narrative coherence. And if they were removed voluntarily, it still might count as a kind of suicide. Consider the great loves and projects of one's own life. Were these to be removed, either voluntarily or involuntarily, it would be hard to imagine oneself as the same, or as even *oneself.* So while the sacrifice of such alters might ultimately be worth it to the fused person, this procedure most definitely plays up the fact that it could indeed be a severe *sacrifice,* one coming very close to narrative death.

On the other hand, the product of fusion here may be a person whose conflicting traits are dealt with in a different way. Derek Parfit, in considering a much more bizarre case of fusion (one wherein two unconscious bodies grow into one overnight), suggests the following possibility:

> Some [of their features] will be incompatible. These, if of equal strength, would cancel out, and, if of different strengths, the stronger would become weaker. These effects might be as predictable as the laws governing dominant and recessive genes. Suppose ... that I love Wagner, and always vote for a Socialist. The other person hates Wagner, and always votes for a Conservative. The one resulting person will be a tone-deaf floating voter.[1]

Suppose this were the process by which alters were fused. Should we have a problem with this? What should the attitude of the alters be to their impending fusion? As an advocate of the IDM view, Parfit thinks we should set aside the question of the identity of the survivor as unimportant. Instead, we should focus on the psychological relation between the pre-fusion and post-fusion persons. One consideration is the strength of that relation: will the fused person bear a great deal of psychological connections to the alter in question? But another crucial consideration will be the *value* to the alter of the psychological features of the fusion survivor. Suppose, for instance, that I am an alter in a DID patient, and I am a math maniac: I've studied and remember all sorts of mathematical theorems, proofs, and so forth, and I love doing what I do—it's become the central project of my life. Now suppose I am fused into other alters, and the survivor retains all of my mathematical knowledge but none of my love of math. Instead, he hates math and enjoys watching reality TV. Even though there are plenty of psychological connections between us, then, the one connection I valued most—my love for math—has been lost, and with it will likely be lost my concern for the survivor of fusion. Instead, I am likely to dread such fusion, and view it as something close to a kind of death.

---

1   Derek Parfit, *Reasons and Persons* (Oxford: Oxford University Press, 1984), p. 298.

On the other hand, if many connections will be lost, but the connections I most value will be preserved, then there may be little reason to dread, and significant reason to look forward to, the fusion. Even if I lose many of my mathematical memories and knowledge, to retain the love for it, such that I'll be able to continue pursuing it, may easily be sufficient to dissolve my worries about the procedure.

As we have seen, then, the issues are once again very complicated. If anything, we have learned that the treatment of those with DID is riddled with moral minefields, and for the patients themselves there is genuine reason to determine so far as one can just what kind of treatment will be conducted, how much psychological continuity might be preserved, and what kind of continuity might be preserved. But we have also seen how the various theories of identity once again have difficulty in accounting for such a case in a fully adequate fashion. We may thus bemoan our lack of theoretical adequacy or we may, with Kathleen Wilkes, worry that in this particular case, "the concept 'person' has fractured under the strain."[1]

And there is one more issue that reveals even more complexity, introduced by a simple question (and here's the monkey wrench referred to above): what if a gross immorality (a murder, say) were committed by one alter in a patient with DID? This sort of thing has actually happened, and the questions that arise are quite difficult to answer. Who, if anyone, would be morally responsible for this action? If the alter were a person, *how* could we hold him responsible? In other words, how might such an alter be punished, without being unfair to the other personalities? What if he were integrated with several other alters before the action were found out? Would the resulting person be morally responsible for his action? These and other related questions reveal just one of the fascinating issues involved in the relation between personal identity and moral responsibility, the topic to which we turn in the next chapter. Hopefully by the end of that chapter we will be in a better position to address these hard questions about DID patients.

---

1   Kathleen Wilkes, *Real People* (Oxford: Oxford University Press, 1988), p. 128.

Conclusion

We have discussed two general ethical issues regarding the end of life in this chapter, and we have come to our usual lack of definitive conclusions. Nevertheless, we have made some genuine progress. It will be worth briefly recapping that progress to remind ourselves that philosophy isn't always just about destruction and befuddlement.

First, this has probably been the most positive chapter for the advocate of the Biological Criterion that we have yet seen. Even though this criterion has had difficulty before in accounting for our practical concerns, it is the only theory of personal identity that comfortably implies that the two human stages in the advanced directive case—the signer and the later patient—are one and the same individual (laying the groundwork for the earlier signer's will to be authoritative over the later patient), and it also does the best in accounting for our intuition that Morton Prince didn't do anything immoral when he "eliminated" various personalities from Christine Beauchamp during therapy (for he was treating one and only one human animal all along). There were problems to be overcome, of course, but they seemed less insurmountable than they have before.

Second, what guided our investigations in both cases were some fairly strong moral intuitions: (a) that the signer of an advanced directive should have her will be authoritative over the demented patient she becomes; and (b) that elimination of various personalities in a DID patient isn't immoral. These seemed to run fairly deep, and it looked as if a metaphysical theory of personal identity lost in plausibility when it implied something that conflicted with these intuitions. While we will probe the nature of this general method more carefully in the final chapter, for now note that it is a method that at least allows us to assess various theories of personal identity against a pretty clear standard, and as a result to come to clearer results than usual. On the other hand, if these intuitions are up for grabs as well, then we may well lose our grip on how to proceed at all.

Finally, it should be clearer than usual by now how the sort of answers we'll get about the morality of various practices will depend on what we take the proper *subjects of those practices* to be. For instance, if we are to focus on the moral issues surrounding ending the lives of *individual human organisms*, then it looks like the Biological Criterion will be most relevant to our investigations. On the other hand, if we are to focus on the moral issues surrounding ending the lives of *persons*, one of our psychology-based criteria will likely be most relevant. But notice that this is not really a *metaphysical* decision; it is, rather, a normative one. For none of our metaphysical theories can tell us what the subjects of our moral practices *ought to be*. Indeed, this fact may open up a number of new possibilities. For instance, one might agree that the Biological Criterion gets the facts right about our essence and thus a certain sort of identity across time, while nevertheless insisting that the proper focus for morality ought to be on *persons*, in which case the relevant metaphysical criterion for their identity across time will be psychological. Or one might embrace the opposite view, that our moral focus ought to be on individual human organisms, even though the Psychological Criterion is the correct criterion of a certain sort of metaphysical identity. But at any rate, progress has been made in revealing this important fact in this chapter, and it is something we will exploit to greater effect in Chapter Eight.

In the meantime, though, we will turn to the interesting and difficult arena of moral responsibility. And while we will eventually get to the thorny issue of the responsibility of DID patients, we will first discuss several interesting everyday cases. As you read through the chapter, pay attention to the role that our intuitions are playing in the general arguments, as well as what the subjects of moral assessment are (or ought to be). This will help prepare you for the much more abstract discussions of our final two chapters.

WORKS CITED OR REFERENCED IN THIS CHAPTER

Buchanan, Allen. "Advance Directives and the Personal Identity Problem." *Philosophy & Public Affairs* 17 (Autumn 1988): 277-302.

DeGrazia, David. *Human Identity and Bioethics*. Cambridge: Cambridge University Press, 2005.

Dennett, Daniel. "Conditions of Personhood." In *The Identities of Persons*, edited by Amelie Oksenberg Rorty. Berkeley: University of California Press, 1976, pp. 175-96.

Dresser, Rebecca. "Life, Death, and Incompetent Patients: Conceptual Infirmities and Hidden Values in the Law." *Arizona Law Review* 28 (1986): 373-405.

Jaworska, Agnieszka. "Respecting the Margins of Agency: Alzheimer's Patients and the Capacity to Value." *Philosophy & Public Affairs* 28 (Spring 1999): 105-38.

Lizza, John P. "Multiple Personalities and Personal Identity Revisited." *The British Journal for the Philosophy of Science* 44 (1993): 263-74.

Luttrell, Steven, and Sommerville, Ann. "Limiting Risks by Curtailing Rights: A Response to Dr. Ryan." *Journal of Medical Ethics* 22 (1996): 100-04.

McMahan, Jeff. *The Ethics of Killing*. Oxford: Oxford University Press, 2002.

Parfit, Derek. *Reasons and Persons*. Oxford: Oxford University Press, 1984.

Prince, Morton. *The Dissociation of a Personality*. London: Longmans, Green, 1906. Reprinted in 1968 in New York: Johnson Reprint Corporation.

Radden, Jennifer. *Divided Minds and Successive Selves*. Cambridge, MA: MIT Press, 1996.

Ryan, Christopher James. "Betting Your Life: An Argument Against Certain Advance Directives." *Journal of Medical Ethics* 22 (1996): 95-99.

Wilkes, Kathleen. "Multiplicity and Personal Identity." *The British Journal for the Philosophy of Science* 32 (1981): 331-48.

———. *Real People*. Oxford: Oxford University Press, 1988.

CHAPTER SEVEN

Personal Identity and Moral Responsibility

Introduction

Recall *Case* 5 from the Introduction, in which Jen still blames her brother Phil for causing her to fall out of a tree thirty years ago when they were kids, whereas Phil thinks this is a ridiculous attitude for Jen to have, given that it happened a long time ago and he's changed so much since then. Theirs is a disagreement over the role personal identity should play (if any) in assessments of moral responsibility, and that is the topic of this chapter. As suggested in the Introduction, it seems there is an obvious principle in play here: one can be morally responsible only for *one's own* actions, where this is taken to mean that one can be morally responsible for some action A only if one is identical to the person who did A. According to this principle, then, personal identity is a necessary condition for moral responsibility. If so, then it looks as if the range of actions for which one is morally responsible actually depends on which theory of personal identity is true. In this chapter, we will investigate whether or not this principle is true, and, if so, what our various theories of personal identity would imply about moral responsibility. As we proceed, you should continue to consider whether or not our theories of personal identity should dictate, or instead answer to, what we think and care about with respect to moral responsibility (and our practical concerns generally).

"Moral responsibility," however, is something of a term of art in philosophy, a technical phrase philosophers use often, but one that most other people rarely, if ever, deploy. Unfortunately, even among philosophers, the phrase is occasionally used to mean different things. As a result, it is very important to stipulate right up front just what will be meant here. The most common understanding of the phrase is what we will employ in this chapter: *to say that agent A is* **morally responsible** *for X (typically an action) is just to say that A is appropriately subject to certain sorts of moral attitudes, like praise or blame, or certain sorts of direct responses, like punishment or reward, for X.* Now this is obviously not a complete definition—what other sorts of attitudes or responses are appropriate, and what makes them fall under the rubric of *moral* attitudes or responses?—but this analysis will serve our purposes sufficiently here. We clearly react to people in certain ways when we think they have done something immoral, or something morally good, and these sorts of reactions are just what moral responsibility is about. Of course, we sometimes react to people in these ways when we shouldn't have. I may blame you for something you "did" in one of my dreams, for example. So what's crucial to the analysis of moral responsibility is that it include the *appropriateness* of these attributions of praise and blame. Just because you *are* blamed doesn't mean it's *appropriate* for you to be blamed.

What, then, makes an attribution of praise or blame appropriate? One condition often given is that the person blamed for some action has to be the same person as the one who performed that action. It is this appropriateness condition we will now begin to explore, starting with the first person to have investigated the issue in any depth.

Locke on Identity and Responsibility

John Locke called "person" a *forensic term*, "appropriating actions and their merit."[1] What he seemed to mean by this was that the term "person" ought to be reserved for the expression of certain sorts of moral and prudential assertions and recommendations, in particular, assertions and recommendations about moral responsibility. Because Locke defined "person" as a self-conscious being—an entity capable of being conscious of its own consciousness—the identity of persons across time consisted, according to Locke, in a preservation of that same consciousness across time, and so "as far as this consciousness can be extended backwards to any past action or thought, so far reaches the identity of that person."[2] As we saw in Chapter One, this backwards-extending consciousness is often thought of in terms of *memory*: X at t1 is the same person as Y at t2 just in case Y remembers X's thoughts and actions.

Locke contrasted the term "person" with the term "man," where the latter referred to a living, organized human body, and so the identity of a man consisted merely in the continuity across time of that living body. (For Locke, "man" referred to humans generally, but I will continue to use Locke's term— rather than the term "human"—in what follows in order to avoid confusion, so forgive what may sound sexist or directed to only one of the genders reading this book.) This distinction thus allowed Locke to say things like the following:

> For should the soul of a prince, carrying with it the consciousness of the prince's past life, enter and inform the body of a cobbler, as soon as deserted by his own soul, every one sees he would be the same person with the prince, accountable only for the prince's actions: but who would say it was the same man? The body too goes to the making the man, and would, I guess to everybody determine the man in this case; wherein the soul, with all its princely thoughts about it, would not make another man: but he would be the same cobbler to every one besides himself.[3]

---

1 John Locke, "Of Identity and Diversity," in *Personal Identity*, edited by John Perry (Berkeley: University of California Press, 1975), p. 50.
2 Ibid., p. 39.
3 Ibid., p. 44.

And later Locke says, "But if it be possible for the same man to have distinct incommunicable consciousness at different times, it is past doubt the same man would at different times make different persons...."[1]

Locke thought, then, that "person," not "man," was the appropriate term for forensic—normative—matters, for our identity-related practical concerns, and the example he discussed repeatedly was moral responsibility. There is, after all, something quite special about those creatures eligible for moral responsibility, and so Locke wants to reserve for them the special name "persons." And what is it that's so special about persons, that is, what is it that enables them to be morally responsible? It is that they are capable of remembering, of being fully aware of their past deeds in the same way they're capable of reflecting on and being fully aware of their current deeds. And just as a person's consciousness of what she is now doing makes that deed her *own* action, so too her consciousness of what she did in the past makes that past deed her own action. This ownership relation is produced only by a memory "from the inside" (extending one's consciousness backwards), which, given the forensic terminology, is also what makes the rememberer the same *person* as the original agent, and which is thus what makes one eligible for moral responsibility for that action. There is, then, the following argument at work here:

1. One is morally responsible only for one's own actions.
2. An action A is one's own if and only if one is the same person as the performer of A.
3. X at t1 is the same person as Y at t2 if and only if Y remembers the actions of X (from the inside).

4. Thus, a past action is one's own if and only if one remembers it (from the inside).

5. Thus, one is morally responsible only for those actions one remembers (from the inside).

---

1   Ibid., p. 47.

This tight connection between moral responsibility and memory is buttressed by a simple thought: how could someone be morally responsible for his actions if he didn't remember performing them? As Locke remarks, if I am punished—held responsible—for the actions of someone whose thoughts and experiences I simply don't remember, "what difference is there between that punishment, and being created miserable?"[1] In other words, imagine that you wake up one day in a prison cell, not knowing how you got there or why you're there. The guards inform you that you murdered your parents, and while this is in fact true of the *man* that you were, you nevertheless don't remember a thing that happened prior to waking up. You're now simply confused and frightened. Now compare that case to the following: suppose that a duplicate of you had been built from scratch, but with no memories of anything that had happened prior to its construction, and then your duplicate had awoken in that prison cell, not remembering a thing. If this latter case would be unjust—and surely it would!—then so would the former, according to Locke, even if the man you are was identical to the man that had committed the crime. If you simply don't remember having performed the crime in question, it seems unfair to hold you responsible for it, even if your DNA matches the killer's.

How adequate is this view, though? It seems initially rather compelling. For one thing, the first premise, as we've said repeatedly, does strike many people as obviously (and deeply) true: how indeed could one be morally responsible for actions that aren't one's own? For another thing, the connection to memory is an important one, and it seems to have real explanatory power. For example, suppose Glen was a career criminal but now has an advanced case of Alzheimer's disease, so he no longer remembers any of his crimes. Is he any longer appropriately subject to blame for those past actions? It would be difficult to maintain that he is, and the Lockean theory easily explains why: Glen can no longer remember those actions and so it is difficult to think of them any longer as *his*—the current "his"—actions. How could it possibly be just or fair to blame him now, as a result, for actions that just aren't his anymore?

---

1   Ibid., p. 51.

Despite its initial plausibility, however, there are some troubling questions about the account. Set aside for now the second premise—the view that identity is necessary and sufficient for ownership—and focus on the first conclusion in the fourth step, that an action isn't one's own unless and until one remembers it. Some people simply won't buy this assertion, for they will fail to care whether or not the target of potential blame can extend his consciousness backwards to the action in question. For instance, try telling the victims of Glen's crimes that they weren't *his* actions, despite the fact that he looks exactly like the killer, and he even shares the killer's DNA! Third-person judgments of responsibility often don't depend on an assessment of how things seem from the inside to the subject of assessment. Instead, what often matters most is physical continuity with the original agent.

Nevertheless, we need to remind ourselves that moral responsibility consists in *appropriate* attributions of blame (or praise), and what Locke is advocating is the view that attributing ownership of actions to those who don't remember them would actually be inappropriate, if the situation were carefully considered. Locke's argument here can be boiled down to a familiar appeal: what if it were *you*? Because you would have no concern or feel any guilt regarding the actions of someone you couldn't remember at all, neither should we, the third-person assessors, maintain that they were your actions or blame you for doing them. That would be, at its root, somehow unfair.

Consider, though, a more common sort of case. Suppose Mel has gotten very drunk and then, when pulled over by the cops, goes on an anti-Semitic tirade against the arresting officer. When he wakes up in jail the next morning, Mel swears he doesn't remember a thing. Should he be held responsible for his tirade the night before? Most people would say yes without hesitation. Locke, however, explicitly says no: if he didn't remember saying what he said, then they weren't *his* actions, and so he's not responsible for them. But this assessment really is completely contrary to our ordinary practices. After all, we hold people responsible all the time for the things they do when drunk. Now Locke actually admits that this is our ordinary practice, and he also admits the *reasonableness* of that practice, but this is only because the blamers in such cases simply have no way of knowing whether or not the subject of blame really has no memory of the events in question or if he's just faking it. So in punishing someone for his drunken actions, say, we can prove the facts of the case against him, but he can't prove to us that he truly doesn't remember, and so, says Locke, we punish him justly in such circumstances—we're simply ignorant of the truth of the matter. "But in the great day," he says, referring to the Day of Judgment, "wherein the secrets of all hearts shall be laid open, it may be reasonable to think, no one shall be made to answer for what he knows nothing of; but shall receive his doom, his conscience accusing or excusing him."[1]

Still, it is very difficult to think that Mel should get off the hook for his behavior—even if he truly blacked out and remembers nothing of the rant—where his being held responsible has nothing to do with our ignorance of his mental state. Indeed, it seems somehow *irrelevant* to his responsibility-status that he doesn't remember what he did, although it is a bit pitiful. "Not only is he blameworthy," we might think, "but he also doesn't even remember the actions he's being blamed for. How very sad." But it would simply strike most of us as outrageous to think that memory loss of this sort could excuse someone from ownership of his actions and thus moral responsibility.

Indeed, there is a further, more troubling point to be made here, stemming from research into criminal behavior. As it turns out, some criminal actions may actually *cause* memory loss. In particular, up to 45% of murderers black out after their crimes and simply lose any memories of the crime afterwards, and this is true of the perpetrators of other violent crimes as well, such as rape and aggravated assault. These are akin, then, to traumatic events for the criminals, and as with other traumatic events in the lives of non-criminals, amnesia often follows. But these seem to be cases in which we also clearly don't want to let the criminals off the hook. It is still appropriate to blame them, we likely want to say, in which case memory loss doesn't excuse one from moral responsibility.

1　Ibid., p. 48.

Indeed, we may have additional reason to reject Locke's view when we think about the flipside of blame, namely, praise. Suppose Jessica is a soldier who jumps on a grenade to save her whole platoon, but by some fantastic luck the grenade only partially detonates, knocking her head against a tree and causing her to forget only this incident, but leaving the rest of her and her memories intact. Would she no longer be an appropriate subject of praise for jumping on the grenade, given that she didn't remember the action in question (making it somehow not her action)? It seems not. Indeed, her suffering an injury like that, however minor, might even increase our praise for her. But if loss of memory doesn't undermine the praising element of moral responsibility, why should it undermine the blaming element?

These examples suggest that an action may be one's own, in the relevant sense, even if one doesn't remember it. In other words, memory of an action isn't necessary for ownership of it (and thus responsibility for it). But as we will now see, it also seems that memory is not *sufficient* for ownership, that is, one might well remember an action that nevertheless is not one's own. Start with a science fiction-type case borrowed from Derek Parfit. Suppose neuroscientists become capable of making a copy in one brain of particular memory traces from another brain. Suppose, then, that Artemis has stolen a car and then (for some crazy reason) agrees to undergo the procedure to have his memory of that action copied into Diana's brain. Diana then wakes up from the surgery and seems to remember furtively looking around an unfamiliar street one night, smashing open a nearby car's window with a tire iron, hot-wiring the car, and driving away. Was that *her* action? Clearly not, even though she now "remembers" it from the inside.[1] Memory, then, isn't sufficient for ownership.

This is science fiction, though. Are there any real-life cases that yield this result? There may be. Suppose Patty has been kidnapped and brainwashed by her captors, so that she comes to "believe" in their cause and helps them rob a bank. Later, when beyond their influence, she "comes to her senses," and while she winds up just as she was before being kidnapped, and

---

1   Some might object to calling this a case of genuine memory, and for those that do, Parfit (following Sydney Shoemaker) suggests calling it "quasi-memory."

so rejects her captors' cause entirely, she does remember being inside the bank and holding the gun on the guard and participating in the robbery. Was that *her* action, then? It sure seems as if it wasn't, that the "real" Patty had disappeared by that point, replaced by a brainwashed person doing things the real Patty would never have done. To now hold Patty responsible for those brainwashed actions would thus seem terribly unfair, even though Patty has full memories of doing those deeds.

The fourth step of the Lockean argument looks, therefore, to be quite flawed, so given that it's a conclusion from three preceding premises, something must have gone wrong there. But where? The most likely place is in the third premise, which gives Locke's criterion of personal identity. We already knew that this criterion was problematic, though, from our investigation of it in Chapter One. And while memory may often be associated with moral responsibility, it's clearly a non-essential relationship, a point revealed by the dispute between Jen and Phil at the outset. Phil actually remembers causing Jen to fall out of the tree when they were kids, but he nevertheless feels no guilt over it and is somewhat irritated by the fact that Jen keeps wanting to attribute that long-ago action to him today. Phil thus urges the inappropriateness of blaming him, despite the fact that he remembers the action in question. On the other hand, Jen's attributions of blame don't depend at all on Phil's remembrance of the action; indeed, she would likely continue to blame him were he to forget the incident entirely.

What this means is that we need to look elsewhere for a more adequate account of the relation between moral responsibility, ownership of actions, and identity. For now we will leave standing the first two premises—that moral responsibility presupposes ownership, and ownership consists in identity—and focus on the third, which is where a criterion of identity would go. What we'll get once we apply different criteria of identity here, then, will produce a new fourth step of the argument, one filling in the following blank: *A past action is one's own if and only if* _____ . The hope, then, is that we'll find a theory of personal identity that can account for the various cases we have discussed, as well as any others we might think up. If so, it might well be the right theory to account for our practical concerns generally.

Before we begin, though, a clarifying note is in order. It is very important to pay close attention to the way the argument proceeds here. We are
going to leave untouched the claim that responsibility presupposes ownership of actions and focus on the criterion for ownership. What makes an
action one's own? That is, what makes an action *properly attributable* to
one? The thought we will be exploring, then, is that the right criterion of
ownership *just is* a criterion of personal identity. But a criterion is simply
a list of necessary and sufficient conditions, so what we will be doing is
exploring examples where (a) identity holds between X and Y but nevertheless X's actions aren't properly attributable to Y, and (b) X's actions
are properly attributable to Y even though identity doesn't hold between
them. The trick, then, will be if we can find a criterion of identity for
which there are no examples of type (a) or (b). So let's begin.

The Biological Criterion

If we apply the Biological Criterion to the main argument, we will fill in
the blank of the fourth step as follows: *a past action is one's own if and
only if it was performed by an individual human organism with whom one
is now biologically continuous.* In other words, some past action was mine
just in case it was performed by the same biological animal I currently am.
Is this right, however?

This view has one distinct advantage over Locke's: it can account for
the anti-Semitic Mel case. We want to say that the drunken tirade was
sober-Mel's action, even though he doesn't remember it, and the Biological Criterion offers a possible explanation, namely, that it's indeed his action in virtue of its having been performed by the same human organism
he is now.

Nevertheless, the view has many flaws. For one thing, cases of Alzheimer's disease and brainwashing cast doubt on the claim that biological continuity is sufficient for ownership of actions. The actions of the
criminal, for instance, no longer seem to be properly attributable to the
Alzheimer's patient he has become. Similarly, brainwashed Patty's bank

robbery no longer seems properly attributable to post-brainwashed Patty, who we would likely think of as the *real* Patty.

For another thing, it doesn't seem *necessary* for ownership of actions that the later individual be biologically continuous with the earlier individual, although it takes a bit of science fiction to see this point. Suppose that I have robbed a bank, and then I have my entire cerebrum transplanted into another body's brain (itself devoid of a cerebrum). Let us stipulate that the person who wakes up will be exactly like me psychologically, that he will have apparent memories of the crime, he will share all of my criminal values, and he will have inherited my intention to go on a spending spree after waking up (and does so). On the Biological Criterion, he will not be me—my human organism is just not his—and so my actions will not be his either: it would thus be a mistake to attribute the crime I committed to him. But this conclusion will strike most of us as itself a mistake. Instead, the psychological relation between him and me is what will make it appropriate to attribute my actions to him (and thus to hold him morally responsible for what I have done). To say that my actions aren't his will be a great joke to him, believing as he will that he's gotten away scot-free with the crime.

Now an advocate of the Biological Criterion might respond, as DeGrazia in fact does, by saying that *"in the world as we know it,"*[1] biological continuity is in fact necessary for the sort of psychological relation on which we seem to be relying. There are no cerebrum transplants available in real life; instead, continuity of one's psychology requires continuity of one's individual biological life, so if moral responsibility really does depend on psychological continuity, biological continuity is actually still a necessary condition for moral responsibility in the real world.

But this reply misses the point. What we're looking for is a criterion of the ownership of actions, a story about what makes various past actions properly attributable to oneself. Biological continuity, even if one necessary ingredient in real-life cases, fails to provide any relevant criterion of what is obviously a *psychological* matter: my ownership

---

1   David DeGrazia, *Human Identity and Bioethics* (Cambridge: Cambridge University Press, 2005), p. 60, emphasis mine.

of an action (and thus moral responsibility for it) has to do with the execution of certain intentions as well as being a legitimate subject of various assessments, that is, being in a position to hear, be receptive to, respond to, accept, and/or reject praise or blame, along with being subject to experiencing various emotions associated with these reactions and judging the fairness or appropriateness of the original assessments. But all of these are psychological states, and they are the only states that could be relevant to a *criterion* of ownership of actions. After all, another necessary condition for ownership of actions in the world as we know it is that the agent be alive at some point and breathe air. But surely the fact that one must breathe air, while of course necessary, adds nothing whatsoever to a relevant explanation of one's ownership of, and moral responsibility for, actions. And, as it turns out, neither does biological continuity.

Now one might insist here that biological continuity is certainly what grounds *legal* responsibility, so why wouldn't it ground moral responsibility as well? After all, it is the *physical* evidence linking a defendant to the crime—fingerprints, facial recognition, and DNA—that is most damning, what we take to be the best indicators of the defendant's guilt, so why shouldn't that sort of physical, biological evidence also determine moral responsibility? The answer is that DNA, for example, is indeed only an *indicator* of the defendant's identity, a sign that he is the owner of the action in question, but as an indicator, it is merely a helpful and generally reliable guide to tracking the sort of identity that matters, namely, the identity of the *moral agent* who committed the crime. So while DNA evidence is a very good tracking system for moral agents as things now stand, suppose one's DNA changed over time, in random ways. Would we any longer think of DNA as any more important for legal responsibility than the color of one's hair, say, or one's current weight? Of course not. For it would now be an unreliable tracker of one's identity as a moral agent, which is a psychological relation. Consequently, we need to look elsewhere for the grounding relation of ownership and moral responsibility.

The Psychological Criterion

The natural move at this point, then, is to embrace the Psychological Criterion. If we insert this criterion of identity into the criterion of ownership, the fourth step in the argument would read as follows: *a past action is one's own if and only if it was performed by some person with whom one is now uniquely psychologically continuous.* This view is a marked improvement over the application of both the Biological Criterion and Locke's view. Even if we restrict our attention to cases "in the world as we know it," the Psychological Criterion is much more directly relevant to ownership than the Biological Criterion, for it is made up of precisely those psychological features ownership of actions must involve, namely, intentions, beliefs, emotional dispositions, and so on. And it is because the Psychological Criterion targets all of these varied relations in its criterion of identity, in *addition* to memory, that it is able to account for some of the cases on which Locke's view founders. Start with the worry that memory isn't necessary for ownership of actions. In the case in which you wake up in prison, not remembering the crimes you—the man—had committed, a case could be made for those still being your actions on the Psychological Criterion, despite the fact that you lack memory of them, given the psychological continuity that nevertheless obtains with respect to all the *other* relevant psychological connections: beliefs, goals, desires, intentions, general character, and so on. This view could also provide an explanation for our intuitions in the drunken-Mel case, for we may again maintain that, even though sober-Mel remembers nothing of his tirade, those were still *his* actions in virtue of the fact that he is psychologically continuous with the drunken-Mel with respect to all the other psychological connections.

Furthermore, when it comes to the worries about the *sufficiency* of memory for ownership of actions, the Psychological Criterion is also an improvement over the Lockean view, at least in one sort of case. If Artemis's memory trace of stealing the car were copied into Diana's brain, the Lockean view implies that it is now Diana's action as well, but this can't be right. The Psychological Criterion helps us see why: recall from

Chapter Two that psychological continuity consists in overlapping chains of *strong* psychological connectedness, which involves the holding of many more than one or a few connections. So Diana would just not be psychologically continuous with Artemis, meaning his action wouldn't be her own, even though she would "remember" it. But now notice that once a significant number of psychological connections are indeed in place—when strong connectedness obtains—the psychological continuity established would then be sufficient to attribute ownership of actions to the psychological continuant, so this view would also explain ownership in the case of the full cerebrum transplant case.

Still, there are two sorts of cases that may give us real pause about applying the Psychological Criterion to ownership of actions. The first is the case of the war hero Jessica, who jumps on the grenade and in so doing suffers a permanent loss of memory of that action. Suppose that what takes place on top of memory loss is a severe disruption of psychological continuity: the person who wakes up from a coma several days later not only doesn't remember jumping on the grenade, but she also has very few other direct psychological connections to the grenade-smotherer, at any rate not enough to provide strong connectedness. Now this may be a harder case to wrap our intuitions around, but I suspect many people would still want to say that the actions of the grenade-smothering Jessica are properly attributable to the post-coma Jessica, and thus that the post-coma Jessica may be morally responsible (praiseworthy) for jumping on the grenade.

There are a couple of points to make here. If the actions of the grenade-smotherer are properly attributable to post-coma Jessica, it looks like we won't be able to account for *why* on this application of the Psychological Criterion to the criterion of ownership, given that the post-coma Jessica is not (by stipulation) psychologically continuous with the grenade-smotherer. This would mean that psychological continuity is in fact not necessary for ownership of actions, that some past action might be yours, say, even though you're not psychologically continuous with the performer of that action.

Nevertheless, an advocate of psychological continuity as the criterion of ownership might still be able to respond to this worry, in one of two ways.

On the one hand, she might simply deny that the post-coma Jessica really did perform the action in question; instead, like Locke, this advocate could say that, because of the significant discontinuity that has occurred, post-coma-Jessica, while the same *woman* as the grenade-smotherer, is not the same *person*, and so the grenade-smotherer's actions aren't properly attributable to her. This would be a case in which the advocate of applying the Psychological Criterion to ownership would be urging us to revise our intuitions in light of the theory, not the other way around (assuming we had the intuition that the post-coma-Jessica was still the grenade-smotherer), and this may be a worrisome methodology to employ. (We'll say more about this in the final chapter.)

On the other hand, the advocate of applying the Psychological Criterion to ownership might agree that post-coma-Jessica didn't in fact perform the grenade-smothering action, but nevertheless insist that post-coma-Jessica *is still praiseworthy.* How might this be possible? To this point, we have been following Locke in talking as if responsibility is entirely and solely about *actions,* that the only things for which we hold people morally responsible are their deeds. But this is false, it seems, for we often hold people responsible for their *characters,* praising and blaming them for the types of people they are, and not just for their actions. So while one might conceivably agree with Locke that Mel, for example, doesn't own and isn't responsible for his specific anti-Semitic tirade (because he doesn't remember it, say), we could nevertheless hold Mel responsible in general for *being anti-Semitic,* for being the type of person from whom anti-Semitic tirades erupt so easily when his inhibitions are lowered while drunk. Similarly, we might also agree that post-coma Jessica didn't jump on the grenade—this wasn't *her* action—while still assessing her as praiseworthy for *being brave,* for being the type of person disposed to jump on grenades to protect others. In other words, perhaps the characters of the grenade-smotherer and post-coma Jessica are sufficiently similar to ground praise for the latter's, even though there aren't enough overall psychological connections of other sorts between them to establish psychological continuity and thus ownership of the action in question. Of course, if post-coma Jessica's character had changed significantly as well, then this assessment would be much harder to maintain about her (perhaps rightly so). But at any rate, this complicated story, divorcing praise for character from ownership of actions, may allow the advocate of psychological continuity as the criterion for ownership to have a way to deal with the Jessica case.

I mentioned earlier, though, that there were *two* cases posing difficulty for the Psychological Criterion, and the second one is much tougher to deal with. It is the case of Patty, kidnapped and brainwashed into performing a bank robbery she later repudiates. Here is a case in which psychological continuity is preserved throughout: the post-brainwashed Patty is psychologically continuous with the brainwashed Patty. Even though the post-brainwashed Patty is psychologically quite *different* from the brainwashed Patty (they don't share many beliefs, desires, or values), nevertheless there has been no disruption to the overlapping chain of strong connectedness that holds between them, and so the advocate of the Psychological Criterion must maintain that they are just different stages of one and the same person. Consequently, if we insert this criterion of identity into the criterion of ownership, the bank robbing action must be *hers*. But as we saw, this seems the wrong answer in this case. Patty repudiates the action, and there seems something right about this: after all, the brainwashed Patty underwent significant psychological alteration, against her will (at least against the pre-brainwashed Patty's will), and so we are inclined to think of the brainwashed actions as not hers, or at least not her *real self's*. But because the Psychological Criterion does not make any distinction between the actions of a person's self and the actions of a person's *real* self, it looks like its application to the criterion of ownership yields the wrong answer in this case, and so looks inadequate to our task.

Narrative Identity

The Patty case, while such a thorn in the side of someone applying the Psychological Criterion to the criterion of ownership, seems tailor made for showing off the strengths of the narrative identity account. Inserting this view of identity into the criterion of ownership, then, we would fill in the blank of the fourth step of the main argument as follows: *a past action is one's own if and only if it is correctly included as an event in the self-told story of one's life.* As Marya Schechtman puts it, "What it means for an action to be part of someone's narrative is for it to flow naturally from the rest of her life story—to be an intelligible result of her beliefs, values, desires, and experiences," and "[t]he more an action seems to stem from a coherent and stable pattern of values, desires, goals, and character traits, the more it seems under a person's control [and so determines the degree of moral responsibility assigned]."[1] Alternatively, the more inexplicable some action—the harder it is to fit within the narrative of one's life—the less responsibility one has for it, insofar as it is difficult to see it as one's own, as flowing from one's genuine self.

The Patty case, then, has an easy diagnosis for an advocate of this narrative view of ownership: the robbery is not properly attributable to post-brainwashed Patty given how inexplicable that action was in the narrative of her life as a whole. It didn't at all flow from the beliefs, values, and desires she currently has, or had prior to the kidnapping, and so is in no way representative of *her*, of the genuine self Patty had developed (and has once more). The action simply can't coherently be included as an event in the self-told story of her life. When she tells that story, the story of the bank robbery will either be excluded altogether, or included as if it happened to someone else by a narrator who is no longer capable of identifying with that agent.

This way of talking is actually quite important, for in talking about what makes an action ours we are inevitably talking about whether or not we can or do *identify* with the action and/or with the agent who performed it. Now "identification" is a very complicated concept, and many important philosophers have wrestled with precisely what it consists in, but for our purposes the idea is rather straightforward: to identify with some past action, say, is simply to *embrace it as one's own*, and so to incorporate it within one's life story; to identify with some past (or future) self is to *embrace him or her as oneself*, as the same subject one now is, as the

---

1   Marya Schechtman, *The Constitution of Selves* (Ithaca, NY: Cornell University Press, 1996), p. 159.

subject of one's narrative. Identification is thus taken to be something one actively engages in, rather than something that merely happens to one. The attitude one takes towards the various events that have occurred is critical to a determination of whether or not they count as part of one's narrative identity. Consequently, the attitude Patty takes towards the bank robbery genuinely matters here: her failure to identify with both the action and the agent in question is essential to their exclusion from her life story. Patty is simply unable any longer to understand what it was like to be that bank robber, and the bank robber's values and goals are so different from her present values and goals as to be those of a complete and inscrutable stranger. She cannot identify with that robber's actions, therefore, because they are completely alien to her.

It is the attitude of identification, incorporated as essential by the narrative identity view, that renders an advocate of its application to ownership able to handle the case tripping up someone applying the Psychological Criterion, and this is because the latter view doesn't privilege one's *attitude* towards one's various psychological connections as making any difference in determining who one is. Instead, on the Psychological Criterion one's identity across time is determined solely by the sheer number of psychological connections that make up psychological continuity, and this is entirely an objective matter. But the narrative identity view maintains that some connections are more relevant to my identity than others, and those that are more relevant are made so precisely by my current attitude to them, making one's identity, recall, a *subjective* matter. This will strike many people as a distinct improvement over the Psychological Criterion, then, which just tallies the various connections indiscriminately.

But while the subjective aspect of narrative identity improves it in one area, it may cause problems in another. Again, the application under consideration is that my current identification with some past experience makes it my own, part of my life story. But identification, as we ordinarily think of it, isn't restricted to just one's own experiences. One might also identify with *other* people's experiences. If you have had an exhilarating epiphany listening to one of your philosophy professors, for example, I can easily identify with you in that regard. Or if you have nearly blacked out on one of those corkscrew roller coasters, I can identify with you. Or if you had your tonsils out at a young age, I can identify with you. Indeed, we do this sort of thing all the time. Those with cancer identify with one another, those who have served in the same branch of the military identify with one another, those who have been civil servants identify with one another, and so forth. In fact, we can even identify with fictional characters in novels. The problem for the narrative view, then, is this: if my identification with some experience makes it my own, part of my life story, then my identification with someone *else's* experience makes it part of my life story as well, but this can't be right. What happened to you as part of your life story surely has no place in mine, as something that happened to me.

One might reply to this worry in a couple of ways. First, one might suggest that, while my identification with some past experience of mine is to embrace it *as* mine, identification with one of your past experiences is to embrace it *as if* it were mine. So I don't make your experience mine when I identify with it; rather, I put myself in your shoes and fully appreciate your experience as I would if it were my own, and this may result in my experiencing certain sorts of emotions in response to it, say, but at the end of the day it's still your experience. I try on your experience and see that it "fits," in a manner of speaking: it's something I can fully understand and appreciate, given my own history—I can *empathize* fully with your experience—but my ability to empathize in this way doesn't make your experience mine.

But why not? If identification is what *makes* an experience mine, part of my narrative identity, then we cannot appeal to which experiences are yours and which ones are mine *prior* to such identification, and yet this is precisely what such a response does. Its criterion of identification presupposes a criterion of identity, which itself presupposes a criterion of identification. A tight circle indeed.

A different sort of reply, then, would distinguish between types of identity—narrative and numerical—and then get out of the circle by deploying both types of identity at key spots in the argument. So one might say that yes, our criterion of identification presupposes identity, but that's *numerical* identity it presupposes. And yes, identity presupposes identification, but that's *narrative* identity doing the presupposing. So the picture would look like this:

Narrative identity

▲

Identification

▲

Numerical identity

On this model, what makes an experience mine—part of my narrative identity—is my identification with it. And while I may identify with all sorts of experiences, the ones that are relevant to my narrative identity are just those that are part of the life of one and the same individual as I am now. This is simply to reiterate the view that narrative identity presupposes numerical identity, stemming from either the Biological Criterion or the Psychological Criterion. But it also suggests once more that neither of these views of numerical identity is going to work as a criterion of ownership (and thus responsibility). For that, one will need something like identification, which (goes the thought) is what narrative identity is all about.

But now we may wonder whether the view is suddenly too *restrictive* again. To see why, consider our Physical Fission case, wherein I split and my two halves re-grow their missing halves, resulting in two people who are exactly similar to me, both psychologically and biologically. Remember that the only remotely plausible answer to this case, from both views of numerical identity, is that I don't survive, that the two fission products are two new individuals. But then if the right kind of identification for narrative identity presupposes numerical identity, neither fission product could identify in this sense with any of my experiences pre-fission. So if I were a criminal, having done lots of bad deeds, and then I underwent fission, none of my actions would be properly attributable to anyone anymore, despite the fact that *two* people seem to remember doing my deeds and having the feeling of having gotten away with it. And if ownership of actions is necessary for moral responsibility, neither fission product would be morally responsible (to any degree) for my actions. This will strike many of us as the wrong answer, however—fission can't be like death!—and so it leaves the advocate of narrative identity in a bind: either the view is too broad, implying that I incorporate the actions and experiences of others into my life story via identification, or the view is too narrow, implying that my fission products aren't responsible for my actions. To avoid this dilemma, then, we may need to deny the importance of identity—either numerical or narrative—to a proper account of the ownership of actions or moral responsibility.

The IDM View

If identity isn't what matters for ownership of actions and moral responsibility, then what does? According to the most plausible version of IDM, what matters in terms of making an action one's own is one's psychological continuity with the original agent, where such continuity doesn't have to obtain uniquely. So in the fission case, where I have engaged in many criminal deeds, *both* of my fission products, being fully psychologically continuous with me, would own my actions and be morally responsible for them. This conclusion thus avoids the problem of fission encountered by the narrative identity view, although it too has its own problems.

The first problem is that the IDM view seems to run into precisely the same difficulties with the Patty case that application of the Psychological Criterion did: if what matters for ownership of actions, say, is just psychological continuity, and post-brainwashed Patty is psychologically continuous with brainwashed Patty, then post-brainwashed Patty owns the bank-robbing action performed by brainwashed Patty, which seems precisely the wrong thing to say. Even though there's an overlapping chain of strong psychological connectedness running from the brainwashed Patty to the post-brainwashed Patty, many of us will want to say that post-brainwashed Patty really had nothing to do with that bank robbery.

One plausible response, though, is for the IDM theorist to combine his view with the narrative identity theorist's and emphasize the importance of *identification* to ownership of actions. Because Patty does not—perhaps cannot—identify with the bank-robbing agent, she takes no ownership of that agent's actions, despite being psychologically continuous with that agent. The problem with this move for the narrative identity theorist was that it opened up the door to my being responsible for the actions of many other people, namely, all those with whom I identify (empathize). But if the IDM theorist couples identification *with psychological continuity* as being what's important, so that identification with some experience makes it mine only when I'm psychologically continuous with the original experiencer, then this worry may not arise, for I won't be psychologically continuous with those many other people with whom I occasionally identify.

A second plausible response for the IDM theorist would be to emphasize the importance of psychological connectedness itself for ownership of actions. Because connectedness comes in degrees (I am more strongly connected to my yesterday's self than my five-years-ago self), perhaps ownership does too, corresponding to the degrees of connectedness that obtain. On this amended view, then, post-brainwashed Patty may have only a very limited degree of ownership in brainwashed Patty's actions insofar as the later stage is very weakly psychologically connected to the earlier stage. And thus, while post-brainwashed Patty would then be responsible for brainwashed Patty's actions, it would be only a very limited degree of responsibility. Of course, figuring out just what it means for there to be degrees of ownership and degrees of responsibility might be difficult, but there is something intuitive about the idea, and it may be worth exploring in more detail.

A second problem with the IDM view has to do with the Jessica case, which posed a problem for an application of the original Psychological Criterion as well. The problem, remember, is that if the explosion caused significant psychological discontinuity, then we are left without a justification for attributing the action to Jessica for which we now want to hold her responsible (as praiseworthy). The IDM theorist may offer the same replies offered by someone applying the Psychological Criterion, however. On the one hand, one may bite the bullet and say that the post-coma Jessica just didn't perform the actions in question: while the same *woman* performed the action, one could say, the *person* who did so no longer exists. On the other hand, one may urge that the post-coma Jessica is responsible, but only for the *character* of the grenade-smotherer, as long as their characters are still quite similar. This would be to say that, even though there were significant psychological discontinuities caused by the explosion, there could still be enough by way of direct psychological connections of character to warrant our praising the post-coma Jessica for being a brave *person*, even though the grenade-smothering wasn't *her* action, given her current failure to remember the deed or have enough of the beliefs, desires, or goals of the original grenade-smotherer.

A third problem of the view seems to attach to one of its straightforward implications, namely, that the principle we have been assuming through-out—"moral responsibility presupposes identity"—is false. In other words, we have maintained all along the second premise of the main argument, that a past action is now one's own if and only if identity obtains between one now and the original performer of the action. But the IDM view denies this premise. After all, if we hold my fission products responsible for my deeds, then we are holding that people may be responsible in the absence of personal identity, that is, that one person may be responsible for the ac-tions of someone else. This result will be deeply counterintuitive to many, however. And it is an intuition that may be buttressed by the fact that, if you were to blame one of my fission products for my action, he is likely to reply, "But *I* didn't do it!" And he will be right. Nevertheless, would this count as a genuine excuse? Remember, both fission products will be exactly like me in every respect, remembering the crime and sharing my glee at pulling it off. It's just that they cannot both be me because of the logical requirements of the identity relation: $2 \neq 1$. But if only one of them had survived, surely my actions would be properly attributable to him, so why should my success at getting *two* people to survive fission undermine those attributions? It might be thought, then, that the successes of the IDM view at dealing with cases the other views found problematic could outweigh the costs of abandoning the assumed principle.

In addition, there is a very subtle point one might make to suggest that the costs of abandoning the assumed principle are in fact quite low. To see why, note again the wording of the first premise of the original

Lockean argument on which we have based our discussion throughout this chapter: one is morally responsible only for one's own actions. This is the platitude that seems overwhelmingly plausible. And this way of putting it pushed us to talk about *ownership* of actions, about which actions are properly attributable to one relative to moral responsibility. But the way we went about filling in our criterion of ownership was by applying various criteria of identity into it, based on the assumption in the second premise of the main argument that an action is one's own if and only if one is the same person as the performer of that action. But why should we assume that? Why, in other words, assume that responsibility and ownership entail identity? It may well seem, of course, that calling an action "one's own," and insisting that one is responsible only for the actions one owns, is just another way of saying that responsibility and ownership entail identity. But the fact that one owns an action doesn't necessarily entail that one owns it *exclusively*, or that one is identical with the original agent. Instead, it just entails that one has a special *ownership* relation with the original agent's action. But given that ownership and attributability aren't necessarily tied to identity and exclusivity—a single piece of property may have many owners, after all—one could claim that the second premise of the main argument is false. Instead of holding, then, that responsibility presupposes identity, perhaps all we need to assume is the principle that responsibility presupposes *ownership*: one person can't be responsible for actions that are not *his or her own*. But if *this* is the only principle we need assume, then the fact that the IDM view denies the so-called principle that responsibility presupposes identity may not be a big deal after all. The IDM view would still adhere to the principle just articulated about responsibility and ownership, and so perhaps that's all that matters.

Preliminary Conclusions

So where do we stand? Each of our four major theories does well in certain respects and does poorly in others, as usual. What we wanted was a single theory that could provide the right criterion of ownership in order to account for all of our cases, cases in which we have fairly strong intuitions, including drunken Mel the anti-Semite, Jessica the grenade-smotherer, Artemis and Diana (where she receives his memory trace), Patty the brain-washed bank robber, and the cases of fission and cerebrum transplants. Now the psychology-based criteria of ownership do markedly better with these cases than does the application of the Biological Criterion, but these criteria are problematic as well: applications of the Psychological Criterion and the IDM view both have difficulty with the Jessica and Patty cases, while an application of the narrative identity view has difficulty with the fission case and cases of over-identification (identification with other people). Now in each case I have suggested possible replies on the part of the various advocates, but it should be clear that more work needs to be done to fully defend the view in question.

So one test of a theory of personal identity here is to see whether or not it can explain the data—our clear-cut intuitions—in cases of ownership and moral responsibility in which such data is available. But the second test of a theory of personal identity is to see whether or not it can help us out by providing a plausible (determinate?) answer in harder cases, cases where our intuitions just aren't so clear-cut. And we have two such cases remaining: responsibility in the DID cases discussed in the previous chapter, and the case of Phil and Jen that got us started off.

Test Case #1: Dissociative Identity Disorder

Sybil suffers a severe trauma in her youth that causes two distinct personalities to arise during her late teens. One calls herself Jan, the other calls herself Joan. Neither Jan nor Joan is conscious of the other, or even aware of her existence. Each "awakens" after losing long periods of time, sometimes days, and honestly has no idea where she has been since last being conscious. Jan is nasty and cruel, and one day while in control of the body she kills an innocent child for fun. When Joan "awakens," she sees blood on her hands and is horrified, so she calls the police, and they soon arrest her for the crime.

There are at least three questions to deal with here, increasing in their degree of difficulty. First, *what is the proper assessment of moral responsibility in this case?* On its face, this question may seem easy to answer: Jan, and only Jan, is responsible—appropriately subject to blame—for the murder. Of course, this answer presupposes that Jan and Joan are two distinct persons, but given our discussion in the previous chapter, this is the most plausible understanding of the case. So if we think Jan, but not Joan, is responsible, it must be because we attribute the murder to Jan and only Jan. If this is right, then the Biological Criterion cannot serve as a criterion of ownership: *Joan's* biological continuity with the murderer doesn't make the murder her action.

This point just reaffirms our earlier conclusion, then, that some sort of psychological relation with the agent is essential for ownership of that agent's actions. But what is the exact nature of that relation? Is it numerical identity constituted by unique psychological continuity? Is it narrative identity? Is it mere psychological continuity (independent of either numerical or narrative identity)? Unfortunately, this case won't help us answer that question, for all three relations are present here, and it's difficult to disentangle them to identify which one, if any, is doing the relevant work. There is one and only one person who is psychologically continuous with the murderer, so both the Psychological Criterion and the IDM view have their conditions met, and Jan identifies with the murder, let's say, so it is incorporated into her narrative identity. Still, it is good to know that each psychology-based view does agree with what we likely think is the right answer here, and does so unequivocally. This harmony may not last for long, however.

To see why, consider our second question: *what would the proper assessment of moral responsibility be post-integration?* Suppose that the patient with DID here were to be brought into extended therapy, where eventually Jan and Joan were integrated into "Sybil." Then suppose the murder were discovered. What should our assessment of Sybil be?

The answer, of course, depends heavily on the nature of integration. We discussed some options in the previous chapter, but what was clear was that it is a matter of real controversy among psychologists just what the goal of integration is, and what in fact happens within the successfully integrated patient. There are at least three options regarding the latter: (a) all but one of the alters has been *eliminated*, so that one alter has been rendered the sole remaining person; (b) the various alters are still present, but are now *co-conscious* with one another, that is, multiple persons remain who are just no longer fully walled off from one another, each having access to everyone else's thoughts and streams of consciousness; or (c) the various alters have been thoroughly *fused*, their various psychological features either agglomerated into one comprehensive psychological set or "edited" down into a manageable and conflict-free set.

Option (a) poses no extra difficulties either for our intuitions or for the three identity-based criteria of ownership still under consideration: if the sole remaining person is just Jan, then the murder is properly attributable to her (and so she's eligible for responsibility for it), given her straightforward psychological relation (which includes identification) to the murderer; if it's Joan, then no one remains in existence to whom the murder is properly attributable (and so no one eligible for responsibility for it), given the lack of the relevant psychological relation between Joan and Jan. Option (b), while posing serious *practical* problems, nevertheless remains metaphysically easy: if Jan is still present, then she owns the murder and is eligible for moral responsibility for it, even if her consciousness isn't walled off from Joan's anymore. The difficulty, of course, would be in how we might *express* our blame to Jan (and not Joan), but this is a different issue, to be dealt with below.

Option (c), however, poses great difficulties for our intuitions. If genuine fusion has taken place (of either sort mentioned above), then what are we to say about the moral responsibility of Sybil for Jan's murder? I confess to being at an utter loss about what to say here. And it is a type of confusion that seems like it should somehow be represented in what our theories say on the matter. If, for example, they yield a clear-cut answer in what is hardly a clear-cut case, this might count as a strike against them, for they would be presenting as simple and straightforward what is obviously not.

Indeed, an application of the Psychological Criterion might be guilty of precisely this. Because Sybil is psychologically continuous with *both* Jan and Joan, she is not *uniquely* continuous with either, which must mean she is neither person and so owns neither person's actions. Nevertheless, we would likely want to say, there is *something* of Jan left over in Sybil, and an application of the Psychological Criterion misses this point by investing so heavily in the uniqueness relation. Is there then no way to represent this missing aspect in our theories?

To know what the narrative identity theorist would say in this case, we need to know more about what Sybil's current attitude is toward the murder. Does she identify with it or reject it as alien to her? This is also relevant for what the IDM view would say here, because in cases of fusion, as Derek Parfit asserted in our discussion last chapter, both the degree of various psychological relations that obtain *plus* the value to the subject of the features that obtain *matter* for determining the degree to which the fused person is related to her unfused predecessors. And the value to her of the features in question may be gleaned from her attitude towards them, whether it's identification or rejection.

At any rate, the details of the case really do matter here, and so there's not much more we may be able to say about Sybil's responsibility without knowing more about her internal life. Still, it is at least heartening to know that two of our theories, narrative identity and the IDM view, are sensitive to these details. This is a very complicated case, after all, and it's good that these two theories, at least, take these complications seriously.

Our third question is *how do we hold anyone responsible in this case?* This might be the most difficult question of all. Note first of all, however, that this is not a question about *whether* or not there is a responsible party here; instead, it's a question about how we might *express* our attributions of responsibility in such a weird case, and this is relevant for both moral responsibility and *legal* responsibility, so let's consider both briefly.

For attributions of moral responsibility, the relevant expressions might be easy. Consider the original *Test Case #1* again, in which the determination of moral responsibility is uncontroversial: Jan is blameworthy. Now how would you express this blame? Obviously, it should be to Jan, not to Joan, for Joan didn't do anything wrong and so wouldn't deserve your chastisement. You should, then, wait until Jan "reigns" in the body before holding the person with that body responsible. Of course, it may be tough to know when that's the case, but that's not our precise problem here, which is instead about how to hold a *properly identified* subject of DID responsible for her actions.

What, though, about holding Jan *legally* responsible? In other words, how should Jan and Joan be treated in a legal context? While holding someone morally responsible may consist in any number of actual expressions—shouting, calm chastisement, a resentful click of the tongue or wag of the head—holding someone legally responsible (blameworthy) calls for a very specific form of public expression, namely, punishment. And while punishment may sometimes consist in a fine, it often consists in a much more sustained public expression of responsibility, namely, imprisonment. Now the point of imprisonment is to restrict the freedom of a person by confining that person's *body* to a very limited domain for an extended period of time. But what shall we do when there is more than one person in a single body, only one of whom is really responsible for the crime?

For the purposes of the law, persons are viewed as indivisible. While ideally we would imprison Jan when she controlled the body and then release Joan when she controlled the body, in practice this would be impossible. There can only be, then, in the eyes of the law, just one person per body. As Jennifer Radden puts it, "It is as wholes that persons are sent to prison or acquitted. It is as wholes they are directed to undergo some psychotherapeutic regimen, even though, as part of that regimen, they may be required to acknowledge their multiplicity."[1] So call the legal person with Jan's and Joan's body "Sybil." Is Sybil legally responsible for Jan's actions, and, if so, what do we do with her?

One might think Sybil should be excused from legal responsibility in such a case, but it is extremely difficult to come up with a reason why. Radden herself considers four possibilities, but finds them all lacking. First, one might attempt an insanity defense on Sybil's behalf, but this is typically a matter of being unable to tell the difference between right and wrong, or having some severe mental illness or cognitive inability that

---

1   Jennifer Radden, *Divided Minds and Successive Selves* (Cambridge, MA: MIT Press, 1996), p. 118.

prevents one from knowing the difference between reality and non-reality, and neither Jan nor Joan, let us say, suffers in this way. The legal person, Sybil, "suffers" from distinct streams of consciousness, but she suffers from neither of the cognitive or moral defects necessary to warrant the insanity defense. Second, one might think that Sybil's action was "unconscious," like that of a sleepwalker, and so she should be excused from responsibility. But unlike a sleepwalker, someone was indeed conscious during the commission of the crime, namely *Jan*, and so there's a serious disanalogy between the two cases. Third, we might try to view Sybil as a "suspended person," like a young child or someone who's mentally ill in being not yet a completed person. But this defense also offers a disanalogy, for far from being an incomplete person, Sybil has *too much* personhood, one might say, consisting in *two* complete persons, and the person who committed the crime is very much unlike a child or someone who's mentally ill. Finally, one might insist that Sybil suffers from a "diminished capacity," an intentionally vague description of an abnormal psychological condition that excuses one from legal responsibility, a condition defined solely in terms of its effects, namely, that it keeps the defendant from being able to form the intent necessary to make what she did a crime. But once again, this cannot be the right excusing condition, for Jan clearly had the relevant murderous intent.

After dismissing these possible defenses, then, Radden concludes that the only plausible option is to judge the DID patient to be guilty, as guilty as a unified person would be:

> Certainly, therapeutic help ought to be provided as part of the sentence for these persons, just as it should for all immature and mentally disturbed criminals, of whom there are a multitude. Through such therapy and after the eventual integration of the multiple's separate selves, one would hope that each self might come to acknowledge and know of the crime for which the multiple is enduring punishment.[1]

But how could this be right? In judging Sybil guilty and punishing her as a result, wouldn't we not only be punishing Jan, the guilty person, but also

---

1   Ibid., p. 140.

Joan, the *innocent* person? But how can punishment of the innocent be warranted? Radden suggests that, when we punish people, there are often others who go through serious hardships as a direct result, namely, friends and family members who suffer right along with the incarcerated person, and we don't call these hardships "punishment." Similarly, then, we might think of the suffering of Joan, not as punishment, but as an analogous sort of hardship and suffering associated with the actual punishment of Jan.

But there's a big difference between these sorts of cases: friends and family, while enduring hardships, just aren't subject to the *imprisonment* administered by the state, whereas in Sybil's case, both Jan *and Joan* would be subject to precisely the same treatment. Suppose, for instance, that the state were to imprison your friends and family, along with you, for your crimes. Surely we would think this to be a wrongful case of punishing the innocent, so it's hard to see how we might think otherwise in poor Joan's case as well.

Nevertheless, it's extremely difficult to know what we might do otherwise in such a case. If the point of a system of punishment is to punish the guilty, and Jan is definitely guilty, then the point of the system would be thwarted if we simply let her go. On the other hand, if the point of the system is punish *only* the guilty, then we also thwart the system by incarcerating Joan. So it looks as if we thwart the system no matter what we do. Once again, we have run into a very difficult case that admits of no easy answers.

Test Case #2: Phil and Jen

We have now come full circle, back to the case that motivated the enterprise, but have we learned anything to help us address this case? Remember the challenge: Jen thinks Phil is still blameworthy for causing her to fall out of the tree thirty years ago, whereas Phil thinks such an attitude is ridiculous, given that so much time has passed since then. Who is right?

The views of ownership and responsibility associated with both the Biological Criterion and the Psychological Criterion would clearly support Jen's case: Phil now is both biologically and psychologically continuous with the Phil from thirty years ago. Phil's case, on the other hand, could generate support from both the narrative identity and IDM views: Phil no longer identifies with either the thirty-years-ago action or the thirty-years-ago agent, and insofar as he is very weakly psychologically *connected* to that long-ago agent, he bears very little, if any, ownership, and thus responsibility, for his actions.

Is this, then, a standoff? Is there no way to settle the issue of whether or not Phil owns the action in question? One avenue of exploration here is to think about the *point* of the exchange between Phil and Jen. Jen seems clearly to be trying to get Phil to *own up to* his actions, that is, to take responsibility for them, to, in effect, identify with them. Phil, on the other hand, is resisting that appeal, maintaining instead that what's relevant is just the low degree of psychological connectedness that obtains between him and that young boy. So we might think of the exchange here as a kind of negotiation: Jen attributes the action to Phil and thinks he should too, whereas Phil thinks Jen's attribution is itself silly, focusing as it does on irrelevant features (his biological and/or psychological continuity with the original agent).

This way of viewing the matter is actually quite revealing. For one thing, it seems to reveal that narrative identity, at least when applied to the case of moral responsibility, is *derivative*, that is, identification itself is grounded in a more fundamental theory of identity. There are two points to explain here. First, identification (or the lack thereof) itself demands justification. Phil does not identify with that past action, but notice that this fact of the matter doesn't settle things; instead, Jen thinks this is a *mistake* on Phil's part, for she thinks Phil *should* identify with the action (or the agent that performed the action), given his biological and/or psychological continuity with the agent. And when Phil resists such identification, he does so by pointing to the low degree of psychological connectedness that obtains between him and that young boy. So both parties (and we, for whom the exchange seems natural) agree that the mere *fact* of identification, in and of itself, is insufficient to establish a fact about ownership of some action; instead, identification itself is either justified or unjustified, grounded on some *other* facts, which themselves establish ownership. This leads to the second point, which is that the narrative identity account of moral responsibility, wherein one's identification with some action incorporates it into one's life story, is at worst mistaken and at best misleading, for it seems like it's actually *justified* identification that does this work, and such justification will likely depend on a more fundamental criterion of identity, be it the Biological Criterion, Psychological Criterion, or IDM view.

A second thing revealed by viewing the exchange between Jen and Phil as a kind of negotiation is that they—and we generally—are simply unsettled on which theory of personal identity is relevant to moral responsibility. Now this could mean that we just don't know which theory is the correct one. But it could also mean that there *isn't* just one correct theory. Instead, one theory could ground moral responsibility in certain contexts, and another theory could ground moral responsibility in other contexts (and a third may ground it in yet other contexts), or there may even be contexts in which no theory is relevant at all. But sometimes the contexts may overlap, or there may be uncertainty over just what context we're in, in which case a negotiation like that between Jen and Phil breaks out over which theory is relevant to responsibility in our particular set of circumstances. So, for example, what grounds my holding responsible my comatose father for his repeated humiliations of me in the past might be his biological continuity with that past humiliator, whereas what grounds my holding responsible sober Mel for his drunken anti-Semitic tirade might be his unique psychological continuity with that tirading person (in the absence of any direct psychological connections), whereas what grounds my holding responsible both products in the fission case for the actions of their pre-fission ancestor is their strong psychological connectedness (in the absence of identity) with that ancestor.

However, when all three relations—biological continuity, psychological continuity, and psychological connectedness—are present to some degree or other, and they imply different things about responsibility, we may find ourselves in something of a jam, as do Jen and Phil. So what we may do in such circumstances is simply negotiate with one another about which theory is most relevant in those circumstances. In such contexts, then, the criterion of ownership of actions could actually depend on the reasons given and accepted in such exchanges. This is a fairly surprising result, but it may be the most accurate portrayal of our actual practices regarding moral responsibility.

Of course, one might simply insist that, if this is what we're doing, we're *wrong* to do so, and that there still is a single answer to whether or not Phil is responsible, say, in this case, and it depends somehow on which theory of personal identity is correct. On this view, the negotiation taking place is just irrelevant to what the truth is, a fact of the matter about whether or not Phil owns the action in question. The question you need to ask yourself once more, then, is which methodology here is more plausible: should we simply try to account for our practices as they are, or should we insist that our practices must depend on the metaphysical truth, whatever that turns out to be? This should by now be a familiar worry, one that looms more and more heavily over our investigation. And for now we will once again set it aside until the final chapter.

WORKS CITED OR REFERENCED IN THIS CHAPTER

Bradford, J., and Smith, S.M. "Amnesia and Homicide: The Padola Case and a Study of Thirty Cases." *Bulletin of the American Academy of Psychiatry and the Law* 7 (1979): 219-31.

DeGrazia, David. *Human Identity and Bioethics.* Cambridge: Cambridge University Press, 2005.

Fischer, John Martin, ed. *Moral Responsibility.* Ithaca, NY: Cornell University Press, 1986.

Frankfurt, Harry. *The Importance of What We Care About.* Cambridge: Cambridge University Press, 1988.

Locke, John. "Of Identity and Diversity." In *Personal Identity,* edited by John Perry. Berkeley: University of California Press, 1975.

Parfit, Derek. *Reasons and Persons.* Oxford: Oxford University Press, 1984.

——. "Comments." *Ethics* 96 (1986): 832-72.

Radden, Jennifer. *Divided Minds and Successive Selves*. Cambridge, MA: MIT Press, 1996.

Schechtman, Marya. *The Constitution of Selves*. Ithaca, NY: Cornell University Press, 1996.

Shoemaker, Sydney. "Persons and Their Pasts." *American Philosophical Quarterly* 7 (1970): 269-85.

Watson, Gary. *Agency and Answerability*. Oxford: Oxford University Press, 2004.

CHAPTER EIGHT

Personal Identity and Ethical Theory

Case 6 from the introduction was about the parents Darren and Samantha, and it involved an ethical dispute about how to distribute the earnings of their cute son Brad, who underwent various sacrifices as a child model. Darren wants to take all of Brad's earnings and give them to their bright son Albert, who will then be able to go to the best schools and make the most of that head start. Samantha, on the other hand, thinks that Brad should get the money: after all, he was the one who underwent the sacrifice, so he should be the one getting the compensating benefit. To do otherwise would be unfair.

While this is a dispute over what the right thing to do is in a concrete case, there are much more general issues afoot here as well. In particular, both parties seem to be basing their specific ethical stances on more general ethical principles. For instance, Darren believes that Albert should get all the money because that particular distribution will bring about the most good, and failing to bring about the most good—even if that failure is the only way to get a "fair" result—is immoral. Samantha, on the other hand, believes that uncompensated sacrifices are unfair, and furthermore that unfairness may "trump" the best outcomes, that is, that unfairness (at least sometimes) ought to constrain our pursuit of "the best": if certain outcomes are unfair, then it wouldn't be right to bring them about, no matter how much good would be produced.

Ethical theory is the study of what makes actions right or wrong, and what makes characters good or bad. And what we really have here is a clash between two long-standing ethical theories regarding right and wrong actions, namely, **consequentialism** and **nonconsequentialism**. Darren is a consequentialist, someone who holds that what makes an action wrong is its failure to maximize the good, that is, its failure to bring about the best consequences. If one is a consequentialist, then, one should always maximize the good. But what is *the good*? It could be any number of things. Consequentialism is a kind of placeholder theory, neutral with respect to a variety of possible valuable things one might maximize. There are, then, a number of more specific versions of consequentialism, but by far the most popular has been a theory called **utilitarianism**, according to which one should always maximize *utility*. Now what is utility? The term has meant various things over the years, but we may adopt its historically most popular understanding: *happiness*. Utilitarians, then, think that we should bring about outcomes with the greatest amount of happiness, and an action is wrong insofar as it fails to maximize such happiness. There are many, many subtle variations of utilitarianism (and consequentialism as well), but this understanding will suffice for our purposes.

Samantha, on the other hand, is a nonconsequentialist, someone who simply denies consequentialism, holding instead that what makes an action right or wrong *isn't always* a matter of whether or not it brings about the best consequences. Sometimes, in other words, whether or not an action maximizes the good is irrelevant to determining its moral status; instead, in such situations, what matters are features of the action itself. Now once more it should be obvious just how general this theory is, and it too has a number of more specific variations, but there's no reason for us to go into those variations just yet; instead, we will introduce them as the need arises throughout the chapter. For now, what matters is just that, for the nonconsequentialist, sometimes considerations of fairness, or of rights, or of respect for persons may legitimately constrain our pursuit of the best possible outcomes.

What, though, does any of this have to do with personal identity? Until the early 1970's, the answer to this question would have been, "Not much." But groundbreaking work begun by Derek Parfit at that time eventually spawned a number of interesting explorations into the relation between identity and ethical theory, and we will attempt to survey some of the most important trends here. In particular, we will look at four topics. First, we will discuss Parfit's own general approach to the issue of personal identity, called reductionism. Second, we will discuss how he applied reductionism to ethical theory by defending utilitarianism from a powerful objection. Third, we will explore how reductionism might be used in support of a few alternative ethical theories. Finally, we will consider two nonconsequentialist objections to appealing to reductionism *at all* when engaged in ethical theory.

REDUCTIONISM

Parfit's general approach to personal identity he called **reductionism**, which is the view that all facts about personal identity simply reduce to, or consist in, more particular facts about brains, bodies, and the ways in which various mental and physical events are related. But what does *this* mean, exactly? Suppose we consider what makes me now the same person as that child in the photo on my mother's coffee table. If one is a reductionist, the fact that I *am* the same person as that child consists entirely in facts about certain physical and mental connections and continuities between us. So to say that I am the same person as that child is just to say that I'm related to that child physically—you could theoretically follow the trajectory from that child's body to mine in space-time—and/or I'm related to that child mentally—there are overlapping chains of psychological connections between the child and me. This is all that personal identity amounts to, for the reductionist.

Now given the four main views about personal identity we have concentrated on thus far, you might well wonder what *else* it could possibly amount to. After all, the Biological Criterion emphasizes only biological facts, facts about brains and bodies, whereas the Psychological Criterion, narrative identity, and the IDM view all emphasize, in one way or another, the relation between mental events. Nevertheless, the view most people still find compelling, despite its overwhelming problems, is the one in which one extra fact is necessary to account for personal identity, namely, a fact about *souls*. For most people, the fact of my being identical to that child doesn't just consist in facts about brains, bodies, and various mental and physical events; it also consists in a fact about my having the same soul as that child. Indeed, this is the way most people think I can survive the death of my body: the possibility of there being a person in heaven who is *me* consists in the fact that that person in heaven will have my soul. This view, that the facts about personal identity don't just consist in facts about brains and bodies, but also consist in some further fact(s) (usually about souls), is what Parfit calls **nonreductionism**.

Parfit gives some powerful arguments both against nonreductionism and in favor of reductionism, but these need not concern us here. After all, we have already discussed some real problems with the Soul Criterion, the paradigm nonreductionist theory, in Chapter One. But there are two things to notice about reductionism. The first is that it is a very *general* view about the nature of numerical identity. As suggested above, it is perfectly compatible with both the Biological and Psychological Criteria, for both are theories of numerical identity according to which the facts of personal identity are facts only about physical and/or mental events. While Parfit himself seems to favor a version of the Psychological Criterion of personal identity, it is also clear that the reductionist view itself is neutral between it and the Biological Criterion. As long as theories of numerical identity appeal to no facts beyond those about brains, bodies, and interrelated mental and physical events, they are acceptable insofar as reductionism itself is concerned.

The second thing to notice about Parfit's reductionism, though, is that it is ultimately a view about what facts *matter* for purposes of our practical concerns. And here is where Parfit actually adopts a version of the IDM view (as discussed in Chapter Three): what matters is not numerical identity at all; instead, what matters are the more particular *psychological* facts and relations in which identity (at least partially) consists. The reason Parfit makes this move is based on the familiar fission case. In considering the scenario where each of my individual brain hemispheres is transplanted into my identical triplet brothers, Parfit concludes that the most plausible answer is that I have not survived—neither of the survivors is numerically identical to me—but that nevertheless this fact is irrelevant to what matters in ordinary survival. Instead, what has happened to me is just as good as ordinary survival, and so all the practical concerns we thought were grounded in personal identity must not be so grounded (for identity doesn't obtain in this case); instead, they must be grounded in psychological connectedness and continuity, for these are the only relevant relations the fission-products even have to me. And so it goes for day-to-day survival as well: what must matter for the practical concerns surrounding ordinary survival are psychological continuity and connectedness, not (numerical) identity.

But does either relation matter *more* than the other? Parfit remains neutral on this point, saying both relations matter. This will mean, then, that when Parfit focuses explicitly on prudential and moral concerns, he has the ability to slide back and forth, suggesting sometimes that what matters is continuity, and sometimes what matters is connectedness. This may be a strength or a weakness of the view, depending on how one comes at it. The main point, though, is that Parfit denies the importance of biological continuity, the central component of the Biological Criterion, to what matters in our practical concerns. This is, strictly speaking, a perfectly legitimate move for the advocate of the Biological Criterion to make as well (as noted at the end of Chapter Six): one might hold that the facts of personal identity are facts about biological continuity, but then deny the *importance* of those facts for our practical concerns, citing instead facts about psychological relations when dealing with those concerns. This isn't what we have taken the advocate of the Biological Criterion to maintain, of course, but it is a legitimate move nevertheless. This should make explicit the fact that a theory of (numerical) personal identity is one thing; a theory of our person-related practical concerns may be quite another indeed.

REDUCTIONISM AND UTILITARIANISM

How, then, does reductionism apply to ethical theory? Parfit thinks it can actually resolve a powerful objection to utilitarianism, bolstering that theory's prospects. The objection comes from John Rawls, perhaps the most important political philosopher of the Twentieth Century, who argued that utilitarianism "does not take seriously the distinction between persons."[1] Utilitarianism is an *impartial* theory: when distributing goods between various parties, the utilitarian looks only to how various possible distributions will maximize happiness, paying no mind to the identities of the various recipients. To illustrate, consider a very simple case. Suppose we have $100 to distribute between two people, Arnie and Barbie. Here are two possible distributions:

Distribution 1	*Distribution 2*
Arnie: $90 Barbie: $10	Arnie: $10 Barbie: $90

Now let's suppose further that Arnie and Barbie are very much alike, getting equal amounts of happiness from the same amount of money. If this were the case, then the total amount of happiness generated by each distribution would be identical: 100 "units" of happiness. But if the happiness generated by each were identical, then the utilitarian would be indifferent between them: it wouldn't matter morally, according to the utilitarian, which way the money in fact was distributed.

Now this result may be jarring to you, given certain background details. After all, suppose this distribution choice gets made every week, and the second distribution is chosen every time, repeatedly giving Barbie the $90 to Arnie's $10. Or suppose Barbie is a downright nasty person and Arnie is a genuine good guy. Or suppose Arnie works ten times as hard as Barbie. In each case, we might think that Arnie actually *deserves* the $90, or that it's unfair that Barbie gets more than him, so that ultimately we think there's a very big moral difference between the two distributions. Not so, says the utilitarian: if Arnie and Barbie would truly get equal amounts of happiness from either, then the question of which person gets what amount is morally irrelevant.

Why might one think such a thing? An answer given by many utilitarians draws from a powerful analogy. We all think it's perfectly acceptable, perhaps even rationally required, to maximize the good within our own lives.

---

1   John Rawls, *A Theory of Justice* (Cambridge, MA: The Belknap Press of Harvard University Press, 1971), p. 27.

This is what we do, for instance, when we go to the dentist for a checkup: we are burdening our present selves with a little pain and inconvenience for the sake of preventing a much greater amount of inconvenience and pain to our later selves. Or when we scrimp and save money now to go on a big vacation next summer, we are sacrificing smaller pleasures now for the sake of a much greater pleasure later. Now it would be silly for someone to say that you are treating your going-to-the-dentist self *unfairly,* or that your scrimping-and-saving self got a raw deal. We view various moments in our lives impartially: *when* a benefit or burden comes is irrelevant, as long as we maximize benefits and minimize burdens in our life as a whole.

Utilitarians, however, apply the exact same reasoning to society, saying that it's morally permissible to burden one person (or group of people) for the sake of a greater benefit to someone else (or another group of people). In other words, just as it's rational for me to maximize across my own life, so must it be rational for us to maximize across lives: for the utilitarian, *to whom* a benefit or burden comes is irrelevant. Indeed, Rawls suggests that this is where the idea of an **impartial spectator** enters into utilitarian thought. The impartial spectator is a device many utilitarians use to reveal right action, by considering what a sympathetic person who identified with the desires and preferences of all people within a society would do. What this spectator would do, then, is adopt all those desires as if they were his own and then maximize in the way each of us does individually, that is, figure out what action would bring about the most happiness, given the variety of competing desires, and then recommend that action as the one to perform.

But this is precisely the point where Rawls objects, saying that this sort of reasoning ignores the fact that the different sources of the impartial spectator's desires are *different, separate persons,* each with his or her own individual life to lead. So yes, it may be perfectly okay to maximize within my own life, but *I'm just one person.* Utilitarians, however, would claim it's perfectly okay to require Arnie to sacrifice himself now for a later benefit to Barbie, and that's simply illegitimate, because it ignores the fact that Arnie and Barbie are different people, whereas me-now and me-later are not. The difference between people is a deep metaphysical difference and should never be ignored. We are all equally deserving, separate individuals, and we all live separate lives. But the lives of everyone should have an equal chance of going well, so one life shouldn't have to be sacrificed for another. What Rawls calls for, then, are **distributive principles**, principles requiring that benefits or burdens be distributed *fairly* among persons. And these will be principles constraining maximization across lives.

In responding to this argument, Parfit straightforwardly admits that utilitarians do in fact ignore the so-called boundaries between lives, and do, as a result, reject distributive principles. But why? Is it because they think of society as like a super-person, one big impartial spectator, so that it is rational to maximize across lives in exactly the same way we maximize within lives? No. Instead of societies being like persons, Parfit argues that *persons are like societies*, that is, individual lives are really like sets of lives. But what does this mean, and how does it help the utilitarian?

To make his case, Parfit appeals to reductionism about persons: there are no facts about persons and personal identity beyond facts about brains, bodies, and mental or physical events. Now what would it mean to adopt this view in practice? One way to think about this is to consider the fact that we're all reductionists already when it comes to other things, like nations and clubs. There's nothing more involved in a nation than its citizens and geographic territory. None of us believe that there's a "soul" of a nation, preserving its identity across time.

But utilitarians, claims Parfit, might easily be reductionists about persons, claiming there's nothing more involved in persons than their various experiences related in certain ways in a particular "geographic" terrain (a body). So just as there's not a deep distinction between nations—as there would be if each nation had a deeply different "soul," say—so also there's no deep distinction between persons. What makes you and me different is just that you've got a different body, brain, and stream of consciousness from me, but that's just not a significant difference between us, and it certainly doesn't call for there to be any deep *moral* difference between us (as there might be if we had different souls). Further, one of the relations within lives—psychological connectedness—holds by degrees, rendering individual lives far less unified over time than they would be if they had souls. Indeed, parts of my past are like the lives of *someone else*, and my retirement-age self may well be more like a stranger to me than my wife or close friends are now. So not only is there no deep metaphysical difference between individuals, there's also no deep metaphysical unity within individual lives. All of this, then, might explain why utilitarians ignore the separateness of persons: utilitarians could be reductionists about personal identity and so believe that persons just aren't that separate to begin with. Sets of lives (societies) thus aren't like a big super-person; rather, individual persons, because of their partial disintegration, are more like sets of lives.

So there is, according to Parfit, an important analogy between individual lives and sets of lives, just not the one Rawls thought there was. But notice that this move could backfire on Parfit, for many of us think that there ought to be distributive principles that hold for sets of lives—distributions of benefits and burdens ought to be constrained by considerations of fairness and desert, say—but if there's this analogy Parfit talks about, perhaps there should also be distributive principles that hold *within* lives as well! If different stages of my life, for instance, are really like different persons, then perhaps it *is* unfair to me if I work now for the sake of my very different, cranky, and old retirement-age self, for he'll reap all the benefits (probably using that retirement money for things I never would, like shuffleboard and Viagra) and I'll get stuck with all the uncompensated burdens.

In other words, reductionism requires treating individual lives like sets of lives. But if reductionism is true, we could apply distributive principles either to *both* sets of lives and individual lives or to *neither*. Utilitarians apply them to neither. But why not apply them to both?

The way Parfit attempts to answer this worry is by asking the question, "What justifies maximization within individual lives?" Critics of utilitarianism believe that we are indeed justified in maximizing in our own lives but maintain that this justification is notably absent across lives, so that distributive principles apply only across lives. What, then, is this special justification?

Parfit considers three options. The first is that I'm justified in burdening my present self for the sake of my future self because both selves are part of *one life*, that is, my various selves are deeply unified into *my* singular life.

So the non-utilitarian thought might be that, if sets of lives were unified in this way too, then we'd be justified in maximizing over them as well, without distributive principles; but they aren't, so we aren't.

But as Parfit has already said, if reductionism is true, then the unity of an individual life is "less deep" than it would be if non-reductionism were true. What he means by this is that the only unities involved are the unities provided by psychological connectedness and continuity, and psychological connectedness doesn't provide unity of a whole life in most normal cases: I have very few direct psychological connections to my ten-year-old self, for instance, and I suspect I'll have few direct connections to my eighty-year-old self. But if these are the only relations that could provide unity (in the absence of a soul), and they don't provide much, then this justification loses a great deal of force. If there just isn't that much difference between individual lives and sets of lives in terms of unity, then it's very implausible to maintain that we can justify maximization only in the former but not the latter.

The second possible justification is that any burdens I undergo can be *compensated* by benefits to me. Compensation, after all, presupposes personal identity: I can be compensated for a burden by a benefit only if that benefit is distributed to me, the same person who underwent the burden. So I'm justified in sacrificing certain things in my own life, simply because *I'll* get the compensating benefit later on: compensation of benefits for burdens is *conceptually* possible only when it's the same person in both instances. But this fact is missing across lives: you simply don't compensate me for a burden if you give a benefit to someone else. And this is Samantha's argument in our original case: Brad just won't be compensated for the modeling work he did as a baby if all his money is given to Albert, even if doing so would maximize utility. So while maximization is justified within lives, it is not justified across lives.

Parfit again disagrees. Yes, he says, compensation does presuppose personal identity, but the justification here puts too much weight on the non-identity between persons. Remember, on the reductionist view, what's involved in personal identity is just less than it would be if we had souls, say, so if the fact of personal identity involves less than we thought it did, then that fact may have less *moral* importance, and so if compensation presupposes personal identity, then *it too* may have less moral importance, and so it may not serve anymore to justify individual maximization at all.

Only one justification remains, then, for individual maximization: the fact that suffering is bad and happiness is good. On this view, I am justified in maximizing within my own life insofar as it brings about less of what is bad and more of what is good. Sometimes certain sacrifices are necessary to bring about better things for me. I go to the dentist now to prevent greater suffering later on. I save money now so that I can enjoy a greater time on vacation next year. What justifies my maximizing in these cases, goes the argument, is that I simply want to bring about more of what's better and less of what's worse, period. Now Parfit thinks this is right, but then notice what it implies: this very same reasoning also justifies maximization across *sets* of lives. It makes no reference whatsoever to identity, after all, so if this is the proper justification for maximization within lives, there seems no more metaphysical reason to block its application across lives.

The upshot of all of this, if Parfit is right, is twofold: (a) there is an important analogy between individual lives and sets of lives, and (b) distributive principles should apply to *neither*. In support of (a), if reductionism is true, then individual lives are far less deeply unified than they would be if nonreductionism were true, making them much more like a collection of experiential moments, each a "life" unto itself, leaving the life of a person as much more like many lives, like sets of lives. In support of (b), if reductionism is true, there aren't any plausible justifications for maximizing within individual lives that don't also apply across lives. So if we think it implausible to apply distributive principles within lives, we should also think it implausible to apply them across lives. As a result, because utilitarianism rejects distributive principles across lives it gains support from reductionism: if reductionism were false, utilitarianism would be less plausible than it is, for there would then be good reason to maintain the disanalogy between individual lives and sets of lives.

So goes the main (and complicated) argument. How plausible is it, though? We may question both (a) and (b). Note first that the analogy between individual lives and sets of lives is based on the claim that reductionism implies the metaphysical disintegration of individual lives. But does it? Not at all. To see why, recall that reductionism is a very general theory. It simply asserts that personal identity consists entirely in bodily or psychological relations across time, and so identity itself doesn't matter for either ordinary survival or our practical concerns. Instead, what matters is psychological continuity and/or connectedness. But this leaves quite a bit of leeway for the precise targets of prudential and ethical matters. In fact, there are three candidates for what we will call the **Morally Significant Metaphysical Units**, or MSMUs, the subjects of ethical theorizing, depending on what particular relation one identifies as being the one that matters:

1. *Persons*: call these the entities unified by psychological *continuity*. Continuity consists in overlapping chains of strong psychological connectedness, so a person would be the unit whose every stage is tied together with every other stage by these overlapping chains. Persons typically come into existence at the psychological birth of a human being and do not go out of existence until the psychological death of that human being.

2. *Selves*: call these the entities unified by psychological *connectedness*. There are two initial worries about talk of selves, though. First, because connectedness is a matter of degree (I may be more or less directly connected to various stages in my past), selves would be entities with very fuzzy—even unknowable—boundaries. Second, we need a conception of what counts as *enough* degrees of connectedness to unify various stages into one self—a very small number of connections wouldn't be sufficient, it seems. These are both difficult issues. One way to address them would be to stipulate that there would have to be a sufficient number of connections for me to *identify* with the stage in question, for me to be able to adopt it and its actions *as my own*. Obviously, if some past stage of mine had very different beliefs, intentions, memories, and character, I would have a very hard time any longer seeing what the world was like for him, or understanding why he did what he did. I would have a very hard time, in other words, identifying with him. So we might think of the ability to identify with some past stage as *revealing* (but not determining) that the sufficient number of connections

between us obtains to unite as part of the same self. This should start to sound a bit familiar: it is the sort of thing we have heard narrative identity theorists say. What distinguishes selves from persons in practice, then, will be their duration: persons will be in existence much longer, on average, than selves. Over the course of my life, for instance, I may have several successive selves, depending on the amount of psychological change I undergo.

3. *Momentary Experiencers, or Person-Atoms*: call these the entities unified only by the duration of a single experience, for whom neither psychological continuity nor connectedness is relevant. These would be entities that come into existence with the start of some new experience, and then pop out of existence at the end of that experience. Obviously, their duration would be much shorter than those of selves or of persons.

To illustrate these three possible units, consider me at the moment I write these words. This experiencer is actually part of (at least) three different units. First, he is a person-atom, a momentary experiencer, who will cease to exist once this particular experience is over. Second, he is strongly psychologically *connected* to many other such experiencers, for he remembers many of their thoughts and deeds, shares their beliefs, carries out their intentions, and continues to have a similar character as them. All of those momentary experiencers, then, are unified as part of the same self. Third, this momentary experiencer and slice of a self is also psychologically *continuous* with an even greater range of experiencers, tracing back ultimately to psychological birth, uniting them all as one person. So even though this experiencer only identifies with stages going back fifteen years or so (the outer limits of his *self*), continuity incorporates many more stages into the person of which he's a part.

Our question, then, is which one is the MSMU, the unit that matters for moral and prudential purposes? Which one should we focus on when talking about the recipients of benefits and burdens, the targets of compensation, the subjects of moral responsibility, and the like: persons, selves, or momentary experiencers? There are various arguments one might give for one or the other, but for our purposes all that matters is that it looks as if, in order for the analogy between individual lives and sets of lives to work, the relevant MSMUs must be *momentary experiencers*: the different moments of our lives must be like different people, and if maximization across those moments is justified, so is maximization across people. On this view, once the deep fact of non-reductionist personal identity is removed—once our souls are taken out of the picture, in other words—we simply become nothing more than bundles of momentary experiences, equally disunified from moment to moment by any relation of moral significance, which leaves us exactly like sets of lives, themselves equally disunified by any relation of moral significance.

The problem, though, is that there are two *other* contenders for MSMUs, and picking either one undermines the analogy, either partially or wholly. Consider selves first. If they were the MSMUs, then we would have to recognize the prudential and moral significance of the fact that some parts of our lives are much more closely connected, and thus more unified, than others. In the realm of prudence, then, this might mean that I have reason to favor the interests of my nearer future stages over my more distant stages, on the grounds that I expect only my nearer stages to be part of my present self, to be part of *who I am now*. And in the realm of morality, emphasizing selves may mean that compensation has its limits, that I can truly be compensated for a burden I undergo by benefits only to those stages with whom I am strongly connected, that is, only with those stages that are part of my present self. And it thus may also mean that what justifies maximization within an individual life is that it is actually taking place *within one self*, and this may provide a relevant disanalogy to sets of lives, which themselves lack the kind of direct psychological connections with one another to warrant maximization without distributive principles to constrain them.

A similar story may be told if we choose persons as our MSMUs. If their unity via psychological continuity is what's morally significant, and sets of lives are not so unified with one another, then this may provide the kind of disanalogy between individual lives and sets of lives that would warrant unconstrained maximization in the former but not the latter.

The analogy between individual lives and sets of lives seems to work, then, only if momentary experiencers are the MSMUs. But reductionism itself is neutral with respect to this issue, allowing that any of persons, selves, or momentary experiencers could be the relevant units. So without some further argument on this score, we are left without much clear defense or support for utilitarianism against the Rawlsian objection. Indeed, if we pick *different* MSMUs, we wind up with support for very different ethical theories, as we shall now see.

REDUCTIONISM AND ALTERNATIVE ETHICAL THEORIES

Suppose *persons* are our MSMUs. In other words, suppose the relation of psychological continuity is the only one that matters in determining the targets of ethical theorizing. This would mean that prudential and moral reasons for action would, in certain circumstances, be determined by the range of psychological continuity. So, for instance, I would have reason to have special concern for all the stages of my life with whom I would be psychologically continuous, but I may have no reason to care about stages of the life of this particular body with whom I would be psychologically discontinuous or that would have no psychology at all. In other words, I'd have no reason to care about my PVS-stage self, or my severely brainwashed self, or the survivor of my severe head trauma (if that trauma caused an abrupt psychological discontinuity). And with respect to ethical matters, I could be compensated for a burden undergone only via a benefit to some psychologically continuous stage.

So far, so good. But what is psychological continuity anyway? It's just an overlapping chain of many direct psychological connections between person-stages, wherein the later stage's mental life is causally dependent on the mental life of the earlier stage. So I have the beliefs, desires, character, intentions, and memories that I do now because my immediate predecessor stages had the beliefs, desires, character, intentions, and memories that they had (and not, say, because these psychological characteristics were hypnotized, brainwashed, or otherwise implanted into me). What connectedness consists in, then, is for the mental life of one stage to have been *shaped* by the mental life of a previous stage. Continuity is just a chain of such connectedness.

Now consider the fission case once more. If I split into two persons, then I will be fully psychologically connected (and continuous) with two different people, neither of whom will be me (because of the logical requirements of identity). So I can clearly be psychologically connected/continuous with other people. But those are people in the future, people with whom my relation is asymmetrical. Would it be possible, though, for me to be psychologically connected/continuous with other *simultaneously-existing* people now, with whom a symmetrical relation might obtain?

David Brink has argued that this could be, and in fact is, the case. Take as an example the relation between loved ones, between friends and family. If connectedness consists in the mental life of one self shaping the mental life of another, then such shaping is rampant among us, for we cause one another to form various desires, beliefs, intentions, memories, or character elements all the time, at least to some extent. Consider your very best friend, and the way in which you finish one another's sentences, nudge one another simultaneously when seeing something you know the other would enjoy as you do, and pursue many of the same interests together. This is strong evidence of the close connectedness between you: you respond psychologically in exactly the same way to various events, believe the same things about the world, want many of the same things, and even adopt one another's physical mannerisms and tics. Because of the time spent around one another, you have each had a significant causal impact on the other person's mental life, so much so that some people think of you has a single unit, a two-headed person. This sort of phenomenon is also very obvious among long-married couples. Call it **interpersonal connectedness**.

But now notice that your best friend or spouse isn't the only person whose mental life you causally influence. You also have a number of other friends and acquaintances you influence, at least to some extent. And there are people besides your best friend—your parents, say, or your teachers or pastors—who contribute to the shaping of your mental life as well. What we have here, then, is a big network of mental shapings, of interpersonal connectedness. But that's not all, for there are other people influenced by your acquaintances whom you'll never meet, but who will nevertheless bear a causal relation to you, for their mental lives were (partially) shaped by mental lives that you *did* shape. But now the extension should be obvious: mental life A shapes mental life B, which shapes C, which shapes D...., which shapes Z. Lives A and Z may have nothing whatsoever in common, though—they may bear no interpersonal connectedness to one another at all—but they are nevertheless related by an overlapping chain of connected mental lives. Call this relation, then, **interpersonal continuity**. I may thus be interpersonally continuous with everyone in the world, given that there are probably at most only six degrees of separation between me and anyone else.

Brink then applies this phenomenon to an ethical theory called **rational egoism**, the view that one has reason to do something only insofar as it contributes to one's own happiness. Another way to put the view is that one should perform only those actions that promote one's own well-being. Now some have doubted that this could even be an *ethical* theory at all, given that it seems to imply a selfishness that is utterly opposed to ethical thinking. So suppose that I save a drowning child, but only for the publicity it will bring me. Or suppose that I don't murder people, but only because I'm afraid of getting caught. Despite the fact that my actions conform, in a way, to the action-demands of morality, many would want to say that I'm not a very moral person at all, and the reason would be precisely that I'm concerned only with my own well-being (or that any concern I have for others would be derived from that primary concern). So many have accepted rational egoism as a *challenge* to morality, but not as an ethical theory in and of itself, precisely because it would call for actions or motivations that seem distinctly immoral (or at least non-moral).

Brink wants to present rational egoism as a distinctly *ethical* theory, though. How so? Consider again the main tenet of the theory: one has reason to perform only those actions that contribute to *one's own* well-being. What counts as "one's own," though? If reductionism is true, then the fact that some future stage is one's own, identical to oneself, isn't what matters in and of itself. What matters instead are the more particular psychological relations that obtain. But which of those relations is of *moral* significance? Brink gives several arguments (which we won't detail here) for why the relation that matters is psychological continuity, and thus for why the MSMUs are *persons*. So I have reason, on reductionist rational egoism, to perform only those actions that contribute to the well-being of just those stages with whom I am psychologically continuous. But now the coincidence of rational egoism and regular morality should be obvious, for if I am psychologically continuous with other people, then their well-being *becomes part of my own*, such that I have reason to perform only those actions that contribute to the well-being of the *persons* with whom I'm psychologically continuous. But now the view is not selfish at all. In fact, it's likely to be a very altruistic view, for I will now have many "other people's" well-being to consider, and so what would have been "my own" demands may often lose out to the more pressing demands of those others.

Now one immediate worry here is that what was formerly thought to be a selfish theory has gone too far in the other direction, counting everyone else's good equally to one's own. But here Brink introduces a very clever qualification: some people's good will count more than others. Why? Because one may be *more strongly continuous* with some people than with others. Some chains are simply stronger or weaker than others because the individual links that make them up are themselves strong or weak. So the kind of continuity I have with some people in Albania, say, will probably be extremely weak, whereas of course the continuity I bear to my best friend will be extremely strong. As a result, the degree of concern I may rationally have for both will be very different: my best friend's well-being will simply count for more than that remote Albanian's well-being, given the disparity in the strength of our respective chains of continuity. What we wind up with, then, is a familiar kind of ethical view: the moral obligations I have to various people diminish in proportion to their "distance" from me, so I have very strong obligations to those in my innermost circle of familiarity and mental influence, but weaker obligations (that is, more easily overridable obligations) the further away from me and my mental influence one gets.[1] Taking persons as the MSMUs, then, in combination with the incorporation of interpersonal continuity, yields a kind of commonsense morality, albeit grounded in an uncommon egoism.

One might wonder, though, about the role being played by psychological continuity here. After all, what gets us different degrees of moral obligation are the different degrees of psychological *connectedness* that obtain. Why not, then, just focus squarely on connectedness as the relation that matters? In other words, why not focus on *selves* as the MSMUs? There are various complicated reasons Brink gives for why we should resist this move, but on its face it seems quite a plausible move to make, so it will be worth exploring just what benefits doing so might bring to our ethical theorizing.

One idea a past self of mine advocated was that targeting selves as MSMUs may enable the defense of a very different ethical theory, **contractualism**, from an important objection. Contractualism is, roughly, the view that one should perform only those actions allowed by principles that would be justifiable to other people on grounds they could not reasonably reject. Now that's certainly a mouthful, but at the root of the theory is simply the idea that what matters morally is *reasonable agreement*, and so what makes an action right, say, is that it is permitted by principles to which all reasonable people would agree, and what makes an action wrong is that it violates such principles.[2] Consider, then, lying. Some ethical theories condemn all lying as immoral. Of course, we have a general need for truth-telling: we have to be able to rely on one another's word to

---

1 This kind of view has very deep historical roots. It was a central part of Confucian ethics, for instance, which goes back to around 500 B.C.E.
2 Contractualism actually has a long and storied history in both political and moral philosophy. Most philosophers drawn to it have applied it to political philosophy as a way of justifying the state (this is what Hobbes, Locke, and John Rawls did, for instance), and so contractualism as a political view (sometimes called "contractarianism") may look somewhat different from the view I've laid out in the text. On political versions, there are often references to states of nature as well as the governmental structures rational people would choose to be authoritative in certain hypothetical circumstances. The view described in the text is more about appealing to agreement to determine the nature of *morality* (which is our topic in this second half of the book), and so makes no reference to governments or the state of nature. Nevertheless, the view described is still rather general and could be taken to accurately describe (with some slight tweaking) all forms of contractualism, including the political versions. (In discussing moral contractualism in the text, I am drawing mostly from the work of T.M. Scanlon.)

get along in the world more effectively. But an absolute prohibition on lying seems crazy, for it would eliminate the possibility of something as trivial and harmless as the planning of a surprise birthday party (where one has to lie to the birthday person to keep him or her in the dark), and it would also yield the absurd implication that one should, in a much more dramatic case, inform the killer where he may find the victim he's inquiring about. We wouldn't all agree to the principle "All lying is wrong," then. What we would agree to instead, though, is a much more nuanced principle, something like "One cannot, without special justification, intentionally lead another to form a false belief about something." Special justification would be needed for the exceptions, of course, but they could be easily forthcoming. In the surprise birthday party case, for example, the subject herself would agree to the exception, given that without it she couldn't have had the special enjoyment from the party she had, and because she'd recognize the good intentions of the "liar." And while the killer may not agree to the exception in his case, he's not reasonable in the first place, so his voice doesn't count; for all other reasonable people, it would certainly be permissible for me to hide the information from the killer (and if the killer *were* reasonable, he'd agree as well, given that he himself might be sought by a killer one day).

One important selling point for contractualism is that it explains **moral motivation** quite well. A story about moral motivation will be a story explaining why it is that people are moved to conform their actions to moral demands, especially when those demands sometimes conflict with self-regarding interests they have. So, for example, when you return the extra change the cashier mistakenly gives you, despite the fact you really want the money, you're typically motivated by the thought that it would be *wrong* to keep it. But the wrongness here, for many contractualists, just consists in the fact that it would be *unjustifiable* to keep the money: you certainly couldn't justify it to the cashier on grounds she could accept— really wanting it isn't sufficient to overcome the cashier's objections to having to make up the lost money out of her own paycheck—and if you couldn't justify it to the victim of the theft (where the victim is reasonable), then it's certainly wrong. But if what motivates you to return the money is the thought that it would be wrong (unjustifiable) to keep it, then this thought must hook up to your motivational center in a powerful way. You must, more specifically, have a very powerful desire to be able to justify your actions to others, and it is this desire that motivates you to act, even against your own interests, in the moral case.

Think about it: when you're going through your day and then you stop short with the worry that what you might be about to do would be wrong, what considerations run through your head? Suppose you're suddenly considering just skipping out on your lunch date with someone, without even calling him or her. What images play in your mind? For many of us, it would be the image of running into that person later, feeling sheepish and terrible. But why? It would be because when that person asks, "What happened to you at lunch?" you wouldn't have a good answer. Attempted justifications like "I just felt like skipping it," or "It didn't seem very important to me" simply won't wash—the lunch date would reject them, and with good reason. Not just any old justification will count, then; it has to be one that would be *acceptable* to a reasonable person. So if that thought—the thought that one wouldn't be able to justify skipping lunch—moves one to keep one's date, one is being morally motivated by the central contractualist desire.

But this account of moral motivation yields a serious worry: what about those who *lack* this desire? Does morality not apply to them? This is a worry about people called **amoralists**, those who just aren't moved to act morally, who simply don't care about morality and so have no desire to act on its demands. If the moral demands of contractualism apply only to those who have the desire to adhere to them, then it looks as if contractualism leaves amoralists without any moral obligations. But that can't be right. Surely, we want to say, morality applies to amoralists, even if they aren't motivated to act on its demands. It may be, however, that appeal to reductionism about personal identity could help out the contractualist at precisely this point.

The main point of contractualism is that a central domain of morality (regarding just our obligations *to one another*) is determined by hypothetical agreement among a certain range of individuals. But who are these individuals? This is precisely a question about the MSMUs: who are the relevant contractors, those to whom I owe justification for my actions? Are they to be persons, selves, or atoms? We have already seen what sort of implications there might be for ethical theory if our MSMUs are atoms (utilitarianism might be favored) or persons (rational egoism might be favored). Let us see what happens, then, if we focus on selves.

What the contractualist wants is to be able to capture the reasonable amoralist in her net. At the very least, then, the amoralist must be *rational*, and if he is reasonable as well, he is likely to be *prudent*. So he will, at the least, be motivated to do what's in his own best interest. But what does such motivation look like? One very plausible model of prudential deliberation has individuals, in effect, bargaining with *themselves*, trying to determine, when choosing among various alternatives, which course of action would be justifiable to the stage of themselves that would have to live through it. After all, we often think, I'd hate to wake up in the morning having done *that* (some bad thing) the night before—*I couldn't live with myself* if I did. So prudentially rational individuals are those who are moved to action by a desire that they be able to justify their actions to the various affected future stages of themselves. The thought that an action would be *imprudent* is just the thought that one couldn't justify it to the stage of oneself that would have to live through it and its consequences.

But now suppose that we go with the "selves" version of reductionism, that is, we maintain that the relation that matters prudentially and morally is psychological connectedness. In the prudential realm, then, this will mean that I am rationally permitted to care less about those far future selves, those with whom I'll bear very little connectedness (so even though I'll be *continuous* with them, that isn't the relation that matters). Thus I'll have less of an obligation to justify my actions to them than I would to those selves more closely connected to me. Indeed, this is how many of us often think—we put off the interests of our distant future selves in favor of the interests of our nearer selves precisely because those distant future selves are likely to be so dissimilar, or unconnected, to us—and this may be an independent reason to focus on selves as the MSMUs.

Thus far, the reasonable amoralist shouldn't object. But now we can reintroduce the idea of interpersonal connectedness, according to which

I now may be psychologically connected to other simultaneously exist-ing selves. Now you should be able to see how the extension in favor of contractualism works. If I am moved by my desire to be able to justify my actions to all the stages of my self with whom I am psychologically connected (to varying degrees), and identity isn't what matters (so the fact that these stages are stages of *my* self is irrelevant), then the scope of that desire ought rationally to be extended to include all the stages of *other selves* with whom I'm also psychologically connected. One way to think of this is that other people are *extensions of me*: to the extent that we are psychologically connected, they should have a voice whose hypothetical objections to my proposed actions are taken just as seriously as the hypo-thetical objections of my future stages when I'm engaged in prudential deliberation. By exploiting the desire at the root of prudential motivation, the contractualist has a "hook" to get the amoralist to see how he's already committed to *moral* motivation as well: if he's moved to be prudent, and selves are the MSMU's, then he ought to be moved to be moral as well, on pain of irrational inconsistency otherwise.

Many details remain to be filled into this account, but on its face it yields an ethical theory that looks at least superficially similar to Brink's extended rational egoism, one in which there are concentric circles of ob-ligation moving outward in degree from the individual. And as mentioned earlier, this is a familiar sort of commonsense morality.

Of course, one thing necessary to any account of the relation between reductionism and ethical theory will be arguments in favor of one MSMU over the others. We haven't considered those here, but various people have offered them. The basic idea behind all of these projects, though, is to establish the truth of the metaphysical view of identity first, to identify the proper MSMUs thereby second, and then to apply the favored overall metaphysical picture to ethical theory third. But there are two general objections one might raise to this method. First, one might object that the metaphysics of identity is just *irrelevant* to ethical theory, that there are certain practical commitments we share that determine the MSMUs for us, and that the metaphysics of identity plays no role whatsoever in this process. Second, one might object that the search for *the* proper MSMUs is a fool's errand, given that there just is no single type of MSMU common to all prudential and moral concerns. The former objection is what we will explore next, whereas the second objection is one we will explore in the concluding chapter.

PRACTICAL COMMITMENTS AND PERSONAL IDENTITY

It is very difficult to believe that reductionism is false. And many reductionists believe that their metaphysics of identity favors an ethical theory like utilitarianism. So how do non-utilitarians reply? One way is to show how reductionism might well favor a different ethical theory, such as rational egoism or contractualism, attempts we saw outlined in the previous section. A second way is more radical. It is to object to the *method* these reductionists use to reach their utilitarian conclusions, which is to apply the metaphysics of identity to the world of ethics. Instead, these non-utilitarians want to say, the right method goes the other way round.

This complaint comes in particular from two different ethical views, namely, **Kantianism** and **communitarianism**. Very roughly, Kantians maintain that our moral duties are really demands of rationality, and Kantians appeal (even more roughly) to the familiar moral question, "What if everyone did that?" The basic thought is that if one couldn't coherently conceive of a world in which everyone were required to act on the intention one is considering acting on, then it would be immoral for one to act on it in one's own life as well. Communitarians, on the other hand, hold (again, very roughly) that the individualist focus of various Twentieth- and Twenty-First-Century moral and political theories is utterly wrongheaded, that the focus of morality, say, should be on communities, on the social networks of selves, as well as on their extension, preservation, and perfection.

The positive details of each ethical theory don't actually matter much for our purposes, though, given that we're really interested in the objections given by their advocates to the direction of argumentation we have seen thus far. For while we have seen various attempts to show how reductionism may be applied to ethical theory, the Kantians and communitarians we will now discuss strongly dispute any relevance of the one to the other. In particular, both want to resist the *disunifying* implications of reductionism. As you will recall, reductionism denies that persons are deeply unified at all, given the nonexistence of anything, like a soul, that could provide such unity. This leaves individuals unified only to some limited extent, either by psychological continuity (such that the MSMUs are persons), psychological connectedness (such that the MSMUs are selves), or not at all (such that the MSMUs are person-atoms). As we will now see, though, one might well question the move from reductionism to any of these more weakly unified MSMUs altogether.

Let us start with the objection from Kantianism. As Christine Korsgaard, the primary advocate of this objection, points out (following Kant), there are two ways in which we might conceive ourselves. The first is as **agents**, as entities which freely deliberate, choose, and perform actions. We all conceive ourselves as being agents when we engage in practical deliberation; indeed, as we'll see, we allegedly can't do otherwise. From this perspective, we are the doers of our deeds, the thinkers of our thoughts, the planners and choosers for our lives. When we consider what to do, then, we can't help but take up what Korsgaard calls **the practical standpoint**.

The second way in which we might conceive ourselves is as a **subject of experiences**, that is, as an entity to whom various experiences occur (and to whom all actions are merely another form of experience). And we all occasionally think of ourselves in this way. Think, for instance, how you might conceive yourself in therapy, trying to figure out the source of your anger at your father, say. As you trace back through your life, you'll view many of your actions as caused by forces out of your control (subconscious desires, say, or deeply ingrained parental influences), and you'll see yourself more as someone to whom things happened, as an object buffeted about by the forces of fate, rather than as someone who *took on* fate, or actively engaged with the world. When we take up this more passive stance, we conceive ourselves from **the theoretical standpoint**.

When we're interested in the *explanation* of our actions, or in predictions of how we might react in various scenarios, we view ourselves from the theoretical standpoint, viewing ourselves as *objects*, as things that are part of the natural causal order. Here, when thinking about what I did, I will notice how some of my desires, say, just weighed more than others and so won out in determining my decisions and subsequent actions. On the other hand, when we're interested in the *justification* of our actions and choices, we occupy the practical standpoint. When, in other words, I'm considering what in fact I *ought* to do, this is the standpoint I occupy, and I conceive myself as an agent. Here I don't feel as if I'm part of the natural causal order; instead, I feel as if I'm a first cause, the prime mover of my actions. I *assign weight* to my various possible options, when taking up this perspective, and then I decide to *act on* one of them.

So which is the correct standpoint? According to Korsgaard, each standpoint is equally legitimate, yet separate. What matters is that we are *forced* to occupy each standpoint at different times for different reasons. We must occupy the theoretical standpoint when we want to explain or predict or understand various experiences that have occurred. And we must occupy the practical standpoint when we are deciding what to do. I *must* think of myself as the originator, the first cause, of my actions when making choices. I can't think of myself as being just another in a long line of caused and determined experiencers. In order to *make* any choices at all, I have to conceive myself as being a free agent.

Now which standpoint is necessary for *moral* deliberation? The practical standpoint. In order to be able to choose which actions I should or should not perform, I must think of myself as the first cause of my action, as a free doer, as an agent. Yet, Korsgaard argues, the reductionist account of persons ignores this practical standpoint in favor of the theoretical one, and so its treatment of the morality stemming from the metaphysics is deeply flawed.

On the reductionist view, persons are seen as mere *locations* of mental events, of desires, beliefs, memories, and the like. They are metaphysical objects, in other words, and so when viewing them (and ourselves) in reductionist terms, we're clearly taking up the theoretical perspective. It is from this perspective, then, that the reductionist insists that we're not deeply unified, that there is no significant relation tying together every part of our lives into a distinct and independent unit in the world.

Korsgaard argues, however, that, while this conclusion may be true from the theoretical standpoint (and so she agrees that reductionism is true as a *metaphysical thesis* about persons), there's another perspective we can take on our actions, the practical standpoint, and from this standpoint we can see that there's a non-arbitrary unity easily found, a unity that is utterly independent of the metaphysics of personal identity. Even if there's no deep metaphysical unity between me and the future occupier of my body, I have to regard that future body-occupier as the same *agent* as me, as unified with me, for entirely practical reasons.

Briefly, the idea comes from consideration of actual deliberation, of what it feels like from the inside when we think about what to do. For Korsgaard, I am practically unified both at one time and across many times. At a single moment, I am unified because I have to act, and because I have only one body with which to perform such actions, I have a practical need to eliminate conflicts in my deliberations and motives in order to do anything at all. Suppose you walked into a convenience store where no one else was around, and you saw the cash register open, with lots of cash you could easily steal. You're broke and need the money, but you also know full well that it's wrong to steal. You have conflicting motives: you want to steal, but you don't want to steal. What happens from the inside as you deliberate? Eventually, you decide on one motive or the other, and then you act on it. Suppose, though, that your conflicting motives in the store remained at a stalemate. You'd be frozen into inaction, unable to go forward or backward. You have to act, though, and in order to do so, your various motives must be unified, or at least ranked, made to cooperate with one another to allow you free rein to move forward.

Across time, practical unity of agency is also presupposed and necessary, insofar as one has only one life to lead and has a rational plan for the living of that life. In order to carry out your life plan, and because you've got only one body with which to act, you have to conceive yourself as deeply unified with all your future stages, with all those stages that will carry out that plan. In other words, in making any long-term choice, I'm identifying with my future self. I am, in effect, *making him me*, in order for my choice to be justified. So in order for me to even have any reasons for action, I must project myself into the future as the very same agent who will carry out my plans.

Remember that reductionists like to compare persons to nations, which consist in nothing more than their citizens and geographical terrain. On Korsgaard's view, though, the identity of agents is like the identity of *states*, not nations. Where the citizens on a territory have organized themselves into a single agent, they have constructed a state, defined by a constitution and deliberative procedures. So they aren't just a group of folks lying about on a particular territory; instead, they do things in one voice, they interact with other states, and they plan for a future. They are unified, in other words, robustly so, and for entirely practical reasons. Moral agents, then, the true MSMU's, are unified for analogous practical reasons, regardless of the truth of reductionism. Indeed, reductionism is just irrelevant to this practical necessity.

What should we say about this objection to reductionism? There are many plausible aspects to the argument, but we might register some skepticism about the so-called *necessity* of practical unity at issue here. Consider first unity at one time. Korsgaard claims that what unites my various experiences at any given moment is my need to act, and so I have a practical need to eliminate conflict among my various motives to enable such action. But one may *do* nothing, and yet one's experiences will still be unified. Suppose you lean back in your easy chair and take in all your various experiences: you may be seeing a computer, hearing birds chirp outside, feeling tension in your shoulders, and smelling the burnt toast from breakfast. These experiences are unified into a single consciousness, *yours*, but they aren't unified *because* of your practical need to act, or to eliminate conflict in your motives. Indeed, you have no motives at all. Instead, these experiences are unified simply in virtue of being the object of a single state of awareness, but this is a fact easily accounted for from the purely theoretical standpoint.

Consider next unity across time. It's certainly true that I have only one life to lead. But why should we think that I'll have just *one* rational plan guiding that life to a single overarching unity? Instead, for most of us, we start off on one plan, and then switch to another, and then another, before (hopefully?) settling into a groove that may or may not last for the remainder of our lives. So the fact that I have one body doesn't yet force on me a single rational plan of life: I may (and probably will) have many, and each of these smaller plans may well necessitate some smaller unities (selves?), but there's certainly no practical necessity that there will be *lifelong* unity.

In addition, there may also be no necessity, practical or otherwise, for unity across one's life *at all*. Recall from Chapter Three the claim of Galen Strawson that some people, including himself, are "Episodics," people who have "little or no sense that the self that one is was there in the (further) past and will be there in the future."[1] Instead, they live their lives with no deep sense of their further futures at all, focusing primarily on the here and now, unconcerned to shape their lives into some rational plan. This seems a perfectly intelligible way of living, one that some of us can easily imagine adopting ourselves. But if it is both intelligible—preserving practical agency—and easily executed (for some, at least), then there could hardly be a *necessity of practical agency* attached to doing otherwise.

Nevertheless, there is something to the Kantian complaint, for it does seem as though, even if there is no practical necessity for life-long unity, there are still shorter-term unities that are indeed practical, independent of the number of psychological connections that hold, say. I *make* some future stage part of me in virtue of planning certain things with respect to it. I establish a special connectedness with that stage, one might say, which is a practical, active uniting, rather than *becoming united* with that stage once a certain number of psychological connections have been established, which would be a theoretical, passive uniting. But while this is true, there seem to be other times when, no matter how hard I try, such active attempts at uniting fail: I "grow apart" from my earlier stage, say, such that his projects no longer interest me, despite the fact that he'd intended for me to carry them out. This is a kind of passive disuniting, and it makes sense only from the theoretical perspective, given that it is an explanation of what occurred to me despite the best efforts of my

---

1   Galen Strawson, "Against Narrativity," *Ratio* XVII (2004): 428-52, p. 430.

practical, active agency. In addition, it seems possible for me actively to set out to *disunite* myself and succeed in doing so, intentionally causing a deep psychological break with my emotionally crippling past, say. Unity, then, may be neither necessary nor even very practical.

Let us turn, then, to the second objection to the method of reductionist utilitarians, this one suggested by the communitarians Alasdair MacIntyre and Charles Taylor. I will focus here on MacIntyre's version of the objection. In his book *After Virtue*, MacIntyre argues that there are three aspects of human actions that yield a practical unity of lives from birth to death, independently of any metaphysical treatment of identity like reductionism. The first aspect is *intelligibility*: in order for our actions to be intelligible, they must be seen with reference to intentions embedded in certain social settings. So consider some piece of behavior: as you eat lunch outside on campus, someone walks up to you and hands you a bible. What would you do? You'd likely immediately try to figure out what was going on and, in particular, *why* this person is handing you a bible. That is, you will try to place that action in the context of a particular intention. Otherwise, *it just makes no sense*. So perhaps the guy was a representative of the Gideons on campus, intending to hand out a bible to everyone he ran across to spread the good news. Or perhaps he was someone who simply saw a pained look on your face and so gave you his own bible, in the hopes it would cheer you up. Or perhaps he was a spy, and he mistook you for the contact to whom he was supposed to slip secret documents (stashed in the bible, of course). But in any event, intelligible actions must be based on intentions, and these intentions will themselves be situated within some institutional or social practice.

The second aspect of human actions, though, is that each short-term intention itself is intelligible only within the context of some longer-term intention, and so on, which ultimately yields a *narrative history*. Right now you're reading this book. But why? Perhaps it's because you intend to do well in a philosophy course. But why? Perhaps because you intend to do well in school and graduate. But why? So that you can get a job doing what you love. But why? So you can enjoy your work life and have enough money eventually to retire in Bakersfield, say. So for each intention, there is a more encompassing, longer-term intention of which it's an instrumental part. Notice, then, that in order to make one's immediate action fully intelligible, one must ultimately view it within the context of a life-long narrative structure.

The third aspect of human actions MacIntyre finds relevant is *accountability*, which is what distinguishes us from other animals: only we can be accountable for our actions. So to identify an action as intelligible is also to be able to hold the agent accountable for it; it's to see it as flowing from the agent's intentions, which themselves are situated in a particular practice.

Consider, then, what we've got so far: intelligibility, narrative history, and accountability. These are all features of our actions, and together they presuppose a significant life-long unity of character. Our lives are constituted by a series of actions: these are things I do for which I am accountable, and each of these actions is made intelligible only from within a particular narrative framework. But this fact implies that our lives are necessarily unified from birth to death by a particular narrative. In order for our individual actions to make sense, they must be seen as part of some history. And in order for our *lives*—the collection of our actions—to make sense, they must be seen as a unity, unified by a narrative structure. We can understand our lives only in terms of the narratives that we live out.

What does all of this mean for reductionism, then? Regardless of the metaphysical facts of personal identity, persons are necessarily unified by narratives and their identity must be treated as all-or-nothing. So MacIntyre agrees (along with Korsgaard) that there's nothing more to us metaphysically than the various psychological relations described by the reductionist. Nevertheless, our lives can only be made *intelligible* by imposing upon them a narrative structure, which presupposes an all-or-nothing unity from physical birth to physical death.

This is essentially an account of narrative identity that is wholly self-contained, insisting upon the utter irrelevance of metaphysical accounts of personal identity to ethics. This makes the two general questions we asked of our narrative identity theorists in Chapter Three particularly pressing once again, though, and worth briefly rehashing. First of all, why *life-long* unity, unity from physical birth to physical death? If it's the intelligibility and accountability of my actions that matters, then it seems that (a) some actions might be intelligible (and have their accountability explained) only with respect to events and experiences pre-birth or post-death, and (b) some actions might be made sufficiently intelligible with respect solely to unities somewhere *in between* the end-points of birth and death (or even with reference to no unities at all).

Point (a) received close attention in Chapter Three, but point (b) deserves some discussion, especially given MacIntyre's specific arguments for narrative identity. For instance, some actions may be perfectly intelligible exclusively within the life of *selves*. As a dramatic example, I may undergo head trauma and enter a fugue state, where I don't know who I am (or think I'm someone else) for several months, after which I return to normal (as occasionally happens to some unfortunate people). The actions during that fugue state will be sufficiently intelligible only within the context of that self. Further, as an example of intelligibility without *any* real unity, suppose I see you running your hand under the water, and I ask you why. Your answer could tell me everything there is to know: "I burned it on the stove." This action is now perfectly intelligible, essentially with respect to an *atom*, a momentary experiencer. If we tried to place this action into the context of your life as a *whole*, we would miss the point in a rather bizarre fashion (indeed, right now the pain may matter a lot to you, but if this moment were viewed instead in the context of your life as a whole, it wouldn't, and shouldn't, matter *at all*!). In the humdrum existence of our daily lives, we rarely engage in the kind of self-exploring and striving for meaning fixated on by MacIntyre. Instead, we fix breakfast, head off to the bathroom, pick up the paper, change the TV station, and so forth. Insisting that these sorts of actions are intelligible only if we refer to their place within the unity of our entire lives seems overly melodramatic.

The second general question we might ask MacIntyre is again one we asked of narrative identity theorists earlier, namely, whether or not the overall view is *descriptive* or *prescriptive*. That is, is the story about narrative unity a description of how our lives actually are unified, or is it meant to be a story about how our lives *ought to be* unified, an ideal of unity towards which we should strive? And again, there is a dilemma. If the view is supposed to be descriptive, then it seems false: our lives often just *don't* exhibit narrative unity from birth to death. Further, if the view is that people have to *conceive* themselves as unified under a narrative structure, the "Episodics" Galen Strawson talks about provide a counterexample once more. On the other hand, if MacIntyre's thesis is prescriptive, urging that narrative unity is an ideal towards which people ought to aim, then it doesn't really constitute an objection to reductionism, for it must allow that people in fact don't live up to this ideal all the time, that people's lives may actually be disunified in the way implied by reductionism. In fact, if unity is truly the ideal, then it really makes more sense to think of persons as disunified, as reductionism suggests. If they weren't disunified, then a directive for them to strive towards unity wouldn't be necessary. Further, a claim about how we ought to be cannot be an objection to the facts about how we are.

All in all, then, it's not clear that either the Kantian or the communitarian complaints against the method of reductionists succeeds, although they both raise important practical points about how we sometimes have to proceed and conceive ourselves in the world. It may be, after all, that reductionism can *incorporate* these practical points and still have the significant kind of bearing on ethical theory discussed earlier in this chapter. At the very least, though, more would have to be said about why these sorts of reductionist attempts to apply the view to ethical theory are undercut.

Conclusion

What we have done in this chapter is simply trace the various attempts to apply conclusions about personal identity to ethical theory, as well as discuss a couple of important objections to that enterprise. As usual, matters are fairly complicated, and it's unclear just what conclusions we ought to draw. We have learned a few things, though. For instance, one common thread running through the more constructive part of the chapter was that the three attempts to apply reductionism to ethical theory do so by appealing to the metaphysics in order to shore up a pre-existing ethical theory, often by defending it from an important objection. In this respect, then, the relation between identity and ethical theory is fairly modest (and thus perhaps more plausible); it certainly isn't about the construction of an entire ethical theory from scratch. This modest "hole-plugging" strategy might also, then, have some appeal in other arenas of the purported relation, for example, for identity and responsibility, or for identity and the various issues in applied ethics.

Another thing we have learned is that very different ethical theories may gain some support from a commonly-held view of personal identity. So, for example, reductionism can plausibly be seen to buttress utilitarianism, rational egoism, and contractualism. But these ethical theories conflict with one another at their very foundations (contractualism, for instance, is distinctly non-consequentialist, as opposed to both utilitarianism and egoism), so what conclusions should we draw from this fact? One might be that reductionism is simply too general to provide determinate support to *any* particular theory. But another conclusion might be that its very generality allows for a few different relations to blossom between metaphysics and ethics, *depending on what one's needs are.* For someone looking to defend utilitarianism, one relation can be found. For someone looking to defend contractualism, another relation can be found. Which relation one finds may thus depend on what one's needs and starting points are. And this may also be a point that survives from our discussion of the Kantian and communitarian critics of reductionism: what really determines the right relation between metaphysics and practical concerns may depend ultimately on what our practical concerns already are. And indeed, this is a central topic of our final chapter on methodology.

WORKS CITED OR REFERENCED IN THIS CHAPTER

Brink, David O. "Rational Egoism and the Separateness of Persons." In *Reading Parfit*, edited by Jonathan Dancy. Oxford: Blackwell Publishers, 1997.

——. "Self-Love and Altruism." *Social Philosophy & Policy* 14 (1997): 122-57.

Korsgaard, Christine M. "Personal Identity and the Unity of Agency: A Kantian Response to Parfit." *Philosophy & Public Affairs* 18 (1989): 101-32.

MacIntyre, Alasdair. *After Virtue*. Notre Dame: University of Notre Dame Press, 1984.

Parfit, Derek. *Reasons and Persons*. Oxford: Oxford University Press, 1984.

———. "The Unimportance of Identity." In *Identity*, edited by Henry Harris. Oxford: Oxford University Press, 1995.

Rawls, John. *A Theory of Justice*. Cambridge, MA: The Belknap Press of Harvard University Press, 1971.

Scanlon, T.M. "Contractualism and Utilitarianism." In *Utilitarianism and Beyond*, edited by Amartya Sen and Bernard Williams. Cambridge: The Press Syndicate of the University of Cambridge, 1982.

———. *What We Owe to Each Other*. Cambridge, MA: The Belknap Press of Harvard University Press, 1998.

Shoemaker, David W. "Theoretical Persons and Practical Agents." *Philosophy & Public Affairs* 25 (1996): 318-32.

———. "Selves and Moral Units." *Pacific Philosophical Quarterly* 80 (1999): 391-419.

———. "Reductionist Contractualism: Moral Motivation and the Expanding Self." *Canadian Journal of Philosophy* 30 (September 2000): 343-70.

Strawson, Galen. "Against Narrativity." *Ratio* XVII (2004): 428-52.

Taylor, Charles. *Sources of the Self: The Making of Modern Identity*. Cambridge, MA: Harvard University Press, 1989.

Conclusion

NOTES ON METHOD

It has not been the aim of this book to make a case for *the* correct theory of the relation between personal identity and ethics. Instead, the aim was to set forth as many of the most significant arguments and positions regarding that relation as possible, and then leave it up to the reader to pursue whatever particular arguments and positions he or she found most intriguing or plausible. In other words, the idea was to introduce the various players and positions in sufficient detail for the reader to jump in and start playing the game as well.

But what are the *rules* of this particular game? What are the permitted approaches and moves one might make as one articulates and defends a particular position on the relation between identity and ethics? This is a question about **methodology**, about the methods one may or should employ when philosophizing about this issue. It is actually a rather difficult question, but in this brief final chapter we will attempt to come to some understanding of the issues involved. We can begin by identifying three serious differences in methodology that may be the source of the disagreements we have run across repeatedly in this book.

The first difference in methodology has to do with the direction one adopts regarding the relation at issue: do we go from personal identity to ethics or vice versa? The standard methodological approach should be evident from its many iterations throughout the book. In it, one works up and defends a purely metaphysical theory of personal identity, and only then does one apply that theory to some prudential or ethical issue. So, for example, David DeGrazia defends the Biological Criterion of personal identity (along with a conception of narrative identity), and then he shows what it implies for the proper definition of death, for certain views of genetic therapy, for advanced directives, for abortion, and so on. Or Derek Parfit, as we saw in the last chapter, defends a very general view of personal identity called reductionism, and then he shows how it may be applied to utilitarian ethical theory (and he also takes some time to talk about reductionism's implications for abortion, euthanasia, promise-keeping, and desert). Or John Locke defends a kind of Psychological (Memory) Criterion, and then shows how it applies to the ethical issue of moral responsibility. In each instance, then, metaphysics seems to be prior to ethics, so that the relation runs in one direction, from personal identity *to* ethics.

But as we also saw in the last chapter, one might well object that this methodology gets things the wrong way round. Instead, as Korsgaard and MacIntyre argued, the relation, if there is one, runs from ethics *to* personal identity. We must start with certain of our ethical commitments, they argue, appreciate how they are genuine *commitments* (necessities), and then see how they must yield a certain practical account of personal identity, one in which we are deeply unified, distinct individuals for all practical purposes, regardless of what some purely metaphysical theory says.

So while the first methodological direction might yield the conclusion that persons are (at least partially) disintegrated, the second methodological direction might yield the conclusion that they can't be. This is a deeply entrenched conflict, but now we can see that the conflict is produced by conflicting views about methodology, about the proper way to approach the articulation of the relation between personal identity and ethics in the first place. So the first methodological question is this: should we start with our metaphysical or our ethical commitments? Different commitments may well yield different theories of the relation between identity and ethics.

The second methodological difference takes place among the members of the first group just discussed, those who think that the right approach is to apply a worked out theory of personal identity to ethics. Here the conflicting views of the relation between identity and ethics sometimes stem from theorists' different motivations for constructing a theory of personal identity in the first place. On the one hand, there are those who are interested in the identity conditions of persons simply because they're interested in the identity conditions of objects *generally,* and persons just happen to be a particularly interesting sort of object to study. Call this a *theoretical motivation*: one wants a purely theoretical understanding of what persons and their persistence conditions across time are, just as one may want to understand what chairs and their persistence conditions are, as part of a larger theory about the nature of the world. Now some of those who approach personal identity from this direction may not have any interest in seeing how the theory they come up with applies to any of our practical concerns. Some will have such an interest, however, and these are the ones who then go on to develop one sort of relation between personal identity and ethics.

On the other hand, one might be motivated to investigate the nature of personal identity precisely because of its potential payoff for our person-related practical concerns. This is to have a *practical motivation*. In other words, one might be interested in the nature of moral responsibility, believe that one condition of the concept of responsibility is that the responsible party must be the same person as the agent who performed the action for which he's now being blamed, and so be moved to investigate the nature of personal identity thereby. Notice that this latter position is different from the "ethics first" methodology of Korsgaard and MacIntyre insofar as this person is ostensibly spurred to look for the correct theory of identity by his interest in ethical issues, but he is not saying that the correct account of identity is actually *determined* or *constrained* by our ethical commitments. So he still thinks that he has to figure out the correct theory of identity *first* in order to apply it subsequently to, say, our practical concerns about moral responsibility.

These different motivations can favor different methods of argumentation, however, which themselves may favor different theories of identity, primarily because different theoretical considerations may count as relevant or significant given the different motivations. For instance, for those with a theoretical motivation, what will be relevant is that the identity conditions of persons not be significantly different from the identity conditions of non-persons, that as just another object in the world what makes us persist across time should be the same sort of thing that makes other objects persist. This may then lead the theorist to posit that our identity conditions aren't really different from nonhuman animals, which is likely to favor something like the Biological Criterion, an animalistic theory of identity.

Alternatively, for those with practical motivations, the theory favored tends to be the Psychological Criterion (or psychology-based variations like narrative identity or the IDM view). The reason is simple: the practical concerns we have discussed are almost always about *persons* (or agents), who are (at the very least) creatures with a robust psychology. It is in this respect, then, that we are very *different* from other animals, and so the identity conditions found by these theorists tend to be less animalistic than psychological. It isn't our similarity with animals, after all, that could possibly explain moral responsibility, a concept that applies only to creatures like us. So what tends to happen is that theorists who have a practical motivation will count it as an advantage of a theory of identity if it accounts for our practical concerns better than others, whereas those with a theoretical motivation may see that consideration as irrelevant.

This is the conflict that has reverberated most often throughout the book. One recurring point of contention between the Biological Criterion and the Psychological Criterion, for instance, was about each one's failure to account for a key feature the other theory accounted for quite well. So while the Biological Criterion accounted for the Essence Problem, regarding our essential natures, the Psychological Criterion did very poorly at it. On the other hand, the Psychological Criterion explained our intuitions about rational anticipation (and other practical concerns) very well, while the Biological Criterion didn't. But now we should be able to see why. The question of *essence* is crucially important in theoretical investigations into the identity of objects generally. Someone with a theoretical motivation would thus deem answering this question to be among the most important tasks of a theory of *personal* identity as well. On the other hand, the question of essence may not be that important to one with a practical motivation, for it's not clear that our essence is even relevant for something like anticipation; rather, what is at issue is clearly some psychological connection between me and the person whose experiences I'm anticipating. Once again, then, we can see how different methodological approaches (spurred by differing motivations) can yield serious disagreements in final results.

A third methodological difference is evident among just the group of theorists with a practical motivation, those moved to an investigation into personal identity by their desire to explain the nature of our practical concerns. The difference here has its sources in *which* practical concerns motivate them in the first place. Many have followed John Locke, for example, in being motivated to investigate the relation between identity and practical concerns by an interest in the nature of moral responsibility. But many others have become interested in the topic by a strong interest in figuring out the possibility of surviving the deaths of our bodies (recall our fictional philosopher of Chapter One, Gretchen Weirob). And still others have been motivated to explore personal identity and its relation to ethics because of their interest in the nature of compensation, or prudential rationality generally, or certain identity-related emotions like pride, guilt, embarrassment, and the like.

Now suppose one is motivated into the project by one's interest in a single practical concern, and then one generalizes the relation one finds to cover *all* practical concerns. If someone else is motivated by an interest in a different practical concern, and he comes up with a different relation between identity and that practical concern that he too generalizes to cover all practical concerns, it is easy to see how yet another set of conflicts will arise between them. To take just one instance, suppose I am motivated by my interest in moral responsibility to investigate the relation between identity and responsibility. I will likely endorse some sort of psychology-based criterion of identity or unity in order to incorporate our strong intuition that the responsible person must be intimately psychologically related to the original agent. Now once I've articulated this sort of relation between identity and responsibility, I may well be tempted to generalize the relation to cover *all* our practical concerns, insisting that a psychology-based relation is also necessary to account for rational anticipation, everyday survival, identity-related emotions (e.g., pride and embarrassment), reidentification (of self and others), and compensation. After all, one might think that if these practical concerns are all identity-related, and one has found the right identity-relation to account for one of them, then they all must get covered by the same relation.

But now suppose one is motivated into the project by an interest in *compensation*. There will be certain instances of compensation one will want to explain by reference to identity, and among these will be cases in which I am compensated for damages inflicted upon me in the womb (by a bad doctor, perhaps), or my PVS-stage self is compensated (via some financial settlement, perhaps) for a head trauma someone inflicted on me earlier. Now here we have cases that can't be explained solely by reference to some psychology-based criterion of identity, for there are human stages in each case that simply *have no psychology*, and yet still seem to be related in the right way to some later or earlier person to warrant compensation. This fact would likely incline one towards a biology-based criterion of identity, a criterion that would explain why compensation in each case is warranted by pointing to a relation of biological continuity that obtains. And then were one to generalize this result to all of our practical concerns (on the same reasoning as above), one would come up with a very different relation between identity and ethics than the theorist who started off with an interest in moral responsibility.

The three methodological differences just articulated are obviously, then, the source of much disagreement in determining the nature of any sort of relation(s) between personal identity and ethics. Are there ways, though, to resolve these disagreements?

A promising first step is to be upfront in tracing the source of the disagreement to these different methodological approaches, as we've just done. Seeing, for instance, that there are alternatives to one's method of approaching the relation between identity and ethics may cause one to be less combative about the differences produced; alternatively, it may cause one to spend more time showing why one's own general *methodology* is preferable to the alternative(s). Very few people in this debate, as it currently stands, either recognize differences in methodology or defend their own approach to the issue in any detail.[1]

In closing, though, I want to suggest another option, which is to become a **pluralist** about the relation between identity and ethics. In other words, one might simply admit *that there is no single relation between identity and ethics*, but instead there are multiple relations, each depending on the methodological approach one takes to the relation. Now this may seem a surprising position to take, but it is at least worth exploring a bit.

The best way to illustrate how it might work is to consider the final methodological difference discussed above, one in which the relation one finds depends on which particular practical concern motivates one into the project. One thing we might say in light of the disagreement produced is just that, when it comes to moral responsibility, say, a psychology-based relation is correct, whereas when it comes to compensation, a biology-based relation is correct. Now of course there can't be two "correct" metaphysical criteria of personal identity that yield two different answers to the question, "Is X at t_1 (one time) identical to Y at t_2 (another time)?" The answer can only be either "yes" or "no," not "yes and no." So the only way pluralism could be plausible is if X and Y referred to individuals *under different descriptions*, depending on the practical concern at issue. So when exploring moral responsibility, we might ask if X at t_1 (the original agent) is identical to Y at t_2 (the person we're now holding responsible), where X and Y refer to *agents*, or persons capable of performing actions for which they might coherently be held responsible. In other words, is *X-the-agent* at t_1 identical to *Y-the-agent* at t_2? Alternatively, were we to be asking about identity motivated by our interest in compensation, we might be talking about X and Y under the descriptions of *human beings*, or as *biological individuals*, in which case a very different set of identity conditions will be relevant. Here, then, we might be asking: is *X-the-human-animal* at t_1 identical to *Y-the-human-animal* at t_2? And things might go similarly for the remainder of our practical concerns.

Now all of this may seem quite complicated. But making this move could allow us to admit the different methodological approaches while dissolving

---

1   For some notable exceptions, however, see the works by Johnston and Schechtman noted at the end of the chapter.

the disagreements they produce. Note that we would not be *resolving* these disagreements; to do that would likely require showing why one's particular methodology was preferable to the alternatives. Instead, we would simply be showing that the so-called disagreements *aren't really disagreements after all*, for they would just be different conclusions one comes to when applying different methodologies to different areas of the debate. And we have seen several points in the book where this was a suggested option. So the relation between identity and moral responsibility may thus just be very different from the relation between identity and compensation, or identity and rational anticipation, etc. In other words, the very title of this book may be quite misleading, for it indicates that the topic of our investigation has been *the* relation between personal identity and ethics, whereas at the end of the day there may be no such (single) relation to be found.

This result may be very depressing to some, for it would leave unsatisfied a deep human desire for a simple and unified explanation of the phenomena in question. On the other hand, it could well be a very liberating result, insofar as it would free us up from the bog we found ourselves stuck in repeatedly throughout the book, with some theories of the relation between identity and ethics in favor at some spots but in serious disfavor at others, or leaving us in great difficulty about how to resolve our many standoffs between multiple theories on specific topics. In addition, this result may open up exciting new avenues of research, in which we could focus solely on the relation between identity and just one strand of our practical concerns, without having to worry about a grander, unifying theory holding up to cover all of them. For example, if we recognize that the form of identity we seek depends on the particular practical concerns we have, we may find that the moral permissibility of abortion, euthanasia, or stem cell research actually varies, depending on what practical concern we find most important.

Again, this is all fairly complicated, messy, and disunified, but it could well be that the truth about the relation between personal identity and ethics, like persons themselves, is complicated, messy, and disunified. But nevertheless, as with persons again, this truth may be deeply valuable and full of grand potential.

WORKS CITED OR REFERENCED IN THE CONCLUSION

DeGrazia, David. *Human Identity and Bioethics*. Cambridge: Cambridge University Press, 2005.

Johnston, Mark. "Human Beings." *Journal of Philosophy* 84 (1987): 59-83.

———. "Human Concerns Without Superlative Selves." In *Reading Parfit*, edited by Jonathan Dancy. Oxford: Blackwell, 1997.

Korsgaard, Christine M. "Personal Identity and the Unity of Agency: A Kantian Response to Parfit." *Philosophy & Public Affairs* 18 (1989): 101-32.

Locke, John. "Of Identity and Diversity." In *Personal Identity*, edited by John Perry. Berkeley: University of California Press, 1975.

MacIntyre, Alasdair. *After Virtue*. Notre Dame: University of Notre Dame Press, 1984.

Parfit, Derek. *Reasons and Persons*. Oxford: Oxford University Press, 1984.

Schechtman, Marya. *The Constitution of Selves*. Ithaca, NY: Cornell University Press, 1996.

Shoemaker, David W. "Personal Identity and Practical Concerns." *Mind* 116 (April 2007): 317-57.

Index